Educationa

Leadership
for 21st Century Learning

BETTER POLICIES FOR BETTER LIVES

This work is published on the responsibility of the Secretary-General of the OECD. The opinions expressed and arguments employed herein do not necessarily reflect the official views of the Organisation or of the governments of its member countries.

This document and any map included herein are without prejudice to the status of or sovereignty over any territory, to the delimitation of international frontiers and boundaries and to the name of any territory, city or area.

Please cite this publication as:
OECD (2013), *Leadership for 21st Century Learning,* Educational Research and Innovation, OECD Publishing.
http://dx.doi.org/10.1787/9789264205406-en

ISBN 978-92-64-18576-0 (print)
ISBN 978-92-64-20540-6 (PDF)

Series: Educational Research and Innovation
ISSN 2076-9660 (print)
ISSN 2076-9679 (online)

The statistical data for Israel are supplied by and under the responsibility of the relevant Israeli authorities. The use of such data by the OECD is without prejudice to the status of the Golan Heights, East Jerusalem and Israeli settlements in the West Bank under the terms of international law.

Photo credits: Cover © Inmagine LTD.

Corrigenda to OECD publications may be found on line at: *www.oecd.org/publishing/corrigenda.*

Foreword

Innovative Learning Environments (ILE) is an international study carried out by the Centre for Educational Research and Innovation (CERI) of the OECD. It is focused on innovative ways of organising learning for young people with the view of positively influencing the contemporary education reform agenda with forward-looking insights about learning and innovation.

The three strands of ILE – "Learning Research", "Innovative Cases", and "Implementation and Change" – describe the organisation of the project, but they are much more than a description. The design reflects the belief that a critical starting point to consider innovative change in the organisation of learning is the close understanding of learning itself. This first research strand resulted in the 2010 publication *The Nature of Learning: Using Research to Inspire Practice*. The next main component in the project design was immersion in what practitioners have actually been working with around the world in their own innovative learning environments – the "Innovative Cases" – that resulted in *Innovative Learning Environments* (2013). Together, this has established a substantial foundation on which to consider change strategies, initiatives and approaches for "Implementation and Change", the on-going third ILE strand.

This volume on learning leadership is the first substantial published output from the "Implementation and Change" ILE strand. It has been carried out in collaboration with the Jaume Bofill Foundation based in Barcelona which has supported the international work while carrying out a contributory study and spearheading a development initiative in Catalonia, Spain.

This work builds on the prominence given to learning leadership in the framework presented in the preceding ILE volume, *Innovative Learning Environments*. It has allowed much more in-depth analysis of what learning leadership means, conceptually and in practice. This volume has also drawn on the network of system co-ordinators of the ILE project to present examples of ways in which learning leadership is being fostered within innovation strategies and initiatives in their particular contexts.

"Learning leadership" as a term is not commonly used but we have chosen it to emphasise how important leading and designing for learning is, yet to distinguish it from related concepts such as instructional leadership. In this report, learning leadership is rooted in the issues covered by ILE. It is specifically focused on the design, implementation and sustainability of innovative, powerful, holistic learning environments aimed at young people. The leadership is exercised through distributed, connected activity and the relationships of a range of formal and non-formal leaders throughout learning systems.

The volume is comprised of a number of specific contributions from individual experts and specialists from different systems, some with theoretical perspectives, some focused on practice. To pull the different threads together, it is introduced by a substantial Secretariat overview, which draws very fully on the different contributions of the report. It is organised around the "5Ws and 1H" framework – Why? What? How? Who? Where? and When?

We are particularly grateful to the Jaume Bofill Foundation in Barcelona which has supported the ILE work on learning leadership so generously. The Foundation has generously provided resources enabling the international study, and it has provided the facilities and organised the local participation at two events in Barcelona. The first was an international seminar held in November 2012 based on early drafts, the second an international conference in December 2013 based on the finalised report. Our particular thanks go to Ismael Palacin, Anna Jolonch, and Valtencir Mendes, respectively the Director, Head of Research, and International Projects Coordinator at the Foundation.

Our thanks go to all those who have contributed specific chapters to this volume: Joan Badia, Clive Dimmock, Anna Jolonch, Dennis Kwek, John MacBeath, Màrius Martínez, James Spillane and Yancy Toh. Thanks also to those who contributed "international examples" for Chapter 5: Lone Lønne Christiansen, Judy Halbert, Linda Kaser, Susanne Owen, Roser Salavert, Per Tronsmo, Dorit Tubin and Tanja Westfall-Greiter. We are grateful to those who contributed to reflections in the preparatory meetings and seminars beyond those mentioned above, in particular Simon Breakspear and Anne Sliwka and those who participated in the seminar in November 2012. Particular thanks extend to Louise Stoll, who contributed throughout and worked with the Secretariat in delineating the main themes and format for the "Overview" chapter and shared its drafting.

Within the Secretariat, this volume was prepared by David Istance and Mariana Martinez-Salgado, with Marco Kools. Lynda Hawe, Iris Lopatta and Isabelle Moulherat worked on the finalisation of the text prior to publication, Sally Hinchcliffe did the copy editing and Peter Vogelpoel the layout of the publication.

Table of contents

Figures

Executive summary

Leadership is critical because it is strongly determinant of direction and outcomes, whether at the micro level of schools or of broader systems. As learning is the core business of education, it provides the paramount form and purpose of leadership focused on creating and sustaining environments that are conducive to good learning. Innovation is an integral part of the exercise of learning leadership in setting new directions.

Learning leadership is thus about setting direction and taking responsibility for making learning happen. It is exercised through distributed, connected activity and relationships. It extends beyond formal players to include different partners, and may be exercised at different levels of the overall learning system. It includes "learning management" in the commitment to transform, persevere and make change happen.

Learning leadership

The OECD Secretariat overview is a substantial and freestanding analysis, while drawing fully on the different contributions of the report. It is organised around the "5Ws and 1H" framework – Why? What? How? Who? Where? and When?

The chapter by James Spillane focuses on leading and managing teaching, for him "the core technology of schooling". He argues that too many analyses dwell on "leading the schoolhouse rather than leading the core work of the schoolhouse" and as a result are only weakly related to teaching, learning and their improvement. He frames and reviews research evidence to inform leadership for that core business.

John MacBeath presents leadership principles – the focus on learning, creating conducive conditions, dialogue, shared leadership responsibility and a shared sense of accountability – and underlines the importance of creating communities of learning. He widens the focus to incorporate non-formal learning arrangements, thereby significantly extending the leadership challenges of design and for practice.

Clive Dimmock, Dennis Twek and Yancy Toh describe an approach that starts with the nature of learning needed for the 21st century and relate that to appropriate teaching and learning arrangements, before delineating corresponding leadership arrangements – a "backward mapping" approach that defines the "learning design model". The model is applied to two Singapore schools.

Chapter 5 presents a selection of the leadership initiatives and analyses gathered through the Innovative Learning Environments project:

- Tanja Westfall-Greiter describes the strategy of creating teacher learning leaders (*Lerndesigners*) in the current Austrian Neue Mittelschule (NMS) reform.

- Judy Halbert and Linda Kaser discuss a leadership programme in British Columbia, Canada that engages the leaders together in a "spiral of inquiry" about learning in their own school and in networked activity.

- The New York City examples described by Roser Salavert cover professional learning communities, leadership coaching, teacher teams, and student "voice".

- Lone Christiansen and Per Tronsmo present Norwegian approaches to leadership and two national programmes, one for school leadership professional development and the other for mentoring principals and local providers.

- The South Australian and Israeli examples offered by Susanne Owen and Dorit Tubin feature the work of particular sections of the respective education ministries looking to drive innovative learning and provide conditions to support it.

Chapter by Anna Jolonch, Màrius Martínez and Joan Badia analyses the origins, methods and impact of collaboration between the OECD and the Jaume Bofill Foundation on learning leadership designed to bring benefits to Catalonia and to the broader international community. This initiative has involved an important research component, with researchers and practitioners looking in detail at six exemplary sites of learning leadership.

Concluding orientations

Learning leadership puts creating the conditions for 21st century learning and teaching at the core of leadership practice. Students' learning is at the heart of the enterprise: the core work is to ensure deep 21st century learning, whatever the environment. Designing and developing innovative learning environments to meet such ambitions requires highly demanding teaching repertoires and for everyone to keep learning, unlearning and relearning.

Continuous learning of all players and partners is a condition of successful implementation and sustainability.

Learning leadership demonstrates creativity and often courage. Innovating, designing, bringing others on board and redesigning all call on the exercise of creativity, and often courage. Deep shifts in mindset and practice and the capacity to keep the long-term vision in view are needed when the aim is transformation, even if the starting point may be incremental. The leadership focus is on deep changes to practice, structures and cultures.

Learning leadership models and nurtures 21st century professionalism. It is exercised through professional learning, inquiry and self-evaluation, and learning leaders are themselves high-level knowledge workers. By engaging in appropriate professional learning and creating the conditions for others to do the same, they model such professionalism throughout their wider communities.

Learning leadership is social and connected. Learning leadership is fundamentally social in nature and interaction is the essence of leadership practice. Learning leadership develops, grows and is sustained through participation in professional learning communities (PLCs) and networks. This means that the "meso" level of networks (rather than as an administrative layer) is critical.

As learning environments innovate, leadership becomes more complex, often involving diverse non-formal partners. The educational leadership literature has been dominated by the "place called school". Increasingly, innovative learning design incorporates non-formal sites and approaches in ways that make growing pedagogical and organisational demands on leadership. The distribution of leadership and the professional learning communities must extend to a range of different professionals, partners, and communities.

Transformative learning leadership involves complex multi-level chemistry. Systemic innovation and sustainability of powerful 21st century learning environments depends on learning leadership at different levels. Initial impetus might come from any level, from within the formal system and from other partners but for this impetus to be sustained at scale it needs corresponding decision-making and action at the other levels.

Learning leadership is needed at the system level. System-level learning leadership may serve to create the initial space for innovation or it may be exercised in response to micro-level innovation. A key policy role lies in creating conditions for facilitating networked professional learning. Governance and accountability systems should align with the ambition of creating powerful, innovative learning environments, or at least should not be pulling in the opposite direction.

Chapter 1

Learning leadership for innovative learning environments: The overview

By the OECD Secretariat[1]

This overview by the OECD Secretariat grounds learning leadership in the wider perspectives of innovative learning environments. Learning leadership is understood to be about actively contributing to the design, implementation and sustainability of powerful innovative learning environments through distributed, connected activity and relationships. It extends beyond formal players to include different partners and may be exercised at different levels of the overall learning system. The chapter presents the "5Ws and 1H" framework for addressing and analysing the different dimensions of learning leadership – Why? What? How? Who? Where? and When? It presents a set of nine points of concluding orientations, accompanied by some questions for learning leaders to enhance the practical application of this overview for those in leadership positions.

The aims and background to this report

Learning leadership is a central theme within the larger Innovative Learning Environments (ILE) study, and occupies a prominent place in the framework developed in the recently-published, preceding ILE volume (OECD, 2013). Leadership is so important because it sets direction for learning within increasingly complex organisations, and is about seeing that through into design and strategy. This suggested the value of giving it much closer scrutiny through analysis and examples: hence, this volume. It is key for another reason: learning leadership provides the natural bridge from analysing individual cases (ILE's second strand of work) and the larger focus on "Implementation and Change" (ILE's third strand).

This is not the first time that OECD has looked at leadership, and studies completed in 2008 and 2009 are summarised in the next section (OECD, 2008a, 2008b, 2009). Those studies already identified the importance of linking leadership closely with learning. In part, this report continues this focus some five years later, and deepens the understanding of what it means to give such an emphasis to the development and promotion of leadership. Emerging as it does from the ILE project, its point of departure are the "micro" level ecosystems of learning and teaching, moving from that to the "meso" focus on networks and communities of practice, and to the "macro" level of systems and policies. It means addressing leadership that can create, develop and sustain innovative learning environments, which may not be located in the familiar settings of schools or classrooms. Educational discussion readily acknowledges that a great deal of the learning done by young people today takes place outside formal classrooms, and that networks and communities of practice are fundamental to learning systems. Nevertheless, the discussion of leadership is still largely dominated by the relatively enclosed world of formal schooling. This report begins to open horizons, and to explore what leadership means in complex environments that mix different players, settings, and styles.

The term "learning leadership" is not in common use. The ILE project has chosen this term to distinguish it from other related, but not identical concepts. It shares many features with other learning-focused forms of leadership, such as instructional leadership, leadership for learning, and learner-centred leadership, but it is distinct. In this report, learning leadership is specifically focused on the design, implementation and sustainability of innovative, powerful learning environments through distributed, connected activity and relationships of a range of formal and informal leaders throughout a learning system.

Starting from where we left off in *Innovative Learning Environments* (OECD, 2013), we offer reflections about learning leadership and discuss key themes that arise. In understanding what the different chapters reveal, we have adopted the "5Ws and 1H" interrogative propositions – Why? What? How? Who? Where? and When? – referred to by MacBeath (Chapter 3) as "a simple but highly generative framework". This framework has been adapted to lay out the different dimensions of learning leadership as discussed and presented in this report, bringing the insights from those different chapters together into one overview. The different 5Ws and 1H, while helpful for disentangling the different dimensions, are largely interdependent. Because of that, they too need to be looked at together. At the end of this chapter we bring together a set of more generic points of synthesis. We are, however, very mindful of the warning of James Spillane (Chapter 2) to avoid simplistic mantras – these are not intended as "what works" recipes.

Building on earlier OECD analyses

This report builds on the insights revealed by earlier OECD work, in ways that are in part complementary to it and in part distinct. Beyond ILE, the OECD undertook a major review of school leadership in its work on Improving School Leadership (OECD, 2008a, 2008b). It reviewed policies and practices to arrive at an overarching framework and policy recommendations, and it conducted specific reviews and case studies around the larger concept of "system leadership". The Teaching and Learning International Survey (TALIS) covers leadership as well as surveying various aspects of teacher preparation, practice, beliefs, and appraisal; the published results to date are based on the 2008 survey (OECD, 2009).

Improving school leadership

The four-way framework designed to inform policy development (OECD 2008a) recognised especially in the first category the importance for leadership to address learning:

1. *Redefining school leadership responsibilities*, especially in terms of improved student learning but also arguing for higher autonomy as part of that redefinition, and for developing larger frameworks for policy and practice.

2. *Distributing school leadership*, arguing for the promotion and support for wider distribution of leadership beyond principals, and for support for school boards as they carry out their tasks.

3. *Developing skills for effective school leadership*, arguing the need to treat leadership development as a continuum and to encourage consistency of provision by different institutions and appropriate variety of effective training.

4. *Making school leadership an attractive profession*, in terms of recruitment, remuneration, professional organisation and career opportunities.

The 2008 case studies (OECD, 2008b), examined promising strategies and developments in five systems: Australia (Victoria), Austria, Belgium (Flanders), England, and Finland. They covered the range of strategies and arrangements for improving leadership in these different systems, but also focused on particular agencies or initiatives such as the Leadership Academy in Austria, or the National College for School Leadership and the Specialist Schools and Academies Trust (SSAT) in England. In addition to the reviews and case studies, position papers were provided by two leading experts – Richard Elmore and David Hopkins.

Richard Elmore (2008) explores the relationship between leadership and accountability and stresses the notion of "leadership as the practice of improvement" (finding an echo in James Spillane's Chapter 2 of this volume). He argues that the practice of improvement calls for strategies for developing and deploying knowledge and skills in schools, leading to high capacity to respond to external pressure, and to high "internal accountability" as coherence around norms, values, expectations, and processes for getting the work done. Many accountability pressures, on the other hand, lead to an under-investment in knowledge and skill and an over-investment in testing and regulatory control. The formative cycle developed in *Innovative Learning Environments* (OECD, 2013), around learning leadership, professional learning, knowledge and evaluation about learning achieved, feedback and subsequent redesign, fits closely with the capacity-building and accountability as argued for by Elmore. Moreover, he maintains that "as improvement progresses, leadership refracts". In the early stages of improvement, organisations rely heavily on role-based definitions of leadership but with improvement these become inadequate and the practices of leadership become substantially more complex as they engage the energy and commitment of people in the organisation.

David Hopkins (2008) is particularly focused on "system leadership", meaning not how systems are led from the top by ministers and others in positions of formal authority at the apex of bureaucratic pyramids, but how school leaders can come to exercise more systemic influence beyond their own particular schools and how this helps to drive system-wide improvement. System leadership calls for "adaptive work", meaning addressing problems for which the solutions lie outside current ways of operating (as distinct from the management needed to tackle technical problems for which know-how already exists). Already, therefore, Hopkins is making a direct link between the nature of leadership and innovation, consistent with the approach of this volume.

Insights from the TALIS survey

The main publication from the first TALIS survey (OECD, 2009; the results from the next survey will be published in 2014), devotes a chapter to leadership. TALIS 2008 examined five aspects of "management behaviour": management of school goals, actions to improve teaching, direct supervision of staff, accountability to internal and external stakeholders, and management of rules and procedures, and these are further reduced to two "styles of leadership" – instructional and administrative.

The majority of the surveyed countries were either above the international average on measures of both administrative and instructional leadership (Brazil, Bulgaria, Hungary, Italy, Mexico and Turkey) or below the international average on both measures (Australia, Austria, Denmark, Estonia, Flemish Belgium, Iceland, Korea, Lithuania and Spain). Few were high on the TALIS instructional leadership measure but low on administrative leadership (Malta and Poland) or high on administration and low on instruction (Ireland, Malaysia and Norway, the latter discussed in Chapter 5 in this volume). A number of countries were borderline on one or other dimension (Portugal, Slovak Republic and Slovenia). Whether because of the insensitivity of the measures, or as a more general reflection of the lack of impact of leadership styles, there were weak or no clear associations between such orientations to leadership and a variety of measures of teacher beliefs, teaching practices, and classroom climate.

While such findings may be very broadly indicative of different national traditions and approaches, it is necessary to delve more deeply into the nature of leadership, especially learning leadership, to gain deeper insights.

The "why" of learning leadership

Why the importance of and interest in learning leadership? The first reason is because **leadership is so influential of direction and outcomes** whether at the micro level of schools and learning environments, or of broader systems. As it is influential, and because of the urgent importance of education, the nature and formation of leadership automatically is also fundamental for anyone concerned with shaping practice and policy. That is, if we are interested in the future of education and learning we must be interested in leadership – its enhancement, and its failures.

This means to be interested in the practice of leadership as it is influential for learning, not in all the tasks that those in formal leadership positions may also perform as part of their remit. Our interest is in "leadership" itself, not in all of what those called leaders happen to do. Such leadership includes others than those who occupy the formal positions (see the "who" of learning leadership), as leadership needs to be distributed to be effective. This does not, however, exclude an interest in management where this is about ensuring the maintenance and sustainability of the directions pursued by the learning leadership – a point emphasised by James Spillane in the opening of Chapter 2 and taken up in the next section.

Second, learning is stressed as an integral part of leadership because **learning is the core business of education**. Hence, this is the paramount form and business of leadership – the leadership that is focused on creating and sustaining environments that are conducive to good learning. Yet, this is not about just any learning. "Learning leadership" should attend to the nature of learning in creating the conditions for "deep learning" to take place as opposed to instrumental or tactical learning (MacBeath, Chapter 3). It is about learning in order to develop the so-called 21st century competences and content, which are central to the treatment and methodology of Clive Dimmock, Dennis Kwek and Yancy Toh in Chapter 4.

Both of these fundamental reasons for attention to learning leadership brings a third, that **innovation is important in setting new directions and designing learning environments** as discussed in *Innovative Learning Environments*. Innovation is a key element of the contemporary agenda, and leadership is necessary to drive and sustain it. Judy Halbert and Linda Kaser, in presenting their Certificate in Innovative Educational Leadership (CIEL) programme in Chapter 5, argue that it is not necessary to decide between competing arguments advocating disruptive innovation or incremental improvement when leader practitioners are faced with choices, as they must attend to innovation in learning and designs in any event:

> Although reformers may like to argue the relative merits of improvement, innovation and accountability, these distinctions are not particularly helpful for practitioners struggling to make learning more engaging and relevant in this moment in their particular context. The stance underlying the CIEL programme is that new approaches to learning *are* necessary and new designs for learning *are* required.

Hence the "why learning leadership?" question joins together a fundamental set of rationales: the necessity of leadership, well exercised, to make change happen; the importance of reinforcing learning as the core business of education while focusing on the nature of learning itself especially in terms of "deep learning" and 21st century content and competences; and the need to innovate if this is to happen. Learning leadership in this report is about fostering and guiding learning change but it is also innovation leadership – promoting, facilitating, organising, and managing the innovation endeavour.

"Why learning leadership?" arises too because in some systems there has been a reluctance for teachers to accept that those with formal leadership position in schools should enjoy authority about the teaching and learning that takes place in the classroom. Lone Christiansen and Per Tronsmo (Chapter 5) maintain: "A great deal of resistance to leadership can be found among teachers, and schools have little tradition for the leader to directly influence the work done by the teacher." Anna Jolonch, Màrius Martínez, and Joan Badia in Chapter 6 express it more generally as: "Introducing the concept of leadership into the world of education still comes up against a lot of resistance." It serves as a reminder that, in the enthusiasm of some to embrace distributed leadership, it may be forgotten that the direction of the distribution often needs to be towards principals and senior managers when the issue is teaching and learning as well as in the opposite direction from those principals towards others.

Christiansen and Tronsmo identify some of the problems that arise with the exercise of learning leadership as generic to "knowledge organisations", in which they include schools but also hospitals, universities, law offices, and consulting firms. They argue that such organisations are especially likely to experience tension between professionals and more senior leaders, with the legitimacy of those leaders being questioned when it comes to core professional activity: for these and other reasons the paradoxical effect may be excessive focus on steering and control. One answer to the "why?" of learning leadership is thus to help address this tension where and when it arises, and the paradox that in knowledge organisations it may be difficult to align all levels of leadership around core business when that business, as in schools, is precisely knowledge, learning and teaching.

Looking at "why?" from another angle, the Norwegian authors Christiansen and Tronsmo (Chapter 5), and MacBeath (Chapter 3) suggest that systems and cultures are not equal in their embrace of the question "why?", referring especially to Hofstede's work on management in different countries (Hofstede 1991). As expressed by MacBeath:

> Geert Hofstede conducted surveys in school systems around the world to gauge the relative uses of institutional power, to measure the extent to which people in positions of leadership were open to challenge and willing to draw on both feminine and masculine aspects of their character.

The importance of inquiry, and developing the capacity to ask (and be asked) searching questions lies at the core of the leadership programme developed in British Columbia (Chapter 5). The importance of self-evaluation as part of the exercise and arming of learning leadership, and of searching inquiry as a key element of that, is also stressed by MacBeath in Chapter 3.

The "what" of learning leadership

We need definitions to establish broad boundaries but we need also to look more closely at the terrain found within those perimeters. As "learning leadership for innovation" is exercised at a variety of levels and settings, by a variety of players, our definition does not assumes that it refers only to those who work in places called "schools". So to demarcate the boundaries of the "what" of learning leadership, we define it as:

> Learning leadership is about actively contributing to the design, implementation and sustainability of powerful innovative learning environments. It is done through distributed, connected activity and relationships. It extends beyond formal players to include different partners, and may be exercised at different levels of the overall learning system.

The different chapters of this volume give insights into aspects of this overall definition. In this section, discussion begins with leadership in general, before deepening into learning leadership within the ILE focus. In this chapter, several of the ways in which learning leadership become manifest that might have been reported here are discussed in the "how" section – developing vision and setting milestones, creating community, professional learning, and so forth – and in the "who" section – the different levels and settings of leadership.

Leadership

In broad terms, leadership is about setting direction for something and taking responsibility for seeing it through. Because this is a creative process, undertaken in dynamic, social situations with others, it has what James Spillane in Chapter 2 describes as an "emergent" quality. It is not simple or predictable, and indeed some, though not this report, distinguish leadership from management precisely in the non-routine nature of leadership. Leadership is not a solo activity but a process involving others, essentially social and interactive that, argues Spillane, "gets beyond individual behaviour and the acts of individuals".

This need to move beyond the acts and qualities of individuals is one reason why this report is focused primarily on leadership rather than on those who lead. In addition, given that leadership is essentially distributed in education and learning and occurs at different levels, to search for individual qualities risks reducing the focus immediately to the familiar terms of individual school leadership rather than the full range of settings, players, and levels that are embraced by our definition. The engaged student or teacher and the senior manager do not necessarily share the same qualities; principalship may be exercised in very different ways; the profile of those who exercise learning leadership in a school district or foundation or ministry of education or in a non-formal programme of service learning may not be the same.

Some generic qualities that mirror the nature of learning leadership are nevertheless proposed by the authors in this volume. John MacBeath refers to the importance of "connoisseurship" as "the ability to perceive what is salient amid the complexity and simultaneity of school and classroom life" (Chapter 3). Adventurous leaders, as MacBeath describes them, need to cultivate their own innovation-friendly habits of mind and skills as well as those of others. Dorit Tubin similarly refers in Chapter 5 to "self-awareness" that includes the ability of leaders to understand their values, motives and effectiveness in influencing others. Jolonch, Martinez and Badia (Chapter 6) include openness to the wider world and a readiness to learn from others among the qualities they noted in the cases they researched in Catalonia, Spain. Learning leaders, for Dimmock, Kwek and Toh (Chapter 4) have the "courageous leadership to engineer changes". "Courage" and "creativity" are frequently mentioned qualities associated with good learning leadership.

Such qualities accord with the strong focus we have given to leadership as creative design, strategising and implementation, as that is mirrored in such qualities as understanding what might be done, awareness of others and of the wider world, courage and the readiness to engage, and openness in seeing options and possibilities. They can inform leadership development programmes and recruitment criteria. Nevertheless, learning leadership itself should not be reduced to individual qualities.

Leadership and management

A common contrast is made between "leadership" and "management". Some stress the creative and inspirational aspects of leadership in contrast with the routine aspects of management that are concerned with maintenance. The two are not identical concepts, and need to be disentangled, but nevertheless may turn out to be more complementary than this suggests. Christiansen and Tronsmo in Chapter 5, for instance, favourably quote Mintzberg's (2009) warning against making an excessive contrast between the two: "We should be seeing managers *as* leaders, and leadership as management practiced well. By putting leadership on a pedestal separated from management, we turn a social process into a personal one". The warning about over-personalising fits our focus on leadership rather than a preoccupation with individual leaders, but our emphasis is somewhat different from Mintzberg's.

In disentangling concepts, one source of confusion is that those nominated formally as leaders often have a range of routine management and administrative duties to perform as well as leading. These tasks often get bundled together to reflect the breadth of particular job descriptions associated with being, say, a school principal. Spillane in Chapter 2 uses the language of "schoolhouse" to help unbundle tasks and definitions: "with some exceptions, many analyses dwell on leading the schoolhouse rather than the core work of the schoolhouse. As a result, descriptions and prescriptions for leading are often only weakly related to the actual work of teaching and leading its improvement." He argues for the complementarity of leadership and management: "The challenge for educators is not simply introducing and implementing change in education systems, but also maintaining changes once implemented. Rather than direct opposites or even enemies, change and constancy are closely related." (Chapter 2)

This suggests that the appropriate contrast is not between leadership and management in general but in those activities directly associated with learning and teaching, on the one hand, and those about the running of the institution and accordance with regulation that may be only very indirectly related to the core business of learning environments. The problem for the design and innovation of learning environments is when particular senior leaders/managers are so preoccupied with the institutional management aspects of the tasks they do that it is to the neglect of leading the core business of learning and teaching.

The focus of this report is on learning leadership, and especially that which is about innovating learning environments, but this is not seen to be achieved only with the creative, inspirational and collaborative acts of design. This needs to be followed up with the capacity and resilience to put those designs into practice and to maintain a far-sighted course through all the messy realities of everyday life. This calls for managing processes and people. The complement to "learning leadership" is "learning management" and both are implied in this report.

They may, however, call for an imposing range of expectations and approaches for the same leaders to do both well. John MacBeath (Chapter 3) and Susanne Owen (Chapter 5) both address this point. For MacBeath:

> The critical and contentious issue for leaders is, in Hampden-Turner's terminology (2007), to understand, and to manage, the "dilemma space" which occurs between the rock and the whirlpool ... The rock values – consistency, reliability, performance, competition and transparency – he counterpoints with the whirlpool values of choice, diversity, dynamism, spontaneity and autonomy.

It is not that learning leadership is all "whirlpool" and learning management is all "rock". Both are valued but they may come into tension and that tension needs to be addressed. Owen makes a similar point in asserting that: "leadership of innovation goes beyond the usual traditional approaches to thinking, strategic change and management that are focused on logic, deductive reasoning and right/wrong results" (Chapter 5). It is to stress that learning leadership involves several forms of leadership and learning management too, making for imposing demands for those mostly actively engaged in it.

Learning leadership for powerful innovative learning environments

The starting point of our deeper analysis of learning leadership is provided by *Innovative Learning Environments*, recently published (OECD, 2013): learning leadership puts learning at the centre of all reform and design processes – students' learning is at the heart of the enterprise, with the core work to ensure deep 21st century learning, in whatever the environment. When the focus is more limited to "instructional leadership", it is centred especially on quality teaching and learning within schools' pedagogical cores, which is only part of the story. When "learning leadership" is understood to be about providing direction to return to traditional learning fare, it lies outside the concept as discussed in this volume altogether.

Learning leadership frequently involves adaptive challenges, requiring responses that go beyond leaders' current repertoires (Heifetz and Linsky, 2002). As noted above, it calls on leaders to be creative, thinking differently, and taking risks as they push themselves out of their comfort zones and experiment with developing and implementing new designs and encouraging others to do the same without fear of failure (Stoll and Temperley, 2009). This is centrally focused on student learning but extends well beyond that. Learning leaders understand that designing and developing innovative learning environments requires everyone to keep learning, unlearning and relearning because continuous learning of all players and partners is a condition of successful implementation and sustainability.

Several delineations of "learning leadership" proposed by authors in this report are within the wider ILE perspective. For Jolonch, Martinez and Badia (Chapter 6), learning leadership is innovative and found in contexts of change and in the endeavour to break with the *status quo*:

> It results from the intersection and accumulation of several leaderships (instructional, organisational, etc.) to take them even further. This leadership continuously and sustainably teaches and creates learning, autonomy and empowerment in the learners and in the community. It aims to identify the transferable theories of change management, of shared, collaborative and team leadership strategies, and the organisations that provide learning, with the value-creation chains which can "read" and interpret the reality – of the classroom in the school, or of the school in the classroom.

Hence they too combine elements of "learning management" with "learning leadership" and see them as multi-dimensional ("several leaderships"). This will often call for deep shifts in mindset and practice, in all members of the learning community and not just the educators.

Dimmock, Kwek and Toh in Chapter 4 offer three defining characteristics of the leadership needed for transforming schools into 21st century learning environments:

> Learning-centred, emphasising leadership of curricula, teaching and learning; distributed so that leadership empowers teachers and builds the capacity of available human capital; and community networked, thereby benefiting from the resources of other schools and the community.

They suggest that to put this into practice and to transform schools at scale require much more than piecemeal tinkering:

> It demands rethinking leadership, and learning-centred leadership in particular, in a more holistic, strategic perspective and with a strong focus on the elements that shape and support innovative 21st century learning environments. It is "strategic" in connecting broader elements that shape the design process itself (especially the aims, goals and outcomes of learning, namely, what are students learning for?) with an understanding of leadership that extends beyond established 20th century institutional models.

A third example of conceptualising "learning leadership" in holistic terms, and set in the context of 21 century change is offered by Tanja Westfall-Greiter in Chapter 5. For one thing, the choice of name for a new role in Austria's *Neue Mittelschule* (New Middle Schools or NMS) exemplifies the ILE focus on leadership as design – *Lerndesigners*. Beyond this, and underpinning the *Lerndesigner* qualification, is the so-called "NMS House" deemed essential for fostering change in learning culture and realised throughout different subjects and lessons. This comprises six development areas that together build the "house" in ways that echo the ILE learning principles: mindfulness of learning, diversity, competence orientation, "backwards design" curriculum development, differentiated instruction and assessment (see Chapter 5 and Figure 5.2).

Different levels and settings

Learning leadership activity varies according to the level of the system in question and the specific learning context in the spotlight. So there is the big picture design of structures, policies and processes, curriculum, governance, etc. which is concerned, as Dimmock and colleagues argue in Chapter 4, with "orchestrating, implementing, sustaining and scaling the transformation process". But there is also the detailed design of what Jim

Spillane describes (Chapter 2) as "the practice of leading teaching", and of other strategies to facilitate student learning. This is micro-level design by teacher and other educator leaders as well as principals in school settings. There is meso-level activity through networks and communities of practice that play their own role of leadership in learning systems, and which need their own particular forms of leadership. There are "hybrid learning environments" (Zitter and Hoeve, 2012), combining very different players and traditions with their own particular leadership challenges. And there are the non-formal programmes discussed by MacBeath in Chapter 3. This variety of levels and setting is discussed especially in the section on "who".

The "how" of learning leadership

In discussing the "how" of learning leadership, we draw on the influential factors shaping the practice of learning leadership that emerge most clearly from the different chapters of this report. They match closely the framework presented in the preceding ILE volume in terms of learning leadership and the "formative organisation", as well as the emphasis given in that report to creating networks and connections across different learning environments (OECD, 2013).

Providing a sense of direction for learning

Several contributions identify the importance of vision, of project, of signposts and accompanying "milestones" – all about offering direction for learning. Dorit Tubin from Israel (Chapter 5) describes educational vision as one of the four conditions for learning leadership:

> ... to offer a "road map" from the unsatisfactory present situation of learning towards a more promising future. The vision should attract partners and followers, and provide them with the motivation, suggested methods, and narratives to explain the importance of such reform for innovative learning. The vision gives meaning to such concepts as "improving", "learning" and "environment" providing the necessary context and relevance that are understood by and attractive to potential partners.

Jolonch, Martinez and Badia (Chapter 6) refer to the "project", formulated in different ways, but a common feature of the six Catalan sites selected as having exemplary learning leadership practice:

> All the learning environments studied have a school-specific project expressly formulated. This reference document acts as a guide to what will be done, with the necessary flexibility to adapt to changing circumstances as needed. All the schools in this sample are acutely

aware that a distinct educational project is being implemented, which will help continuous improvement and which involves challenge for the school's educational community as a whole.

Dimmock, Kwek and Toh (Chapter 4) in presenting the "school design model" incorporating the backward mapping methodology, begin with the importance of identifying "the main elements of a school that are fundamental to its redesign as a 21st century learning environment". For this vision to guide learning leadership, it must be understandable in terms of the learning to be achieved, not only the institutional transformations involved.

Translating vision into strategy

However important visions and projects may be, they need to be translated into strategies of design, and those strategies need to be implemented. Tanja Westfall-Greiter (Chapter 5) quotes Barth (2000) to illustrate how easy it is to espouse an ideal but how much harder to turn that ideal into reality:

> "Our school is a community of learners!" How many times do we see and hear this assertion, now so common in public schools? This is an ambitious promissory note, indeed. The promise, is, first, that the school is a "community," a place full of adults and youngsters who care about, look after, and root for one another and who work together for the good of the whole – in times of need as well as times of celebration. I find that precious few schools live up to this mantle of "community." Many more are simply organisations or institutions. As if "community" were not enough to promise, a "community of learners" is much more.

So much revolves, therefore, around implementation, and the factors associated with success in doing that. Spillane in Chapter 2 refers to the importance of the "performative" as well as the "ostensive": that is, what is actually done to put the ideal into practice. MacBeath describes it as the challenge of "enactment", in Chapter 3 in relation to teachers and their practice:

> As Joyce and Showers (2002) point out, it easy for teachers to know what they should do, harder for them to be able to do it, and most difficult of all for them to embed it into their daily practice. This is characterised by Mary Kennedy (1999) as "the problem of enactment" – the difficulty teachers face in translating into effective practice and coherent action the ideas they may have embraced yet struggle to make the connection between what seems is right in theory and principle and what is right in the circumstances.

The same might be said of applying research findings in general where "knowing" a research finding on teaching and learning as a fact may be mistaken for knowing what it means for practice in context, and even more to embed it in practice, by individual practitioners and in learning communities at large. But it is equally relevant to the broad challenge of learning leadership in moving from vision to implementation

Various supportive conditions and factors are referred to in this report. Owen (South Australia) and Christiansen and Tronsmo (Norway) and Dimmock and colleagues (Chapter 4) refer to the cultivation of cultures of "positivity", of developing the readiness to have a go and take risks rather than timidity or pessimism. A readiness to experiment and to "bend rules" in the interest of learning innovation is also mentioned by Susanne Owen (Chapter 5) and by MacBeath in Chapter 3 ("self-confessed rule breakers, driven by their conscience and what they believed to be right … in full knowledge of the risks and consequences of defying policy mandates"). The second of the five "leadership for learning principles" presented by MacBeath is that putting learning front and centre presupposes a culture able to nurture learning for everyone, affording opportunities to reflect on the nature, skills and processes of learning and the physical and the social spaces that stimulate and celebrate it. Owen also emphasises how important it is to ensure that the vision is actually shared, as well as having a common language to characterise the innovation, for which collegial professional learning is seen as essential (see also the section on professional learning).

Organisational strategies and infrastructural change

The ILE framework refers to learning leadership operating first on the "pedagogical core" of the core elements – learners, educators, content and resources – and the organisational structures and dynamics that link those elements together. The four organisational dynamics that feature in *Innovative Learning Environments* are how teachers and educators are grouped beyond the "single-teacher classroom" model, how learners are grouped, how learning time is used, and pedagogy and assessment.

James Spillane devotes a great deal of attention to these aspects in Chapter 2. He emphasises the importance of leadership as diagnosis and design in order to maintain learning at the core of the organisation and to innovate accordingly, and then to deploy an array of organisational structural tools and devices ("One way to think about this social structure is as an infrastructure for the practice of leading teaching.") Altering the conditions for learning via organisational routines features prominently not only in Chapter 2 but also in an earlier ILE analysis he wrote with Lauren Resnick, Pam Goldman and Elizabeth Rangel (Resnick et al., 2010). In that case they focused on "kernel routines" designed to disrupt comfortable behaviour maintaining fragmented organisations in favour of highly learning-focused, collaborative routines. As he discusses in Chapter 2, a key challenge in transforming any vision for learning into practice is that often school organisational structures are so familiar and well established as to seem invariable and inviolable, thereby blocking room for more powerful learning environments to emerge. Organisational routines themselves can seem to be the main problem whereas, argues Spillane, it is not the existence of such routines but rather the well-entrenched, invisible ones that hinder professional learning and collegiality:

> Organisational routines are staples in schools and include teacher evaluations, teacher hiring, school improvement planning, grade-level meetings, and student assemblies. Organisational routines have a bad rap in organisational theory and school reform literature, more often than not blamed for inertia and preserving the *status quo* in the face of change efforts. However, organisational routines are essential for organisations to function, enabling co-ordinated action, reducing conflict about how to do organisational work, and providing continuity in the face of changing personnel.

Hence, the issue is not how to get rid of organisational routines *per se* but for the diagnostic work of leadership to clarify how the taken-for-granted routines block powerful learning, and how these can be supplanted by other more powerful ones like the "kernel routines" or those underpinning Lesson Study or Learning Study in Asia and the United States (Cheng and Lo, 2013). However much this relies on the engagement of a range of teacher leaders, it is likely to call for the active promotion of the formal leaders with the legitimate authority to be able to argue for an end to long-standing but learning-unfriendly school practices.

It might be hoped that such organisational transformations might happen naturally as a generational matter, as one cohort of teachers comes to replace another. But this is to underestimate the resilience of those existing routines and "grammars" of schooling (Cuban, 1995), and MacBeath is pessimistic in Chapter 3 about the transformative power of teacher education: "The perennial problem is that these neophyte teachers are 'insiders' (Hoy and Murphy, 2001), their views of teaching shaped by their own experience, so that they return to the places of their past, complete with memories and preconceptions often unaffected by their higher education or training college experience". Hence, as well as organisational changes, it is important for leadership to address the views and understandings of what teaching and learning should be that new teachers bring with them as they start their careers. There is the broader policy question of how to ensure that teacher education exercises a sufficiently powerful influence to disturb the assumptions and expectations derived from student teachers' experience of their own earlier schooling.

Spillane also identifies five characteristics of the ostensive, or formally defined, infrastructure arrangements that will impact on how they will be interpreted and put into practice. These are not specific to learning leadership, but represent ways of correcting blockages and mismatches that the leadership can use to smoothing advance to becoming more clearly learning-focused:

1. *Anchoring in and aligning with teaching* and how the infrastructure for school leadership connects with teaching.

2. *Cognitive adequacy:* referring to an organisational infrastructure's accuracy in describing and understanding itself in ways that can be easily applied in different situations (Stinchcombe, 2001, p.18).

3. *Communicability, corruptibility, and correctability*: ostensive representations of infrastructure must be transmissible, and able to withstand being easily changed in practice and yet keep pace with practice on the ground.

4. *Consistency* within any one component (e.g. a particular organisational routine) and across components is needed if the formal organisational infrastructure is to influence practice.

5. *Authority* of the school organisation's infrastructure refers to the weight it carries for organisational members, which is especially relevant at times of redesign and change.

Dimmock, Kwek and Toh in Chapter 4 focus on a set of organisational dimensions and tools very similar to those identified in *Innovative Learning Environments* (OECD, 2013) in the quest for transformation: "New curricular, learning and pedagogical practices are presaged on sympathetic changes to organisational structures, especially to teacher grouping, the timetable, and classroom layout (including use of physical space, technology and equipment)." They go much further than that in terms of the "how" of learning leadership and propose a full "school design model" based on five key characteristics:

First, the model identifies the main elements of a school that are fundamental to its redesign as a 21st century learning environment. Second, it recognises interconnectivity, in that change in one element requires concomitant change in the other elements that functionally inter-relate with it. Third, it is strategic in the sense that, with many changing elements, it is imperative that the process has some order and rationale. Fourth, leadership is the key agency for securing and achieving the school redesign in its completeness, and fundamentally, it is the school design process and the nature of the new learning environments themselves that help to reconceptualise the new leadership that is presaged. Fifth, the model is underpinned by an explicit methodology, known as "backward mapping".

The authors present the example of two Singapore schools, whose transformation trajectories are presented within the school design framework. At one level, it offers an analytical device to focus on key dimensions and to better understand transformation processes. At a more practical level, they argue that this framework can be applied to help practitioners make a complex long-term process clearer conceptually and more manageable organisationally, as opposed to piecemeal innovations without the design model to engineer the connections between the key elements.

Professional learning

How to put the design process into action? The most widely-shared agreement on this in the chapters of this volume centres on the importance of teacher and leadership learning and professional development. Widespread educator learning does not happen by chance: it depends on serious investment in the best kinds of professional and leadership learning.

The numerous international literature and reviews on effective professional learning and development for teachers and leaders (e.g. Timperley et al., 2008; Darling-Hammond et al., 2009; Dempster, Lovett and Flückiger, 2011; Huber, 2010, 2011) are largely related to classroom and school environments, with an increasing interest in the impact on student learning outcomes. Clearly, the more that the relevant learning environments include non-school settings, the more this evidence base should be widened, and the deeper will be the reflection that leaders need to give to their own impact, recognising that their own transformation is likely to be a necessary part of the change (Robertson, 2013). One way of widening focus is to focus on recognised adult learning principles that apply to many different contexts. These are beginning to underpin more recent professional and leadership learning efforts, highlighting the importance of blending theory and practice, with opportunities for practical experimentation and projects, and learning from these experiences and through feedback.

Even in this short report, there are numerous examples related to professional learning, including several in Chapter 5. A characteristic of the innovative sites described by Susanne Owen regarding South Australia is the nurturing of leadership skills for all members of these professional learning teams, supported by the school/preschool leader through the provision of time and/or funding for professional learning. Leadership coaching is a feature of today's most accomplished organisations, argues Roser Salavert in Chapter 5, and she presents the example of the Harlem school in which the principal, in partnership with the coach, guided her staff in the development of a shared vision, established the conditions for a rigorous and collaborative culture, and effectively implemented distributive leadership. The professional learning organised by and with the *Lerndesigners* in the Austrian case, who themselves help to identify the learning needs for the other members of the school and learning communities, is a notable feature of the programme including a whole calendar of *Lernatelier* courses and events. This is backed up by an online platform enabling communication and exchange of ideas and innovations.

The national programme for leadership training and development in Norway, set up in 2008 after the 2006 national reform and in response to a Norwegian "PISA shock", is for all newly employed principals at primary and secondary level. There is a strong emphasis in the training on schools being well-managed and goal-oriented and covers five main areas, of which the most important is judged to be the first: *1)* learning outcomes and learning environment; *2)* management and administration; *3)* collaboration, organisational development and the supervision of teachers; *4)* development and change; and *5)* the leadership role. To date, the leadership development programme has been positively evaluated and seems to have led to a shift in attitudes about leadership and capacity development.

Jolonch, Martinez and Badia (Chapter 6), identify the shared high and constant interest in professional development in the six exemplary sites chosen to study learning leadership in Catalonia, Spain. This generalises to the desire for permanent learning in places where learning leadership is shared, and such a desire is indispensable for the leadership to be exercised and the wider project realised. Moreover:

> The desire for learning that comes about through practices of leadership shared by an increased number of actors provides a context for building capacity, while also showing a horizon of innovation and research that is very healthy for the wider education system.

For Dimmock, Kwek and Toh in Chapter 4, writing about Singapore but arguing that the framework and dimensions apply universally, learning-centred leaders place teaching and learning at the heart of their leadership, and this requires a continuing process of learning for the leaders. They need to possess the knowledge, skills and dispositions to lead in adopting innovative curricular, pedagogical and assessment practices, and in building close professional relationships and communication with their colleagues. Learning is necessary both to sharpen the strategic vision to improve learning and to address the orchestration and organisational operations to implement transformation.

Inquiry, self-evaluation and research

Building knowledge within learning environments as a collective endeavour means to understand learning progress and identify direction and implementation to feed back into a cycle of design and redesign and occupies a central part of the ILE framework. Elmore's brilliant analysis

(2008) calls for strategies for developing and deploying knowledge and skills in schools as fundamental to any serious improvement or innovation. MacBeath in Chapter 3 identifies promoting dialogue as one of the five "learning for leadership principles": talk between colleagues helps transform tacit knowledge (what is known but not articulated) into explicit knowledge and the social process involved helps to create new shared knowledge (Nonaka and Takeuchi, 1995) – in this case, the design of innovative learning environments. Dialogue is fundamental to creating and sustaining a culture of active collegial inquiry and of learning in which leadership practice is made explicit, discussable and transferable.

Roser Salavert in Chapter 5 offers an example of inquiry and self-evaluation that is directly linked to practice and strategising:

> The Collaborative Teacher Team inquiry model that is implemented in the New York City public schools is an adaptation of the Scaffolded Apprenticeship Model (SAM) of School Improvement through Leadership Development (Talbert and Scharff, 2008) … teachers learn to analyse and triangulate data from different sources as they look closely at instructional practices and their alignment to the needs of the target students. Together, they drive the implementation of strategies that can work for their particular students and evaluate their impact towards achieving ambitious end of year learning goals. The outcomes of these teams then inform the instructional and/or organisational practices of the school thus creating the conditions for an innovating learning environment, and a school culture that promotes evidence-based student achievement.

Inquiry is also central to the British Columbia programme presented in Chapter 5 in which the core concept is the "spiral of inquiry" (see also Halbert and Kaser, 2013). Educators in the programme "engage in a disciplined approach to collaborative inquiry designed to assist them to gain the confidence, the insights and the mindsets required to design new and powerful learning environments – indeed to transform their schools and their systems" (Chapter 5). The "scanning process" is worth describing in some detail. It is a process designed for each learning environment to gain a deeper understanding of the experience of the learners in ways that extend well beyond available achievement data or results from satisfaction surveys. Scanning also means to ask questions designed to focus on implementation of the seven ILE learning principles; for example:

- Do learners see and understand themselves as learners? Are they self-regulated? Are they becoming increasingly meta-cognitive?

- Do learners see and understand the connections across content areas?

- Are learning professionals tuned into the emotions of learners – and the connection between emotions and motivation?

- Do learners receive high-quality focused feedback that provides clear directions for improvement?

- Are learners confident and comfortable in both giving and receiving feedback with their peers based on co-constructed criteria?

- Are all learners stretched through demanding, engaging and challenging work?

- Are learners engaged in high quality, well-organised co-operative learning on a regular basis?

- Is the prior knowledge that learners bring to the setting respected and valued?

- Are learners at the centre of every decision made in the school?

Leaders take responsibility for ensuring that all teachers are researching and evaluating their practice. Educators and other members of the learning environment share ideas and work to research and collect evidence on new improved teaching practices and their implementation. Synergies are achieved across the learning environment, with prominence given to peer learning from tacit knowledge, and promotion of shared teacher decision making on the adoption of evidence-informed practices. The leadership is exercised by and informed through the process of inquiry.

Creating capacity through learning communities

A recurring theme in the different chapters is the importance of creating community as a vehicle for learning leadership and as a means to make it more effective. This is not argued principally in order for community members to feel more positive about themselves through a sense of belonging (though that may be a very welcome spin-off and help to reinforce the positive educational benefits), but as a means for shared strategies and visions to emerge within learning environments, and for developing appropriate expertise through sharing. In the language of Andy Hargreaves and Michael Fullan, there is need for both individual and team work but team work should be prioritised: "social capital trumps human capital" (Hargreaves and Fullan, 2012).

Hence learning leadership is both about creating community (what) and is exercised through the community so created (how) (as well as the "who", as communities are always made up of people). MacBeath's (Chapter 3) principles of leadership for learning include the creation and maintenance of community in stating that "leadership for learning practice involves the sharing of leadership in which organisational structures and procedures support participation". He refers to Pasi Sahlberg's discussion of Finland's educational success (2011) in which Sahlberg points to the critical nature of the teacher collective and their openness to addressing and changing their practice together:

> The best-performing educational systems all have built their change strategies on systemic approaches that rely on collective professional and institutional (or social capital) development, enhanced conditions for teaching and learning for all, and more equal educational opportunities within their education systems.

The collaborative climate is extended, for MacBeath, to a "shared sense of accountability", echoing the "internal accountability" stressed by Elmore (OECD, 2008b) and collective responsibility, which is at the heart of professional learning communities (PLCs) (Stoll et al., 2006). As a reflection of the distributed nature of learning leadership when well exercised and as a means to the achievement of powerful, dynamic, innovative learning environments, therefore, the "how" of learning leadership importantly includes the creation of learning communities. Learning leadership develops, grows and is sustained through participation in professional learning communities: it is a team endeavour and depends on carefully crafted collaborative activity to deepen, spread and maintain the learning. This mirrors the ILE principle that is founded on the social nature of student learning that actively encourages group work and well-organised co-operative learning (Dumont, Istance and Benavides, 2010).

Building larger communities and networks

Learning leaders who have larger horizons may start small, but they think big. They intend that their vision and commitment will ultimately be shared by many educators in diverse contexts. They devote energy and effort to deepening their understanding and practice of all of the elements of innovative learning environments (Hargreaves and Fink, 2000). These are "system leaders" as described by Hopkins (OECD, 2008b), who build communities and synergies beyond their own particular school. In this report we have focused more on "leadership" than "leaders" in order to avoid personalising the functions and linking them too closely to individuals and those occupying particular positions. An important vehicle through which the wider leadership can function, over and above that provided by such players as ministers, superintendents and the like, is through networked professional communities.

While "professional learning communities" frequently refer to groups of educators within a school or whole school staffs, and "networks" apply to teachers or leaders in different locations, the terms are often used interchangeably. PLCs and networks are the means by which the vision, inquiry and other forms of collaborative learning, and distributed leadership are all brought together, supported by the glue of trusting relationships and structures. They connect numbers of educators together as they gain access to research evidence, develop new knowledge and practice, and share this around the community or network. The leadership and benefits flow in both directions – from the wider community into the single learning environment and from the different sites outward to the learning system as a whole.

Several of the chapter authors make both the general case and illustrate how this is being put into practice. Dimmock, Kwek and Toh in Chapter 4 add to the defining characteristics of leadership "for transforming schools into 21st century learning environments" not only that it should be learning-centred and distributed, but also that it should be "community networked, thereby benefiting from the resources of other schools and the community". Dorit Tubin (Chapter 5) argues that "sustainable innovative learning reform at scale needs to have a learning network embedded in its very structure, promoted by the learning leadership, and providing information about the learning taking place in the innovation venues among the participants system-wide." Thus whether starting from the benefits to the individual learning environment or from the success of innovative learning reform, the importance of robust meso-level networked communities of practice is underlined, that together should add up to an intertwined, interconnected infrastructure at the system level.

The chapters offer more specific illustrations, whether or not they use the terminology of communities of practice. The graduates of the CIEL programme in British Columbia (Halbert and Kaser, Chapter 5) can also: "continue to extend their learning and deepen their connections ... through on-going involvement in the networks of inquiry and innovation. This layering of networked learning opportunities helps to sustain and extend their leadership influence." Owen from South Australia summarises the benefits of the system-wide networked innovation in Chapter 5 as: "through an on-going and expanded Innovation Community of Practice, individual site leaders and their communities are able to use their experience and influence to work collaboratively to shape those future directions and ensure that the new department has innovation as a predominant aspect of its work." The careful building of a system-wide community of stakeholders in Catalonia, Spain supported by research and by connection to international expertise, is described in detail in Chapter 6.

James Spillane in Chapter 2 argues both the need to look at different levels beyond the school or learning environment and observes, for the United States at least, that "system-level infrastructure for supporting classroom teaching is fragmented and impoverished". School autonomy, as commonly advocated, may indeed exacerbate the problem of inadequate social and human capital at the meso and macro levels if autonomy is mistaken for isolation. When the aim is to build the larger communities of practice and system-level infrastructure, the stimulus may come either through the networking of different learning environments or through the policy support helping to create and maintain such infrastructure.

Tanja Westfall-Greiter illustrates the latter in Austria in Chapter 5 in the education ministry support for the *Lerndesigners* through the national qualifications and capacity building to add necessary status and skills, and through the funding and willingness to organise the *Lernateliers* that bring together the *Lerndesigners* from around the country. Tubin and Owen both refer to system-level identification and support for networks of innovative schools in Israel and South Australia, respectively. The South Australian department draws parallels with the Austrian and Israeli examples: "the work of the innovative schools across the South Australian public education system has been supported through a small team operating in the department's central office".

Roser Salavert describes as a "major organisational breakthrough" in New York City schools a decade ago "the requirement that principals had to join a network of their choice". This is also interesting in raising the question of the balance of the mandatory vs. voluntary nature of engagement. Several authors insist on the voluntary nature of their programme (such as the Advisory Team in Norway) but the requirement that there is engagement by leaders in wider communities of practice (while leaving open the nature of that engagement) is an interesting example of system-level learning leadership.

Finally, Dorit Tubin in Chapter 5 explicitly discusses conditions that enhance leadership and the exercise of influence at the system level:

> Learning leadership can usefully be understood as the ability to influence others to accomplish common goals of improving the learning environment(s) within and beyond the classroom. This definition contains four elements that represent the conditions for learning leadership to flourish at scale: *1)* social position; *2)* the ability to choose a common goal and develop a vision; *3)* the capacity to influence others and create a structure; and *4)* the ability to evaluate and provide feedback.

This places more emphasis on improvement around common goals than our definition, but helpfully identifies conditions for system-level leadership, bringing in a sociological understanding of the nature of influence.

The "who" of learning leadership

Addressing who leads in schools and education is at once to engage in contested terrain. We have deliberately focused in this volume more on leadership than on leaders. A great deal of the literature has stressed that leadership does not depend on formal position, which usually means the position of school principal, but instead may and should be exercised by a much wider range of influential players in a distributed way. But while it is surely correct that leadership does not depend on formal position this is not only because others are involved but because formal position is no guarantee that leadership will be exercised.

Leadership is about providing direction and taking responsibility for making it happen, a responsibility and task that may or may not be carried out by those in authority. As we know from previous work (e.g. OECD, 2008a), and as Spillane reminds us in Chapter 2, education systems differ widely concerning the expectations associated with particular role positions so that what may look at first sight to be the same formal post (e.g. school principal) can turn out to be very different positions in practice depending on the setting and system.

Even within systems, sharing similar cultures and traditions, some occupying a particular authority position may choose to exercise leadership whereas others shy away from the task. MacBeath (Chapter 3) reports the typology of headships he and colleagues developed in an earlier study in Scotland to illustrate that there is no automatic match between formal position and how that is exercised in practice. The five categories in MacBeath et al. (2009) are: the "dutifully compliant", the "cautiously pragmatic", the "quietly self-confident", the "bullishly self-assertive, and the self-confessed "defiant risk-takers". By definition, the "dutifully compliant" will not provide active leadership. MacBeath generalises this by reference to the distinction between explicit and implicit leadership:

> Leadership may be made plainly visible in the hierarchy of the school or, alternatively, may not be easy to perceive because it is dispersed, less invested in institutional authority than in shared endeavour, enacted spontaneously by those who singly or in concert take responsibility for their fellow beings. These two forms of leadership, explicit and implicit, often exist in tension, defined by the structural order or expressed in the flow of activity in which members of the school community are engaged.

Assuming any simple correspondence between formal position and the exercise of leadership is thus hazardous both because those in the same formal authority position may exercise leadership very differently *and* because leadership is never vested in one single individual but is always distributed to some degree.

At this point, it is helpful to return to our project focus on learning environments. An important reason for adopting this lens and terminology is precisely to start with the nature and organisation of learning, rather than to start with the institutions within which this takes place. Both matter, of course, but how questions and solutions are framed depend critically on the starting point. To use Spillane's language (Chapter 2), we are focused on the core activity of what goes on inside the "schoolhouse" (as well as other settings) rather than on the "schoolhouse" itself.

With this starting point, it is obvious that formal institutional position is insufficient by itself to understand learning leadership. It becomes an empirical matter to establish who is influential in decision making over learning, rather than rely on the assignation of position in institutions, however important these may be (see below). As discussed in relation to the "what" of learning leadership, it is necessary, following Spillane, to see leadership as people in interaction, not just their individual actions, and this too is to move beyond the individual occupants of particular positions. We noted Elmore's (2008) assertion that progress brings more complex forms of leadership, less defined by formal roles. The increased organisational complexity of innovative learning environments, as they extend ambitions and partners, argues similarly for more complex forms of leadership.

In this section, therefore, we can look at different insights about who is engaged in learning leadership drawing on the different chapters, starting with schools but extending the focus beyond, both in terms of different partners and players (the "breadth" of learning leadership) and in terms of the level of operation in systemic terms (the "depth").

Principals and senior school managers

James Spillane in Chapter 2, himself internationally known for his work on distributed leadership, seeks to correct any misunderstanding that to accept the importance of distributed leadership must somehow diminish or come at the expense of the role of principals and senior school management. As he puts it:

> … the "heroic leader paradigm" is challenged (Yukl, 1999), and instead we seek to understand how responsibility for leadership and work gets distributed across multiple individuals on the ground. Such recognition, contrary to popular writing on distributed leadership, in no way

negates the important role of the principal in school leadership. Indeed, empirical work from a distributed perspective (as distinct from armchair theorising) consistently points to the critical role of the school principal (Camburn, Rowan and Taylor, 2003; Spillane and Diamond, 2007).

As well as leading learning strategies themselves, a number of the school-based cases make it clear that, even when teacher leaders are the central focus of efforts, the learning leadership of principals is also fundamental, giving permission and space and rallying the wider team. This is repeated throughout the different chapters:

> The management team is another key element with a central role in every case, although the distributed nature of leadership and collaborative leadership, based on the participation of the members of the team itself or on the creation of broader co-ordination teams, are also given recognition. In many cases, the team creates conditions that give rise to leadership in small teaching teams for a cycle or linked to a project. (Jolonch, Martinez and Badia; Chapter 6)

> Distributing leadership places even greater onus on senior school leaders, especially principals, to orchestrate and secure alignment, consistency and coherence of policy and leadership practices across the school. Flatter structures bring principals and senior leaders into closer functional relationships with classroom teachers. (Dimmock, Kwek and Toh; Chapter 4)

> The school leader's role in supporting professional learning teams cannot be overestimated. Teachers working together in teams, focusing on particular student groups and sharing leadership and responsibility for the learning of others, need to be supported by leaders who not only provide time and funding for professional learning to occur, but who support the establishment of teams as "deliberate structures where people can challenge each other about the level at which they do that work" (Owen, 2012: Leader Interview 3). (Owen; Chapter 5)

The creation of community, as discussed above as part of the "how" of learning leadership, will often depend critically on the activities and permission of principals and senior managers.

Therefore, exercising the potential opened up by dint of occupying a formal leadership position means that "principals matter". It is just as fallacious to assume that "position doesn't matter" as it is to assume that "position defines everything". We noted Spillane's endorsement of the critical role of principal; Dorit Tubin, in her analysis of the conditions for the exercise of learning leadership (Chapter 5), includes "social position" and "the capacity to influence others and create a structure", both of which are facilitated (but not guaranteed) by occupying a formal position of authority, wherever in the system that might be. Jolonch, Martinez and Badia (Chapter 6), however, warn of the dangers of "saturation of, or excessive dependency on, a small number of people" when it means that there is an insufficient foundation or spread of leadership within the organisation that it endangers continuity or sustainability in the medium or long term.

The distribution of distributed leadership

Spillane in Chapter 2 discusses findings from the United States about how many people and who is engaged in leadership work in schools, in describing what "distributed" means. A substantial number are so engaged even in primary schools, and still more might be expected to be active leaders in the more complex learning environments of secondary school-age learners:

> A study of over 100 geographically dispersed elementary schools, for example, found that responsibility for leadership functions was distributed over teams of leaders, typically ranging from 3 to 7 people including principals, assistant principals and coaches. Further, while principals tended to take responsibility for work that spanned all aspects of leadership, coaches and other specialists tended to focus on leading teaching (Camburn, Rowan and Taylor, 2003). Another study including all 30 elementary schools in one urban school district found that, including the school principal, the average number of full-time formal leaders per school was 3.5 (Spillane and Healey, 2010; Spillane, Healey and Kim, 2010). Factoring in individuals who had classroom teaching responsibilities as well as leadership responsibilities increased this number substantially … Exactly how leadership is distributed across multiple individuals appears to depend on various factors, such as the type of leadership function or routine (Camburn, Rowan and Taylor, 2003; Heller and Firestone, 1995), the subject matter (Spillane, 2005), the school's size (Camburn, Rowan and Taylor., 2003), the school type (Portin et al., 2003), and whether the school's leadership team is well established or new (Copland, 2003; Harris, 2002).

Many of those involved in distributed leadership are teacher leaders. Teacher leadership, whether formal or informal, is generally exerted by teachers with expertise who participate in efforts to develop the quality of teaching and learning within schools and support colleagues' development (York-Barr and Duke, 2004). Tanja Westfall-Greiter from Austria (Chapter 5) describes a specific set of roles for teacher leaders that has been created with the view of enhancing learning design through agents of change. The Austrian example of *Lerndesigners* adopts language that fits entirely with that of the ILE project; they are nominated from among the existing teachers:

Lerndesigners are teacher leaders with specific expertise in areas of curriculum and instructional development related to the reform goals of equity and excellence. Each NMS site designates a teacher to be the *Lerndesigner,* who attends national and regional *"Lernateliers"* as well as local networking events. Ideally they act as change agents in a shared leadership dynamic with school principals and other teacher leaders (subject co-ordinators, school development teams, etc.).

Especially at the beginning of the reform, there were many questions about what this new role was, and in any event this is not an official function inscribed in school legislation with corresponding salary structures so that each *Lerndesigner* creates his or her own role, with their colleagues, in their own context. This illustrates the characterisation of learning leadership as "emergent" and "co-produced" (Spillane, Chapter 2). The identified need for explicit, newly-defined change agents which is particular to the Austrian reform drive relates back to the "how" of learning leadership.

The Norwegian example offered by Christiansen and Tronsmo (Chapter 5) shares some parallels with the Austrian one in respect of the creation of a particular role for change agents in which staff are specifically selected, the nature of the work is voluntary and varied and dependent on local circumstances, and it is part of a deliberate policy strategy of innovating to raise quality. But the examples are by no means identical: the Norwegian Advisory Team personnel are recruited primarily from among the groups to which the guidance will be directed – those from administration and senior school leaders/managers. Their role is seen as one of guidance, identifying development needs, planning the development project, and offering guidance to put it into practice.

The purpose of this section has not been to rehearse the range of arguments in favour of distributed leadership – an argument that is widely accepted even for relatively traditional schools, let alone more complex and innovative learning environments – but to give some content to what this means in practice in fleshing out the "who" of learning leadership. Obviously, this is not meant to be a review, let alone a comprehensive one, of the different participants that may engage in distributed leadership but draws primarily on the sources available in this report. This also anticipates the next section ("where"), in which we engage with the dominant assumption that the settings and partners are well established and centred around schools. The more that settings are widened and different partners engaged as part of the innovative extension of learning environments, the more complex and varied will be those who join the cast list of distributed learning leadership.

Students in learning leadership

A school that focuses on learning seeks the involvement of all its constituencies, including its students (Salavert, Chapter 5, referring to Leithwood, et al., 2004). The notion of "learning communities" would be strangely incomplete if it excluded those whom the learning is for, first and foremost – the young people. The impact of students in a formal role should not be underestimated, argues Salavert, and her own experience has been to guide principals to establish academic advisories, as well as student councils, or other forms of student governance. With the active participation of students in strategies to improve learning, it fosters responsibility for their own learning while demonstrating their ability to contribute to sustaining effective learning environments.

Similarly, in all of the innovation sites in Catalonia, Spain (Chapter 6), it was clear that the learners should assume leadership responsibilities for their learning, and assist with collective learning by contributing to group participation and teamwork often stemming from problems or projects proposed by the learners as a group. MacBeath (Chapter 3) argues that attending to student "voice" has been a growing feature in a number of countries over recent decades. He points towards the example of New Zealand, where students are seen as playing a key role in evaluating the quality of their school, and where staff have equipped their students with the skills and vocabulary to talk about pedagogy and what makes for good learning.

Later in Chapter 3, MacBeath returns to the role of young learners exercising leadership, in relation to non-formal programmes that depend on the very active engagement of the young people. For example, discussing the Children's University: "As children's participation and commitment continue to increase, they begin to play a more proactive role in generating ideas for future activities and grow greater confidence in assuming leadership".

Calling for young people to assume leadership of their learning should be understood from the distributed perspective of sharing leadership with others. Simply creating possibilities for access and handing over responsibility to students to make all the relevant choices and avail themselves of those possibilities – the more extreme advocacy of non-formal provision – is to abrogate the responsibility that all others in the leadership constellation should exercise. The ILE project has deliberately avoided such perspectives, arguing instead that environments always involve educators and that they should apply the learning principles in which professionals exercise powerful responsibilities of leadership and design. MacBeath, while advocating learner leadership, makes the same point in concluding: "The more children and young people assume control of their own learning the greater the pedagogic insight and adaptability it will require of teachers and teacher leaders".

Far from young people's active role in learning leadership meaning a diminution of that exercised by important others, it means instead that those leaders and educators exercise even more demanding professionalism and leadership responsibility.

Learning leadership at different levels

Learning leadership is not confined to the immediate participants in micro-level learning environments. Creating the conditions for learning leadership and innovation to flourish on the ground calls for leadership to be exercised elsewhere. Of course, sometimes the exceptional school and learning community may be able to "go it alone" but that is scarcely a recipe for driving and sustaining deep learning change at scale. There needs to be some contribution from other partners at other levels, most obviously (but not exclusively) the leadership that comes from the top of formal education systems.

Even more than within schools, the exercise of learning leadership by others cannot be defined by position or formal authority. In some circumstances and systems, the central authorities may exercise very little leadership over learning but leave that to players and stakeholders much nearer to students and classrooms. Such leadership when it is exercised is through such ways as deliberately developing the capacity to sustain quality learning, curriculum guidelines, and the incentives and disincentives of accountability systems and funding, or it may involve specific initiatives to foster innovative learning environments. The general point is made by Spillane in Chapter 2, referring in particular to teaching as the practice that most influences the learning that takes place:

> A teacher and her pupils co-produce teaching, but their practice is enabled and constrained by arrangements beyond the immediate classroom (Cohen, 2011). The particular school in which the classroom is situated together with local, state, and national education government arrangements as well as an array of other agencies (e.g. textbook publishers, teacher preparation programmes and testing agencies) in the education sector are all critical to understanding leadership for teaching.

It is necessary here to recall the focus on innovative learning environments and the discussion under the "what" of learning leadership: our interest is not in the learning leadership provided by the politician who insists on a "back to basics" agenda or educational agencies who drive systems with accountability criteria embodying very limited interpretations of the knowledge and skills that young people need in today's world. Instead, our interest is in the leadership emerging from other levels in learning systems giving direction and fostering conditions on the ground to facilitate deep learning, develop 21st century competences, and apply such principles as those of OECD's *The Nature of Learning* (Dumont, Istance and Benavides, 2010).

Hence, two aspects of wider learning leadership may be underlined. First, learning systems are just too complex for leadership to be restricted only to one (school) level and to that exercised by formal leaders. Second, the leadership in question that we are addressing is that exercised in the promotion of contemporary agendas of powerful innovative learning, not any learning agenda and certainly not those that argue for a return to the traditional fare of a century ago.

Several chapters refer explicitly to the kind of system learning leadership that is exercised from the higher reaches of the education system, as summarised in the section on "how". Examples from Austria, Catalonia, New York City, Norway and South Australia in Chapters 5 and 6 all discuss the role of system-level players and agencies setting agendas, creating conditions, and offering support to initiatives to innovate learning. Some (Austria, Israel) mention the leadership provided by the individuals at the top (ministers, senior system managers). Tubin suggests: "Public education systems as bureaucracies, however, tend to have only few directors at the top and even fewer innovators. Thus, it is usually one person, sometimes together with a small leading team, who initiates and leads such reform". Just as in schools, however, it is necessary to be wary of the personal "heroic leader paradigm", and to recognise that others are involved, including specialist departmental teams as outlined for Austria, Israel and South Australia in Chapter 5.

Two more points are relevant to this section. First, the distinction between the macro system level and the meso network level is not a clear-cut one in the exercise of learning leadership. A strategy may be the creation of a network or learning community that itself operates as an arm of system leadership – macro in its origins, meso in its operation, systemic in its ambition. The NMS schools in Austria or the South Australian Innovation Community of Practice (Chapter 5) are such examples. The initiative outlined in Chapter 6, in Catalonia, Spain, is another impressive example of creating a meso-level network of chosen stakeholders, yet which is intended to influence practice system wide.

The Catalan example introduces the second relevant point here. The leadership of this development and research leadership initiative is a foundation (the Jaume Bofill Foundation), not the formal education authorities. Hence, not only are learning environments inclusive of organisations and partners outside the conventional system, but also learning systems include such partners who may come to exercise a significant role of leadership and support. Foundations are exercising this role in many education systems; certain large corporations and social movements have taken on similar leadership roles as well. This is not a particularly recent phenomenon: the

OECD/CERI "Schooling for Tomorrow" study on networks of innovation identified and discussed several examples a decade ago (OECD, 2003).

OECD's ILE project as a contributor to learning leadership

The examples discussed in this report give several direct examples of how OECD's Innovative Learning Environments project has contributed through stimulus, support and legitimation of locally based activities. It has thus played its own contributory role of learning leadership.

The CIEL programme in British Columbia is a year-long graduate programme for formal and informal leaders (Chapter 5). Both Canadian and international perspectives are central to the curriculum, and it uses the OECD report *The Nature of Learning: Using Research to Inspire Practice* (Dumont, Istance and Benavides, 2010) as a basis for in-depth study with educational leaders:

> The seven concluding learning principles from *The Nature of Learning* act as a set of cognitive tools in the leadership programme. CIEL participants study the research, explore each principle individually, enact inquiries to actualise the seven principles in their contexts, and present the results of their inquiries to their colleagues in a final presentation. In addition – and this is extremely important to transforming leadership practices – participants experience all seven of the learning principles as a deliberate part of their own learning in the programme. (Chapter 5)

The CIEL programme also calls for the exploration of the case studies from the OECD/ILE "Inventory" (see OECD, 2013) as a way of prompting new thinking and action based on experiences in other parts of the world. This is an example where the international learning project has provided the inspiration and starting materials for leadership development in a particular schooling system.

Networking around engagement in the OECD ILE project has happened in South Australia (Chapter 5), in which a state-wide Innovation Community of Practice was established around the learning environments selected to be part of the international project, but now with a life of its own well beyond this original purpose.

> During 2011, seven South Australian Department for Education and Child Development (DECD) schools, preschools and early learning centres were accepted into the OECD Innovative Learning Environment (ILE) project, having met the criteria for significant innovation. An additional 8 sites have since been identified by the department as being significantly innovative; with all 15 now

being recognised and operating within the state-wide Innovation Community of Practice (CoP) ... being part of a systems approach within a community of practice has benefits and the importance of connection to the innovation work of the OECD is acknowledged.

However, the most profound example of the influence of this international project reported in this volume is in the work that has led to this research and report on learning leadership, i.e. the collaboration with the Jaume Bofill Foundation in Spain. This is described in detail in Chapter 6. It details how a multi-stakeholder partnership was established, together with a supporting research programme on learning leadership, under the drive and leadership of the Foundation. The engagement and collaboration with the OECD enabled international frameworks and expertise to be accessible, and provided legitimacy as well as inspiration. The example in essence involved the creation of a high-level community of practice, combining local and international participants, supported by research, seminars, and feedback in such ways as teacher education. The benefits are reciprocal: the example has led to as much development work at the international level as the international project has fed into regional and local-level development.

Naturally, it is to be hoped that such an influence may continue in a more diffuse way internationally with the publication of this report.

The "where" of learning leadership

A substantial overlap occurs between the "Who" and the "Where" of learning leadership. Our discussion above about the different players at different levels who are an integral part of learning leadership might equally have been included in this section. Combining different players, levels and locations adds up to a complex layering of learning leadership. For instance, Halbert and Kaser in Chapter 5 refer to the key role of networks and communities of practice but also to creating special spaces and their own learning leadership role in British Columbia as establishing: "'third spaces' outside the rhetoric of conflict where educators can engage in inquiry, experience new learning and try out new practices that will benefit their learners".

A recurring theme in the chapters of this report is the importance of context. This means a lot more than geographical location. Systems differ significantly in terms of traditions, rules and opportunities. Wide socio-cultural and economic variations exist within each country and system that impinge sharply on the possibilities for different leadership strategies. Context matters, but, as James Spillane cautions in Chapter 2, this is simpler to state than to grasp in its implications:

Social structure makes human interaction possible. The particulars of this social structure both enable and constrain how individuals interact with one another, and in this way define practice. The mantra "context matters" is overused and under-understood in education. It is often treated by school reformers as a nuisance and by researchers as a "catch-all" variable for why interventions fail or succeed. Both are unfortunate because more sophistication is essential in thinking about the situation as it relates to practice.

Context is not something that is just external to schools and learning environments. Social context comes right inside schools and classrooms, most obviously via the learners themselves, who arrive each day with a raft of beliefs and experiences formed in families and communities. It is precisely when context enters directly into the learning environment that it becomes so important for learning leadership. MacBeath in Chapter 3 suggests that higher expectations and professionalism in the schools of the 21st century mean that there is now greater onus on management and teachers to respond appropriately to the variation that inevitably accompanies sensitivity to context. He quotes Mayer, Pecheone and Merino, who write: "Challenging curriculum expectations and more diverse learners mean that teachers have to be more sophisticated in their understanding of the effects of context and learner variability on teaching and learning." (2012: 115)

Learning environments provide their own context for learning to take place. Leadership strategies to design and redesign such environments are ways of altering the context for the educators and the learners in ways that are more engaging and more nearly meet their needs and interests. One of the most important extensions of the terrain of learning leadership that stems from moving beyond the institutional parameters of "schools" and "classrooms" is discussed next through incorporating the non-formal, also representing some of the most challenging aspects of leadership and governance.

Learning leadership incorporating informal and non-formal settings

The project on Innovative Learning Environments has taken for granted that not all the learning of interest takes place within places called schools, while recognising that schools remain absolutely core institutions in contemporary societies. As schools innovate they often draw on partners and sources of knowledge outside the traditional school boundaries (OECD, 2013). New non-school learning environments are also created, with particular appeal for young people. Even more complex, the learning environments being created for young people involve combinations of such approaches and settings for learning – partly school-based, partly non-school based – as increasingly mainstream developments.

The extension of, and challenges to, approaches to leadership that have predominantly assumed that both the people involved ("who") and the setting ("where") are school-based are clear. The design and leadership challenge is of a new order when it means to bring together the formal and non-formal, the school-based and the community-based, different human and learning resources with different professional cultures. This has also been explored in ILE work, albeit less in terms of leadership, through analysis of "hybrid learning environments" (Zitter and Hoeve, 2012).

The chapter of this report that deals with this most directly is that of John MacBeath (Chapter 3). In part, the leadership challenge is to create the structures and capacities to absorb the different kind of learning that is informal into designed formal programmes. He characterises informal learning as more social, spontaneous and exploratory: "Learning to swim, ride a bicycle, play the piano, read a map, navigate unfamiliar terrain, lead a team, solve a problem, all benefit from certain common features – they are embedded in relationships, learner-centred, concerned with skills and dispositions, contextualised, enjoyable but risky, supportive but challenging, relaxed but alert, age blind."

MacBeath describes examples of non-formal programmes that are organised outside mainstream school settings, building on the benefits of informal learning as described above yet in ways that are reproducible and with quality assurance. They include the Other Learning Experiences (OLE) in Hong Kong, the Parkway model in Philadelphia, the Learning School in Scotland, and the Children's University in the UK that seeks to offer innovative learning activities to 7-14 year-olds outside normal school hours. For MacBeath, such examples hold considerable promise in ways that are yet to be properly realised: "The potential of sites for learning ('construction sites') is still largely unexplored but have a major contribution to make in bringing learning to life".

MacBeath further argues that, as learning environments change and become more innovative by absorbing larger non-formal elements, the demands on learning leadership increase:

> The greater the opportunities that arise to exploit learning sites beyond the classroom the more it will demand of leaders of learning. It will require them to help teachers to extend their repertoire, individually and in concert. The more children and young people assume control of their own learning the greater the pedagogic insight and adaptability it will require of teachers and teacher leaders. The more children and young people become independent and interdependent learners the greater the strategic resourcefulness it will imply for those who lead and shape children's learning.

Understanding the complexities involved in these and similar examples has scarcely begun in a literature that has been so dominated by the "place called school". The pedagogical demands are seen to grow through incorporating non-formal sites and programmes, yet many of those teaching in non-formal settings will not be trained for such demands nor belong to the kinds of "learning communities" that are discussed repeatedly in this volume as an integral part of developing learning leadership. So long as these examples remain outside the main programmes and provisions of mainstream education, the learning leadership rests with those who run them and the young people and their parents who take part.

Yet, the scope for change and innovation is greatly enhanced the more that they cease to be marginal activities for weekend or vacation learning, but become increasingly integrated within learning designs incorporating formal learning as well. And then the leadership and management challenges increase significantly. MacBeath recognises that the "alternative" nature of the programmes he presents are at once their appeal but also their limiting factor as regards the scope for wider innovative change: "However, as long as the Children's University is seen as a contrast, a counterbalance or an alternative to school the less scope there is for systemic change". These represent important extensions of the discussion of learning leadership, management and governance. They arise the more young people are not just learning in school but in innovative learning environments, incorporating a range of different professionals, volunteers, partners, communities that both reinvigorate their "pedagogical core" and extend their boundaries outwards via a range of partnerships (see OECD, 2013).

In conclusion, the "where" (and "who") of learning leadership have been relatively neglected through assuming that the settings and partners are familiar and centred around schools. The more that settings are widened and different partners engaged as part of the innovation of learning environments, the more the leadership complexity and issues arising should be addressed and clarified.

The "when" of learning leadership

As the chapters of this report emphasise, there is no particular time for learning leadership and the creation of innovative learning environments: they should be constants not choices. Arguably, they are particularly necessary in circumstances in which educational organisation and administration has become routine rather than dynamic, or in which learning outcomes are worryingly low. By the same token, such circumstances might be expected to be especially hostile to the practice of good learning leadership.

However, even if we would argue that learning leadership should be a constant, time is a key dimension as illustrated in the chapters of this report.

The impetus to innovate, and the readiness for new learning leadership to get behind the drive to do so, can emerge especially in the face of severe pressure to respond to new circumstances. This is most vividly expressed in Chapter 6 by Jolonch, Martinez, and Badia:

> … the beginning of the change can be clearly identified: a milestone, a situation or a realisation of the need for change. The schools and projects analysed achieve the desired change at a particular moment, which the collective itself is able to identify. The schools analysed arrived at that call for change via various routes; some examples include: a sustained decrease in enrolments, a change in the characteristics of the management team and its mandate, an awareness of the school's deteriorating image within the neighbourhood, a continued decline in academic results, or the creation of a new school from the division of an existing one. These processes lead to a "breaking point" or a point of change from the previous stage for the learning environment.

It need not be a full crisis, but the costs of trying to maintain the *status quo* or of doing nothing becoming greater than the perceived benefits of business as usual. Dimmock, Kwek and Toh in Chapter 4 present innovative case study schools in Singapore where there was no urgency to change as the schools could understandably have rested on the laurels of conventional high performance. Nevertheless, due to courageous leadership and the perception that what is high performance in the first decade of the 21st century may well not suffice by 2020, the leadership of the schools embarked on new trajectories even when the external pressure to do so was low. Setting milestones and establishing visions, necessarily means looking out ahead into the future and being ready to activate changes over time. It is Dimmock, Kwek and Toh (Chapter 4) who focus most on time in this volume. They do it in at least two different ways.

First, their approach to learning leadership as "backward mapping", consistent also with Elmore and others such as Wiggins and McTighe (2005), deliberately introduces future planning into the leadership process – determining where one wishes to be at a fixed time ahead, and then working out strategies to ensure one has at least a chance of reaching those large objectives. This parallels the futures thinking that has inspired a great deal of earlier OECD/CERI work under the heading of Schooling for Tomorrow (see for example OECD, 2001, 2006). The authors of Chapter 4 refer to a dictum attributed to Covey (1989): "successful people begin with the end in mind". Anticipation is also about continuation of those able to drive the learning project, as Jolonch, Martinez and Badia emphasise in Chapter 6 in identifying the mindfulness of senior leaders in their innovation sites to recruit those who will continue the good work.

Second, Dimmock, Kwek and Toh emphasise in their model and in their two cases of learning leadership in practice how transformation takes time (up to a decade), how trajectories are needed in which certain things must be done before others in terms of context and realising the vision, and how the visions and strategies themselves can change over time. The ILE framework with its cycles of leadership, design, learning, evaluation and feedback, and redesign are based on the passage of time and the possibility to see the impact of leadership decisions on patterns of learning and to make organisational decisions accordingly. Professional learning takes time. Establishing trust and developing partnerships take time. Recognising the importance of time is not to give up on the urgency of innovation and change; it is simply that, with the best will in the world, learning environments cannot be created or modelled overnight.

Concluding orientations on learning leadership

Learning leadership is critical for reform and innovation. It is so important because leadership is so influential of direction and outcomes, whether at the micro level of schools and learning environments or of broader systems. Learning is the core business of education and so this is the paramount form and business of leadership – the leadership that is focused on creating and sustaining environments that are conducive to good learning. Innovation is an integral part of the exercise of learning leadership in setting new directions and designing learning environments.

Learning leadership is about engaging in the design, implementation and sustainability of powerful innovative learning environments. It is about setting direction and taking responsibility for making it happen. Learning leadership is exercised through distributed, connected activity and relationships. It extends beyond formal players to include different partners, and may be exercised at different levels of the overall learning system. It includes "learning management" in the commitment to transform, persevere and make change happen.

Learning leadership puts creating the conditions for 21st century learning and teaching at the core of leadership practice. Students' learning is at the heart of the enterprise; the core work is to ensure deep 21st century learning, whatever the environment. Designing and developing innovative learning environments to meet such ambitions require highly demanding teaching repertoires and for everyone to keep learning, unlearning, and relearning. Continuous learning of all players and partners is a condition of successful implementation and sustainability.

Learning leadership demonstrates creativity and often courage. Innovating, designing, bringing others on board, and redesigning all call on the exercise of creativity. Deep shifts in mindset and practice and the capacity to keep the long-term vision in view are needed when the aim is transformation, even if the starting point may be incremental. The leadership focus is on deep changes to practice, structures and cultures – not just tinkering – and ensuring that the supporting conditions are in place. This often calls for the exercise of courage as well as creativity.

Learning leadership models and nurtures 21ˢᵗ century professionalism. Through professional learning, inquiry and self-evaluation, learning leaders are themselves high-level knowledge workers. By engaging in appropriate professional learning and creating conditions for others to do the same, they demonstrate and spread a similar professionalism throughout their wider communities. Professional learning blends theory and practice, with opportunities for practical experimentation in teaching and organisation, and learning from these experiences and through feedback.

Learning leadership is social and connected. Learning leadership is fundamentally social in nature; interaction is the essence of leadership practice. A team endeavour, it depends on carefully crafted collaborative activity to deepen, spread and maintain the learning. Learning leadership develops, grows and is sustained through participation in professional learning communities and networks. This means that the "meso" level (of networks rather than as an administrative layer) is critical, to be nurtured through learning leadership and with its own challenges as an arena for the exercise of learning leadership.

The more learning environments innovate, the more learning leadership will come from diverse non-formal partners, requiring much greater attention to their roles and capacities. The educational leadership literature has been dominated by the "place called school". Increasingly, innovative learning incorporates non-formal sites and approaches in ways that make growing pedagogical and organisational demands. Learning leadership and professional learning communities must incorporate and extend to a range of different professionals, partners, and communities.

Transformative learning leadership involves complex multi-level chemistry. Systemic innovation and sustainability of powerful 21ˢᵗ century learning environments depend on learning leadership at different levels. Initial impetus might come from any level, from within the formal system and from other partners. For this impetus to be sustained it needs leadership to be exercised in the other levels and settings to nurture that initial drive.

Learning leadership is needed at the system level. This may be to create the initial space for innovation or it may respond to micro-level innovation. There is a key policy role in creating conditions for networked professional learning to take place. It may require courageous leadership to ensure that governance and accountability systems align with the ambition of creating powerful, innovative learning environments, or at least are not pulling in opposing directions.

Questions for learning leaders

Learning leadership, in the terms outlined in this chapter, is challenging for practice and not a quick fix. For many starting out, it may be a long journey, but it is one that is essential in our view to realise innovative learning environments for 21st century effectiveness.

Having read this chapter, you may wish to reflect on or use the chapter to engage in a conversation in your learning community about the following questions:

- What has resonated with you?

- What has challenged your thinking?

- When you think of your own examples and experiences of learning leadership, how do they map on to the interrogative framework – Why? What? How? Who? Where? and Who?

- What other reflections do you have on learning leadership?

- How might you use, adapt and/or take forward these ideas?

Here are some further questions for reflection and dialogue as you read the expert contributions and international cases in the following chapters:

- What interested you most and why?

- What is similar or different in your experience and contexts?

- How might you adapt any of the international examples for development in your contexts?

- What further reflections do you have on learning leadership?

Note

1. The chapter has been drafted by David Istance, of the OECD Secretariat, and Louise Stoll, of the Institute of Education, University of London, drawing heavily on the inputs of the other authors of this volume.

References

Barth, R.S. (2000), "Foreword", in P.J. Wald and M. Castleberry (eds.), *Educators as Learners: Establishing a Professional Learning Community in Your School*, ASCD (Association for Supervision and Curriculum Development), Alexandria, VA, www.ascd.org/publications/books/100005/chapters/Foreword.aspx.

Camburn, E.M., B. Rowan and J.E. Taylor (2003), "Distributed leadership in schools: The case of elementary schools adopting comprehensive school reform models", *Educational Evaulation and Policy Analysis,* 25(4), 347-373.

Cheng, E.C.K and M.L. Lo (2013), *The Approach of Learning Study: Its Origin and Implications*, OECD CERI Innovative Learning Environments project, OECD, Paris, www.oecd.org/edu/ceri/Eric Cheng.Learning Study.pdf.

Cohen, D.K. (2011), *Teaching and Its Predicaments,* Harvard University Press, Cambridge, MA.

Copland, M.A. (2003), "Leadership of inquiry: Building and sustaining capacity for school improvement", *Educational Evaluation and Policy Analysis, 25*(4), 375-395.

Covey, S.R. (1989), *The Seven Habits of Highly Effective People,* Free Press, New York.

Cuban, L. (1995), "The hidden variable: How organizations influence teacher responses to secondary science curriculum reform", *Theory into Practice*, 34(1), 4-11.

Darling-Hammond, L. et al. (2009), *Professional Learning in the Learning Profession: A Status Report on Teacher Development in the United States and Abroad,* NSDC (National Staff Development Council), Dallas, Texas.

Dempster, N., S. Lovett and B. Flückiger (2011), *Strategies to Develop School Leadership: A Select Literature Review,* Australian Institute for Teaching and School Leadership, Melbourne.

Dimmock, C. (2012), *Leadership, Capacity Building and School Improvement: Concepts, Themes and Impact,* Routledge, London.

Dimmock, C. (2000), *Designing the Learning-Centred School: A Cross-Cultural Perspective,* The Falmer Press, London.

Dumont, H., D. Istance and F. Benavides (eds.) (2010), *The Nature of Learning: Using Research to Inspire Practice,* OECD Publishing, Paris. http://dx.doi.org/10.1787/9789264086487-en.

Elmore, R. (2008), "Leadership as the practice of improvement", in *Improving School Leadership, Volume 2, Case Studies on System Leadership*, OECD Publishing, Paris. http://dx.doi.org/10.1787/9789264039551-4-en.

Halbert, J. and L. Kaser (2013), *Spirals of Inquiry: For Quality and Equity,* BCPVPA (British Columbia Principals' and Vice-Principals' Association) Press, Vancouver.

Hampden-Turner, C. (2007), "Keynote address", Leadership of Learning Seminar, Peterhouse College, Cambridge, April.

Hargreaves, A. and D. Fink (2000), "The three dimensions of education reform", *Educational Leadership*, 57(7), 30-34.

Hargreaves, A. and M. Fullan (2012), *Professional Capital: Transforming Teaching in Every School,* Routledge.

Harris, A. (2002), "Effective leadership in schools facing challenging contexts", *School Leadership and Management*, 22(1), 15-26.

Heifetz, R.A. and M. Linsky (2002), *Leadership on the Line: Staying Alive through the Dangers of Leading,* Harvard Business School Press.

Heller, M.F. and W.A. Firestone (1995), "Who's in charge here? Sources of leadership for change in eight schools", *Elementary School Journal, 96*(1), 65-86.

Hofstede, G. (1991), *Culture and Organisations*, McGraw-Hill, London.

Hopkins, D. (2008) "Realising the potential of system leadership", in *Improving School Leadership, Volume 2, Case Studies on System Leadership*, OECD Publishing, Paris. http://dx.doi.org/10.1787/9789264039551-3-en.

Hoy, A. and P. Murphy (2001), "Teaching educational psychology to the implicit mind", in B. Torff, and R. Sternberg (eds.), *Understanding and Teaching the Intuitive Mind: Student and Teacher Learning,* Lawrence Erlbaum Associates, Mahwah, NJ.

Huber, S.G. (2011), "Leadership for learning – learning for leadership: The impact of professional development", in J. MacBeath and T. Townsend (eds.), *Springer International Handbook on Leadership for Learning,* Springer, Dordrecht.

Huber, S.G. (ed.) (2010), *School Leadership: International Perspectives*, Springer, Dordrecht.

Joyce, B. and B. Showers (2002), *Student Achievement through Staff Development,* 3rd edition, Longman, New York.

Kennedy, M.M. (1999), "The role of pre-service teacher education", in L. Darling-Hammond and G. Sykes (eds.), *Teaching as the Learning Profession: Handbook of Teaching and Policy,* Jossey Bass, San Francisco.

Leithwood, K., K. Seashore, S. Anderson and K. Wahlstrom (2004), *How Leadership Influences Student Learning,* Center for Applied Research and Educational Improvement, Ontario Institute for Studies in Education, Toronto.

MacBeath, J. et al. (2009), *The Recruitment and Retention of Headteachers in Scotland,* Scottish Government, Edinburgh.

Mayer, D., R. Pecheone and N. Merino (2012), "Rethinking teacher education in Australia", in L. Darling-Hammond and A. Lieberman (eds.), *Teacher Education around the World,* Routledge, New York.

Mintzberg, H. (2009), *Managing,* Prentice Hall.

Nonaka, I. and H. Takeuchi (1995), *The Knowledge-Creating Company,* Oxford University Press, New York.

OECD (2013), *Innovative Learning Environments,* OECD Publishing, Paris. http://dx.doi.org/10.1787/9789264203488-en.

OECD (2009), *Creating Effective Teaching and Learning Environments: First Results from TALIS,* OECD Publishing, Paris. http://dx.doi.org/10.1787/9789264068780-en.

OECD (2008a), *Improving School Leadership, Volume 1, Policy and Practice,* OECD Publishing, Paris. http://dx.doi.org/10.1787/9789264044715-en.

OECD (2008b), *Improving School Leadership, Volume 2, Case Studies on System Leadership,* OECD Publishing, Paris. http://dx.doi.org/10.1787/9789264039551-en.

OECD (2006), *Think Scenarios, Rethink Education,* OECD Publishing, Paris. http://dx.doi.org/10.1787/9789264023642-en.

OECD (2003), *Networks of Innovation: Towards New Models for Managing Schools and Systems,* OECD Publishing, Paris. http://dx.doi.org/10.1787/9789264100350-en.

OECD (2001), *What Schools for the Future?* OECD Publishing, Paris. http://dx.doi.org/10.1787/9789264195004-en.

Owen, S. (2012), "'Fertile questions,' 'multi-age groupings', 'campfires' and 'master classes' for specialist skill-building: Innovative Learning

Environments and support professional learning or 'teacher engagers' within South Australian and international contexts", Peer-reviewed paper presented at World Education Research Association (WERA) Focal meeting at the Australian Association for Research in Education (AARE) Conference, 2-6 December, University of Sydney, Australia, www.aare. edu.au/papers/2012/Susanne%20Owen%20Paper.pdf.

Portin, B., P. Schneider, M. DeArmond and L. Gundlach (2003), *Making Sense of Leading Schools: A Study of the School Principalship,* Center on Reinventing Public Education, Washington University, Seattle.

Resnick, L.B., P.J. Spillane, P. Goldman and E.S. Rangel (2010), "Implementing innovation: From visionary models to everyday practice", in *The Nature of Learning: Using Research to Inspire Practice,* OECD Publishing, Paris. http://dx.doi.org/10.1787/9789264086487-14-en.

Robertson, J. (2013, in press), "Learning leadership", *Leading and Managing,* 19(2).

Sahlberg, P. (2011), *Finnish Lessons: What Can the World Learn from Educational Change in Finland?* Teachers College Press, Columbia University, New York.

Spillane, J.P., and K. Healey (2010), "Conceptualizing school leadership and management from a distributed perspective", *The Elementary School Journal, 111*(2), 253-281.

Spillane, J.P., K. Healey and C.M. Kim (2010), "Leading and managing instruction: Using social network analysis to explore formal and informal aspects of the elementary school organization", in A.J. Daly (ed.), *Social Network Theory and Educational Change*, Harvard Education Press, Cambridge, MA.

Spillane, J.P. and J.B. Diamond (2007), *Distributed Leadership in Practice,* Teachers College Press, New York.

Stinchcombe, A.L. (2001), *When Formality Works: Authority and Abstraction in Law and Organizations*, University of Chicago Press, Chicago.

Stoll, L. et al. (2006), "Professional learning communities: A review of the literature", *Journal of Educational Change*, 7(4), 221-258.

Stoll, L. and J. Temperley (2009), "Creative leadership: A challenge of our times", *School Leadership and Management*, 29(1), 63-76.

Talbert, J. and N. Scharff (2008), *The Scaffolded Apprenticeship Model of School Improvement through Leadership Development,* Center for Research on the Context of Teaching, Stanford University, California.

Timperley, H. (2011), *Realising the Power of Professional Learning*, Open University Press, Maidenhead.

Timperley, H., A. Wilson, H. Barr and I. Fung (2008), *Teacher Professional Learning and Development: Best Evidence Synthesis Iteration*, New Zealand Ministry of Education and University of Auckland.

Wiggins, G. and J. McTighe (2005), *Understanding by Design,* 2nd edition, ASCD, Alexandria, VA.

Yukl, G. (1999), "An evaluation of conceptual weaknesses in transformational and charistmatic leadership theories", *The Leadership Quarterly,* 10(2), 285-305.

York-Barr, J. and K. Duke (2004), "What do we know about teacher leadership? Findings from two decades of scholarship", *Review of Educational Research*, 74(3), 255-316.

Zitter, I. and A. Hoeve (2012), "Hybrid learning environments: Merging learning and working processes to facilitate knowledge integration and transitions", *OECD Education Working Papers,* No.81, OECD Publishing, Paris. http://dx.doi.org/10.1787/5k97785xwdvf-en.

Chapter 2

The practice of leading and managing teaching in educational organisations

James P. Spillane[1]

Northwestern University, USA

This chapter by James Spillane focuses on leading and managing teaching, described as "the core technology of schooling". He argues that too many analyses dwell on "leading the schoolhouse rather than the core work of the schoolhouse" and as a result are only weakly related to learning, teaching and leading their improvement. The chapter begins with consideration of the nature of teaching. It discusses the diagnosis and design work of leadership as the practice of leading teaching. It then focuses on diagnostic and design work centred on the school's organisational infrastructure: organisational routines; tools (e.g. classroom observation protocols); and formal positions, departments or sub-units (e.g. school subject departments and grade levels). The chapter focuses mostly on the school level, but it argues for a more comprehensive approach that goes beyond any one level of an education system to consider the multiple components and how (or not) they operate together.

Introduction

This chapter focuses on leading and managing classroom teaching, the core technology of schooling. While much of the work in this domain focuses on leadership and change, here the focus is intentionally on both leadership and management. Management is about maintenance (Cuban, 1988). This usage of the term differs from the more popular, and often pejorative, usage that focuses on running the schoolhouse rather than leading improvement efforts in teaching. The challenge for educators is not simply introducing and implementing change in education systems, but also maintaining changes once implemented. Rather than direct opposites or even enemies, change and constancy are closely related. While leadership and management are both critical, for readability purposes this chapter will only use the term "leadership", though in doing so, both leadership and management is implied (Spillane, 2006).

Teaching and efforts to lead it are central to this chapter's argument and essential rather than incidental for three reasons. First, with some exceptions, many analyses dwell on leading the schoolhouse rather than the core work of the schoolhouse. As a result, descriptions and prescriptions for leading are often only weakly related to the actual work of teaching and leading its improvement. Second, when researchers do attend to teaching in their investigations of schoolhouse leadership, it is frequently treated as a dependent or outcome variable and rarely considered an explanatory variable that would help us get inside the work of leading. Third, if teaching does figure in these accounts, it more often than not figures as a generic activity. Throughout the chapter the importance of anchoring work on leadership in teaching is underscored.

While teaching needs to be central in leadership work, its centrality has to be situated in the school organisation and the broader education system that structure teaching practice inside classrooms. A teacher and her pupils co-produce teaching, but their practice is enabled and constrained by arrangements beyond the immediate classroom (Cohen, 2011). The particular school in which the classroom is situated together with local, state, and national education government arrangements as well as an array of other agencies (e.g. textbook publishers, teacher preparation programmes, and testing agencies) in the education sector are all critical to understanding leadership for teaching. State and local government, together with universities, who prepare most teachers, can fundamentally influence their intellectual capability through pre-service and in-service training, certification requirements, hiring, and tenure decisions. In turn, the intellectual capability of the teacher fundamentally shapes the quality of teaching. Still, research syntheses and meta-analysis suggests that school leadership, as mediated through school-level conditions, is associated with the quality of teaching, and has an indirect and significant effect on student learning (Hallinger and Heck, 1996a; Leithwood et al., 2007; Lieberman, Falk and Alexander, 1994; Robinson, Lloyd and Rowe, 2008; Louis and Kruse, 1995; Rosenholtz, 1989).

Thus, a close analysis of leadership and learning at the school level is an important starting point for informing system-level considerations about leading teaching and its improvement. Readers should of course be mindful that schools reside in education systems that differ in ways that are consequential for classroom teaching and thus have implications for the work of school leaders. School leaders who work in systems that manage to recruit the best and the brightest to teaching face rather different leadership challenges than those who work in systems that exercise little quality control. This chapter considers leadership for teaching and learning, focusing on the school level (while cognisant of the broader system in which schools reside), and anchored in teaching.

This chapter offers no five-step or twelve-step approaches to educational leadership, and avoids simplistic mantras. To do so would be to offer simplistic solutions to what is a difficult and complex challenge in the education sector; it is a challenge that, while sharing some similarities across national borders, also differs in important ways that often go ignored in the never-ending quest for easy global solutions. I would readily offer a simple solution if I thought it existed, with something approaching solid empirical evidence of its efficacy. It does not! Worse still, peddlers of the "one best solution" (and there is no shortage) contribute to, rather than ameliorate, the problem.

This chapter is organised according to the following. First, teaching, and specifically the nature of teaching, is considered. Second, diagnosis and design work on school leadership has to engage the practice of leading, and that practice is framed in a particular way that has consequences for both how one researches and develops the phenomena. Third, in the implications of this framing of leadership practice for efforts to improve it, there is a need to focus on diagnostic and design work centred on the school's organisational infrastructure. While this chapter dwells mostly on the school level, much of what is discussed *1)* has to be situated in school systems whose arrangements and organisation have consequences for both teaching and school leading practice; and 2) can be applied to organisations at other levels of the "education system" (local government, state government, federal government) and indeed to "extra-system" organisations such as charter school providers. Even more importantly, a system-level approach is necessary in order to go beyond an exclusive focus on any one level of an education system and its extra-system components to consider the multiple components and how (or not) they operate together.

Teaching: the essence of leadership work

Classroom teaching should be central in diagnosis and design work on school leadership. That might seem easy to agree to, but one should carefully consider the implications of such a stance. This call to arms involves much more than studying the *effects* of leadership on teaching and learning, though that is important. Teaching is not simply a dependent variable in diagnosis and design work on school leadership but it is also an important explanatory variable. Treating teaching as an explanatory variable affords new insights into the nature of leadership.

What are the consequences of taking teaching seriously for diagnosis and design work?

Teaching as the subject of leadership

Teaching is more than just the object of leadership; it is also the subject of the work. While work in the instructional leadership tradition (Hallinger, 2005; Heck, Larsen and Marcoulides, 1990) put teaching on the map in research and development work on leadership, it offered limited insights into how principals (let alone other school leaders) actually accomplish this work – the daily practice (Hallinger, 2005; Hallinger and Heck, 1996a, 1996b; Heck and Hallinger, 1999). Factoring teaching in as a key explanatory variable involves moving away from views of teaching as a monolithic or unitary practice. This means to acknowledge that the school subject and the dimension of teaching (e.g. content coverage, teaching strategies and materials), are necessary considerations in diagnosis and design work related to leadership.

The school subject matters not only for how teachers teach, but also for how leaders lead teaching. Secondary school teachers differ in their conceptions of the subjects they teach on dimensions that include definition, scope, sequencing of material and whether the subject is static or dynamic (Grossman and Stodolsky, 1995). These differences are consequential for teaching practice, such as teachers' control of content and curriculum coordination and standardisation, and in turn mediate the influence of educational reform on classroom teaching (Ball, 1981; Grossman and Stodolsky, 1994; Little, 1993; McLaughlin and Talbert, 1993; Siskin, 1991, 1994). Although elementary school teachers tend to be generalists rather than subject-matter specialists, they also tend to think about the work of teaching differently depending on the school subject matter (Stodolsky, 1988), and these differences are important considerations in teachers' responses to efforts to reform classroom teaching (Drake, Spillane and Hufferd-Ackles, 2001; Spillane, 2000).

If teachers' conceptions of teaching differ by school subject, then the work of leading teaching is likely also to differ depending on the school subject and there is empirical evidence to suggest that it does. Some research also suggests that the cognitive scripts of school leaders (school principals and other formally designated school leaders) differ depending on the school subject (Burch and Spillane, 2003). If this is right, then the work of leading instruction will differ in some respects depending on the school subject. The available evidence suggest it does: while school leaders work at re-coupling both language arts and mathematics teaching with school leadership and government policy, the coupling mechanisms were different depending on the school subject (Hayton and Spillane, 2005; Spillane and Burch, 2006).

We can sharpen the analysis beyond the school subjects that teachers teach and leaders lead by engaging with the multiple dimensions of teaching practice: school leadership for the most part does not entertain the multiple dimensions of teaching – content coverage, teaching strategy, material usage, student grouping arrangements and so on. More sophisticated conceptualisations of teaching are necessary in diagnosis and design work that seek to understand relations between leadership practice and teaching practice.

Understandings of teaching and leadership practice

The subject matter and dimension of teaching aside, there is also the matter of how teaching practice is construed in an education system. As some commentators have pointed out, most notably Janet Weiss (1990) and Brian Rowan (1990, 2002), teaching as a practice is socially constructed and how it is defined has implications for how the work might best be led. In some systems at some times, teaching is socially defined more as a complex social craft whereas in other systems and other times, teaching is socially defined more as a well-defined, relatively invariable, technical endeavour. If teaching is socially constructed more as a complex craft, then leadership arrangements that involve teachers in decision making with network structures that promote professional control and collegiality among teachers are more likely to be effective. If, on the other hand, teaching is socially defined as a relatively invariable technical practice, then a standardised system of input, behaviour and outputs controlled and monitored by administrators may be more effective. In most school systems, teaching is socially defined as some hybrid of craft and technical practice, with some systems privileging one definition over the other depending on the time period (Rowan, 2002).

Seeing teaching as a social practice

Regardless of how teaching practice is defined in place and time, we grapple with teaching as a social practice. Popular images and conceptions of teaching portray it as a relatively straightforward solo practice, roughly equivalent to a teacher's actions in the classroom. But such conceptions are limiting as they fail to recognise that teaching is co-produced by teachers and their students with particular intellectual and physical material (Cohen and Ball, 1999; Cohen, 2011). Teaching depends not only on the teachers' skill and knowledge but also on the knowledge and skill of the students who co-produce teaching with their teachers.

Acknowledging the social nature of teaching practice has consequences for diagnosis and design work. Relations between leadership and teaching are often cast too narrowly on connections between school leaders' work and teachers' classroom work, rather than involving multiple routes including not only interactions with teachers, but also students and the materials they use in teaching. Thus, leadership activities may connect directly not only with teachers but also with students and teaching materials. Or, leadership may connect with different combinations of these core elements that define teaching practice, such as with both teachers and students or teachers and curricular materials.

In sum, teaching has to be front and centre in any diagnosis and design work on leadership, not just as object but also as subject. Some may worry that starting out with an extended analysis of teaching is putting the cart before the horse. It is not and is done intentionally to counterbalance the dominant treatment of teaching in much of the work on leadership. Further, as this section has illuminated, making teaching the subject of leadership work is neither simple nor straightforward: teaching practice is a complex phenomenon – multi-faceted, social, and differently defined in place and historical time.

So how might one lead this complex phenomenon called teaching?

Focusing in on the practice of leading teaching

Over the past decades several reformers and researchers have developed and applied what is broadly referred to as a "distributed perspective" to frame diagnosis and design work on school leadership (Gronn, 2000, 2002; Spillane and Diamond, 2007; Spillane, Halverson and Diamond, 1999, 2001). Drawing on distributed cognition, activity theory, and micro-sociology, a distributed perspective presses for attention to leadership not only as an organisational quality (Ogawa and Bossert, 1995; Pitner, 1988), but also as practice (Spillane, 2006). Framed this way, the practice of leading is the key unit of interest.

A central argument in this chapter is that education leaders' diagnosis and design work must focus on the practice of leading teaching. Practice must be the anchoring concern in diagnostic efforts and its improvement must be the target of design efforts. The practice of leading teaching is where school leadership meets classroom teaching. Leadership positions, roles, responsibilities and structures matter, but they matter to the extent to which they contribute to improvement in the everyday practice of leading. Creating new leadership positions or redefining the responsibilities does not guarantee change, let alone improvement, in the practice of leading. Hence, our diagnosis and design efforts have to be centred on practice.

It is easy to agree that practice should be a central concern but the devil lies in the details of what this means. Three things are essential in taking a distributed perspective in diagnosis and design efforts related to leadership agreement: *1)* to attend to people in interaction, not just their individual actions; *2)* to get beyond an exclusive focus on the chief executive or denotative leader at the top of the organisational hierarchy; and 3) that people depend on aspects of their situation in order to interact, aspects that are too often taken for granted as simply a stage or backdrop for practice.

Beyond the actions of individuals: getting to interactions

Researchers have studied leadership behaviour for a half century or more (Fiedler, 1967; Hemphill, 1949), and conceptualising practice as behaviour has allowed scholars to observe what individual school leaders (typically the school principal) do, and to report on it. However, framing practice as behaviour fails to recognise that in the real world, people do not act in social isolation; someone acts and someone else reacts and practice takes shape in the interactions between them. Thus, practice must be framed in a way that gets beyond individual behaviour and the acts of individuals.

Viewed from a distributed perspective, leadership practice takes form or shape in the **interactions** among people – teachers, administrators, specialists, and one might also add in students, parents, and others external to the organisation such as school district officials, school inspectors and so on – and their situation. Individuals act, but they act in relation to others and these everyday interactions are the essence of practice. Practice then is co-produced in the interactions among school staff. Efforts to understand practice and improvement efforts have to get to these interactions rather than simply focusing on practice from a narrow psychological perspective, where it is seen as a product of an individual leader's knowledge and skill. Interactions, rather than just individual behaviours, are critical.

If practice lies in interaction, the **emergent** property of practice must be acknowledged: individuals may, more or less, plan to act in particular ways, but it is often difficult to anticipate how others will react: Person A acts, Person B reacts, and Person A or C reacts. This is what the social psychologist Karl Weick calls the "double interact" – "the basic unit for describing interpersonal influence" (1979: 89). Human interactions, the building blocks of practice, then depend on reactions or interactions that are emergent rather than pre-determined individual plans or scripts. While social norms and formal positions (among other aspects of the situation) serve as scripts for human interactions in particular situations, they provide broad scripts that cannot cover or anticipate the particulars of each interaction. Thus, people have to improvise in their interactions with one another.

Beyond the heroic leader

When practice, framed as social interactions, becomes the central unit of analysis, then it is necessary to go beyond an exclusive focus on the behaviours, actions or even styles of individuals with formally designated leadership positions such as the school principal. In doing so, the reliance of the field on the "heroic leader paradigm" is challenged (Yukl, 1999), and instead we seek to understand how responsibility for leadership and work gets distributed across multiple individuals on the ground. Such recognition, contrary to popular writing on distributed leadership, in no way negates the important role of the principal in school leadership. Indeed, empirical work from a distributed perspective (as distinct from armchair theorising) consistently points to the critical role of the school principal (Camburn, Rowan and Taylor, 2003; Spillane and Diamond, 2007).

From a distributed perspective, the challenge involves not only identifying who does the work of leading teaching but also how responsibility for the work is arranged among or stretched over teams of school leaders. A study of over 100 geographically dispersed elementary schools, for example, found that responsibility for leadership functions was distributed over teams of leaders, typically ranging from 3 to 7 people including principals, assistant principals and coaches. Further, while principals tended to take responsibility for work that spans all aspects of leadership, coaches and other specialists tended to focus on leading teaching (Camburn, Rowan and Taylor, 2003). Another study including all 30 elementary schools in one urban school district found that, including the school principal, the average number of full-time formal leaders per school was 3.5 (Spillane and Healey, 2010; Spillane, Healey and Kim, 2010). Factoring in individuals who had classroom teaching responsibilities as well as leadership responsibilities increased this number substantially. Other studies show that teachers with no formal leadership position, as well as school district personnel and external consultants, also take responsibility for leadership work (Harris, 2005; Heller and Firestone, 1995; Leithwood et al., 2007; Portin et al., 2003; Timperley, 2005).

Exactly how leadership is distributed across multiple individuals appears to depend on various factors, such as the type of leadership function or routine (Camburn, Rowan and Taylor, 2003; Heller and Firestone, 1995), the subject matter (Spillane, 2005), the school's size (Camburn, Rowan and Taylor, 2003), the school type (Portin et al., 2003), and whether the school's leadership team is well established or new (Copland, 2003; Harris, 2002). A distributed perspective on school leadership thus presses us to focus on how leadership practice is stretched over multiple leaders as well as followers, not just that it is.

Acknowledging that leadership practice is stretched across leaders involves recognising that no one individual in a particular school will necessarily have the requisite knowledge or skill to execute a particular leadership task well, so engaging two or more individuals may be necessary to carry out the leadership task. For example, imagine a primary school working to lead the introduction of an inquiry approach to science teaching. An outstanding first-grade teacher who has a deep conceptual knowledge of science content and pedagogy may be a natural to lead such efforts, but may lack the requisite skills to facilitate deliberations among colleagues about their teaching. Given these circumstances, finding one or more school staff members to co-perform the task of leading change in science teaching at this school is essential. It also involves recognising that in their interactions with one another in performing a leadership task – as they share information and deliberate – school leaders may generate new knowledge and skills, contributing to the improvement of the leadership practice. In this way, and consistent with work on distributed cognition, the expertise for performing the task lies in between the individuals rather than being possessed by any one individual. It does not involve, as some would have us believe, silly and simplistic prescriptions that everyone is a leader or that the more leaders involved in a leadership task the better. Too many cooks can, and indeed do, spoil the broth!

Situations: defining practice from the inside out

As argued above, social interactions are key to understanding practice, and people are crucial to such interactions. But people don't interact with one another in a vacuum. As sociologists remind us, human interactions are only possible because of what they refer to as "social structure". Things often taken for granted, such as language, social norms, organisational routines, work conventions and tools of various kinds, are the means through which people interact with one another in the world. Social structure makes human interaction possible. The particulars of this social structure both enable and constrain how individuals interact with one another, and in this way define practice. The mantra "context matters" is overused and under-understood in education. It is often treated by school reformers as a nuisance and by researchers as a "catch-all" variable for why interventions fail or succeed. Both are unfortunate because more sophistication is essential in thinking about the situation as it relates to practice.

The situation of practice is not simply a stage or a place in which individuals interact with one another; rather, it includes such things as formal positions, organisational routines, norms and protocols that focus and centre on who, what and how individuals interact with one another, and in so doing define everyday practice. Of course, work on leadership, such as that done by contingency theorists, has long recognised the importance of situation to organisational leadership, but they have mostly treated the situation as influencing leadership from the outside, in great part because they have equated practice with individual behaviour or actions, and typically those of the school principal. A distributed perspective differs in its treatment of relations between practice and its situation: aspects of the situation do not simply "influence" what people do or plan to do from the outside in; rather, they do so from inside practice, i.e. they are not external to leadership practice. These aspects of the situation contribute to defining how people interact with one another, enabling some sorts of social interactions while inhibiting or constraining others, thereby defining practice from the inside. In this way, aspects of the situation do not simply moderate the impact of what people do on some outcome variable, but rather are a core defining element of practice in much the same way that people are (Spillane, 2006). Consequently, aspects of the situation, more often than not taken for granted and thus unnoticed and unacknowledged by those in it, fundamentally define practice.

In this way, leadership practice is not only stretched over people but also stretched over aspects of their situation such as norms, organisational routines and tools. In a world in which notions of heroic leadership prevail around "great men" and sometimes "great women", grasping the significance of the situation to practice is difficult. Practice – be it the cardiology team performing heart surgery or a secondary school leadership team working to lead a curricular change so that literacy skills are taught across the secondary school curriculum – is fundamentally shaped by the situation. New technologies are not simply accessories that make practice more (or sometimes less) effective and efficient, they fundamentally transform the very nature of practice. Individuals see and interact with others, using tools such as checklists, protocols (e.g. classroom observation protocols, rubrics for grading teacher or student performance) and student achievement printouts. These tools, often taken for granted, fundamentally shape how one sees, what one sees, and what one deliberates about in interactions with colleagues. In doing so, they define everyday leadership practice in schools from the inside out, rather than external contingencies that shape practice from the outside in. Thus, there is a need to engage the situations seriously from the inside in diagnosis and design work, diagnosing how practice is defined and then redesigning accordingly.

A different mindset must be developed with respect to relations between practice and its situation, one that takes seriously how everyday things contribute to defining everyday practice. The things that are used in order to interact with others define interactions by focusing and framing them on some things and not others, with some people and not others. While aspects of the situation contribute to defining practice, by enabling and constraining who interacts with whom, about what, how, and when, these same aspects of the situation are defined in practice. Things within one's situation, such as norms of trust or an organisational routine for supervising teachers, are reproduced and sometimes transformed, either incrementally or dramatically, in everyday practice (Sherer and Spillane, 2010; Spillane, Parise and Sherer, 2011). Aspects of the situation provide scripts, albeit very broad ones, for how one might interact in particular situations, but these scripts can never cover all contingencies, so improvisation is essential in practice.

So how do we work to improve the practice of leading teaching?

Diagnosis and design: organisational infrastructure and practice

If emergence and improvisation are key properties of practice, then practice cannot be designed. We can give a school principal scripts, manuals, professional development, and protocols for how to conduct a teacher evaluation or facilitate a school improvement planning effort, but if we take seriously the emergent property of practice and the necessity of improvisation in human interactions, these efforts will not design leadership and practice. But we can design **for** practice (Spillane and Coldren, 2011).

Specifically, we can design and redesign aspects of the situation or social structure so as to influence the practice of leading in particular ways including organisational routines, norms, formal positions, tools and so on. One way to think about this social structure is as an infrastructure for the practice of leading teaching. Infrastructure is essential for all spheres of human activity. Policymakers and economists constantly remind us that cities' and states' infrastructure – roads, trains, electrical supply, banks, water, sewage and so on – are essential to economic productivity. It shapes how we work. Organisations such as schools also have an infrastructure that shapes how people in them work. This includes the building, organisational routines (e.g. teacher evaluation), tools (e.g. curriculum, student assessments, protocols for evaluating teachers, and student report cards), and regulations (e.g. attendance policy). The organisational infrastructure, especially for veteran organisation members, is more often than not mundane, residing behind the scenes. Indeed, it is only when the infrastructure fails or is suddenly changed due to some exogenous shock that what was taken for granted becomes apparent. Organisational infrastructure – for good and bad – contributes to defining everyday practice in schools by more or less defining with whom one interacts, where, when, and about what.

Infrastructure design and redesign provide traction on the task of improving the practice of leading teaching. Diagnosis is essential in such work. Diagnosis is about figuring out and constructing an argument about the nature or cause of something that forms the basis for prognosis in which one defines goals and identifies ways of attaining these goals. Design is about moulding aspects of one's situation in purposeful ways in order to attain these goals. Though design is typically thought of as a rather grandiose pursuit, it is an everyday activity (Norman, 1988).

Arguing that diagnosis and design are essential for improving the practice of leading, the section below does two things: First, through organisational routines – a staple in schools, and in all organisations for that matter – it examines the dialectic relationship between infrastructure and practice. Second, other elements of the school organisational infrastructure are identified, advancing the argument that we can think about these elements using the same framework proposed for organisational routines, and as they relate to the practice of leading teaching.

Infrastructure and practice: the case of organisational routines

Organisational routines are staples in schools and include teacher evaluations, teacher hiring, school improvement planning, grade-level meetings, and student assemblies. Organisational routines have a bad rap in organisational theory and school reform literature, more often than not blamed for inertia and preserving the *status quo* in the face of change efforts. However, organisational routines are essential for organisations to function, enabling co-ordinated action, reducing conflict about how to do organisational work, and providing continuity in the face of changing personnel. Organisational routine refers to "a repetitive, recognisable pattern of interdependent actions, involving multiple actors," (Feldman and Pentland, 2003).

Analytically, and especially important for understanding relations between infrastructure and practice, we can think about organisational routines as having both "ostensive" and "performative" aspects (Feldman and Rafaeli, 2002). While the ostensive aspect refers to the "routine in principle" or the idealised version, the performative aspect refers to the routine in practice in particular places and time.

The ostensive aspect of organisational routines can structure practice in organisations by patterning interactions among school staff. As a broad script, the ostensive aspect of a routine such as grade-level meetings enables and constrains interactions among school staff (e.g. teachers in the same grade are more likely to interact with one another) about particular things (e.g. materials to use rather than teaching approach). What is important to recognise here is that the ostensive aspect of organisational routines, by design or otherwise, embody cognitive representations of key aspects of school work such as teaching, learning, leading, and student success. The material (e.g. classroom observation protocols) and abstract things that staff use to interact with one another (e.g. ostensive script for an organisational routine) embody "inter-mental models", representing key aspects of their work in particular ways. To the extent that school staff use these things, what they notice and how they interpret what they notice are not simply a function of their individual intra-mental, inside-the-head knowledge or schemas but also the inter-mental models embodied in what they use to interact with one another (Hutchins, 1995).

At the same time, each enactment of an organisational routine – the performative aspect – allows for changes in everyday practice as people improvise in the moment, filling out, modifying, or changing an ostensive script in its enactment in some fundamental way that may or may not get encoded into the formal school infrastructure. The everyday co-practice of organisational routines necessitates improvisation in the moment from those in the situation because scripts are too broad and abstract to guide work in multiple diverse situations. While the ostensive aspect of an organisational routine guides school leaders' and teachers' interactions with one another, their performance at a particular time and place are broadly, rather than particularly, influenced by those co-performing the practice (Sherer and Spillane, 2010). Over time, incremental and often unplanned changes in performance of a routine may lead to the ostensive aspect of that routine also being changed. At the same time, unsatisfied with how a particular routine is working on the ground, school leaders redesign the ostensive aspect so as to improve its performance (Spillane and Diamond, 2007). So, while the ostensive aspect of routines frames particular performances of them, it is in the performance that the ostensive script is reproduced and at times transformed (Sherer and Spillane, 2010; Spillane, Parise and Sherer, 2011).

The design and redesign of organisational routines was one common response by school leaders to the emergence of high-stakes accountability policy. They designed new school organisational routines to transform school leadership practice so as to make it more responsive to both government policy and classroom teaching (Sherer and Spillane, 2010; Spillane, Parise and Sherer, 2011). These routines, once institutionalised, transformed work practice in schools, increasing interactions among school staff about teaching in core school subjects (Sherer and Spillane, 2010; Spillane, Parise and Sherer, 2011). But these routines were not neutral with respect to teaching. Responding to state tests in mathematics and literacy, school leaders designed these routines and their accompanying tools to embody particular representations of learning and student success (e.g. descriptive words, vocabulary) and neglect other representations (e.g. originality). Thus, while interactions among school staff about teaching increased these interactions, they were focused on some school subjects (e.g. literacy) and not others (e.g. science), and on particular ways of thinking about teaching.

We can work to change, and hopefully improve, the practice of leading teaching, then, by designing and redesigning the ostensive aspect of organisational routines. Such work will involve diagnosing the performative aspect of routines and developing prognosis to inform design efforts.

School organisational infrastructure: components and characteristics

Organisational routines are but one aspect of a school's organisational infrastructure. Other components include tools (e.g. classroom observation protocols), formal positions (e.g. deputy principal, mentor teacher), and departments or sub-units (e.g. school subject departments and grade levels). The ostensive and performative frame can be applied to these other components of the school's organisational infrastructure, in much the same way as is done above for organisational routines.

School leaders and teachers design some components of their school's infrastructure whereas other components are designed, and their use sometimes mandated, by external agencies (e.g. government agencies and extra system providers). Consider student achievement data on standardised tests that have, over the past several decades and as a result of government policies, become a prominent feature of work in American schools. School leaders and teachers are pressed by government policies to use these data in decision making. Over time, reporting requirements for achievement data have evolved with states having to disaggregate data by particular groups of students. These shifts in the policy environment are not just new pressures on schools to use student test data, they also involve a shift in how learning, and by extension teaching, is represented in school practice. Just like organisational routines, these data embody particular representations of student learning, drawing attention to some aspects of learning and not others, simplifying at the individual student, classroom and school levels the complex terrain of student learning and classroom teaching by assigning numerical values to what students have learned and by extension to what (and perhaps how) teachers have taught (Sauder and Espeland, 2009). To the extent that school staff notice and negotiate meaning with these particular representations of learning in the form of test score data, they come to see teaching and learning in some ways and not others.

In this way, tools such as standardised test data, embodying particular representations of what it means to learn and teach, are an integral and defining component of leadership practice. Whether a function of design, emergence, or some combination of the two, a school's organisational infrastructure more or less supports the practice of leading teaching. And through the design and redesign of infrastructure, leadership practice can be changed. School organisational infrastructure makes a difference with respect to the practice of leading teaching. Recent work, for example, suggests that, controlling for teaching advice and information ties from prior school years, teachers are more likely to seek advice and information about teaching from teachers in their same grade (Spillane, Kim and Frank, in press). Similarly, teachers are more likely to seek advice and information about teaching from colleagues with formally designated leadership positions (Spillane, Kim and Frank, in press).

Infrastructure is typically invisible in everyday practice, except in times of change (e.g. a new school leadership team or government policies that disrupt business as usual in schools). Though essential and constitutive of practice in schools once institutionalised, infrastructure is "invisible though ready to hand" (Star, 1998). Defining practice from the inside, the transparency, taken-for-grantedness, persistence, and reach of infrastructure makes it difficult for organisational members to notice and diagnose. Still, careful diagnosis is essential for infrastructure design and redesign.

A concern in any diagnostic or design work on infrastructure is what characteristics of the ostensive aspect of an organisational infrastructure make it more or less effective in enabling and constraining the performative aspect. A tentative list is outlined below, drawing on work on educational systems (Cohen and Spillane, 1992; Floden et al., 1988), as well as work in sociology on the conditions under which formalities work (Colyvas, 2012; Stinchcombe, 2001). This list is meant to be suggestive rather than comprehensive. Five characteristics of the ostensive aspect of an organisation's infrastructure are identified, that I hypothesise are likely to influence its relations with the performative aspect.

1) Anchoring in and aligning with teaching. One consideration is whether and how the infrastructure for school leadership connects with teaching. We cannot assume that a school's leadership infrastructure connects with teaching, and various studies have captured how teaching has been loosely coupled or decoupled from the school's infrastructure and from government policy (Meyer and Rowan, 1977; Weick, 1976). If the infrastructure is anchored in teaching, how it is anchored should also be examined and through which elements of teaching – teachers, students, and the material. As discussed earlier in this chapter, teaching is co-produced by teachers and students interacting with and about particular material. Framed this way, it should be expected that an organisational infrastructure and leadership practice that works on each of these elements of teaching – teachers, students, and materials – and attends systematically to them in interaction, rather than in isolation, is more likely to enable improvement in teaching.

2) Cognitive adequacy. Another characteristic of the ostensive aspect of the school's organisational infrastructure that is likely to influence how it constrains and enables the performative aspect – practice – is its "cognitive adequacy" (Colyvas, 2012; Stinchcombe, 2001). Cognitive adequacy refers to an organisational infrastructure's "*accuracy* in description, their *sufficiency* to grasp all that is necessary to govern the action, their *cognitive economy* that makes them easy to work with, and their *scope* so that they can govern a wide variety of situations" (Stinchcombe, 2001: 18). While the ostensive may not govern or determine the performative, cognitive adequacy has traction for thinking about the ostensive aspect and resonates with the notion that the infrastructure embodies cognitive representations of leading, teaching, and learning. Cognitive adequacy stresses the need to diagnose the extent to which the ostensive aspect of a routine represents the practice of leading teaching, classroom teaching, and student learning. To what extent do the abstract representations of the work of leading teaching in the school's organisational infrastructure accurately, economically, and sufficiently represent that work? If the representations of work practice in the ostensive aspect of a school's infrastructure are inadequate for everyday usage by practitioners in schools, they are unlikely to guide their practice.

3) Communicability, corruptibility and correctability [drawing on Stinchcombe (2001) while adapting several of his categories]. The representations of practice in the ostensive aspect must be transmissible so that they get taken up in the performative aspect. If this is absent, these representations are unlikely to enable and constrain practice in particular places at particular times. Further, the ostensive aspect of the organisational infrastructure must be able to withstand being corrupted in performance or practice. If the ostensive aspect of an organisational routine is susceptible to corruption, such as school staff going through the motions of a grade-level meeting but missing or avoiding its purpose, the ostensive aspect is ineffective in enabling and constraining the performative. Finally, a critical concern is whether the ostensive aspect has a way of correcting itself – correctability. This is essential so that the ostensive remains relevant, usable and useful in the performative. The school's infrastructure has to keep pace with practice on the ground, and doing so entails being in touch with daily practice in schools and somehow tapping into and using that knowledge to correct and repair as needed.

4) Consistency. Consistency within any one component (e.g. a particular organisational routine) and consistency across components are important if the ostensive aspect of a school's organisational infrastructure will be influential in enabling and constraining practice. Inconsistencies within or across components of the organisational infrastructure are likely to undermine its influence on the performative.

5) Authority and power. The authority and power of the school organisation's infrastructure refers to the weight it carries for organisational members. This can be a function of formal authority, such as that associated with the position of the principal or, as noted above, some aspects of a school's infrastructure required by government regulation (e.g. formal positions and who is eligible to hold them, some organisational routines). At the same time, the authority and power of an organisation's infrastructure can also be a function of the sense of ownership of it by organisational members (Spillane and Anderson, under review). Authority and power are likely to be especially relevant at times when the organisational infrastructure or parts thereof are being redesigned and changed.

Conclusion

This chapter has focused on leading classroom teaching – the core technology of schooling. Most of the examples in this chapter focus on leadership practice for teaching at the school level because leadership, as mediated through school-level conditions, is associated with the quality of teaching and has significant indirect effects on student learning (Hallinger and Heck, 1996a; Leithwood et al., 2007; Lieberman, Falk and Alexander, 1994; Robinson, Lloyd and Rowe, 2008). Accordingly, close attention to relations between leadership and learning at that school level is an important point of departure for informing organisation and system-level considerations about leading teaching and its improvement.

At the same time, it is important to consider carefully how schools in a particular education system are situated with respect to the government of classroom teaching. Education systems differ widely on such arrangements. Several commentators classify such differences as centralised versus decentralised systems, a classification which, though minimally helpful, also glosses over some of the most important differences between education systems when it comes to guidance for teaching (Cohen and Spillane, 1992). To be mindful that schools reside in education systems that differ in ways that are consequential for both teaching practice and, therefore, school leading practice, is important when it comes to taking a distributed perspective to diagnosis and design. Many schools in the United States and quite possibly elsewhere are in a context where the system-level infrastructure for supporting classroom teaching is fragmented and impoverished, often sending contrary and underdeveloped messages about teaching and its improvement to schools (Cohen and Moffitt, 2009). Under such arrangements, schools are often left to figure out largely on their own how to reach externally imposed improvement metrics. Other education systems, in contrast, provide more consistent and elaborated guidance about teaching to schools as well as constraining more who can enter the teaching profession and how they are prepared to teach. A systematic discussion of differences across education systems in instructional governance arrangements and their consequences for leading teaching and its improvement at different levels of the school system is beyond the scope of this chapter. But they are important when elaborating on the arguments advanced here.

Taking a distributed perspective to leading teaching, as discussed in this chapter, can be applied with some careful and thoughtful adaptations to any level of an education system (e.g. local educational authorities, ministries of education) and indeed to extra-system agencies (e.g. charter school networks or Comprehensive School Reform providers). It is problematic to consider any one level of an education system in isolation, because what happens at one level with respect to leading teaching is interdependent with what happens at other levels – local, state, and federal – and indeed with extra-system agencies. School-level efforts to lead teaching are interdependent with efforts, or the lack thereof, at other levels of the education system.

Organisations at any one level of an education system should be considered in relation to the institutional sector more broadly. This is essential for at least three reasons. First, leadership of teaching at any one level is more or less dependent on leadership of teaching at other levels. Thus, in order to understand and work on improving leadership at the school level, one must not only be cognisant of the interdependencies with other levels but also explore these interdependencies.

Second, there is a need to understand leading teaching at the level of education systems and their extra-system components – an institutional analysis. This is a challenging but necessary task. Furthermore, work on understanding systems should not be conflated with looking from the highest level (e.g. federal or state government) down to get a sense of the lie of the land on the ground. Such top-down diagnosis and design work will generate few insights that are useful and usable if the improvement of leadership for teaching is a key goal. Instead, systems must be understood from the top down and the bottom up, as well as from the outside in and the inside out.

Third, adopting a system or institutional approach is essential to interpreting work on leading teaching from different countries. Findings from empirical work on school leadership in one country or world region can only be understood and appreciated in another when one seriously entertains the education system in which that work was conducted. This permits fair cross-system comparisons to be drawn and valid inferences generated: we can learn from the work of leading teaching in other education systems as long as we are careful in translating these lessons across diverse education systems.

Note

1. Spencer T. and Ann W. Olin Professor in Learning and Organizational Change at the School of Education and Social Policy at Northwestern University.

References

Ball, S.J. (1981), *Beachside Comprehensive: A Case Study of Secondary Schooling,* Cambridge University Press, Cambridge, UK.

Burch, P. and J.P. Spillane (2003), "Elementary school leadership strategies and subject matter: Reforming mathematics and literacy instruction", *The Elementary School Journal,* 103(5), 519-535.

Camburn, E.M., B. Rowan and J.E. Taylor (2003), "Distributed leadership in schools: The case of elementary schools adopting comprehensive school reform models", *Educational Evaulation and Policy Analysis,* 25(4), 347-373.

Cohen, D.K. (2011), *Teaching and Its Predicaments*, Harvard University Press, Cambridge, MA.

Cohen, D.K., and D.L. Ball (1999), *Instruction, Capacity, and Improvement,* CPRE Research Report Serries RR-43, Consortium for Policy Research in Education (CPRE), Philadelphia, PA.

Cohen, D.K., and S.L. Moffitt (2009), *The Ordeal of Equality: Did Federal Regulation Fix the Schools?* Harvard University Press, Cambridge, MA.

Cohen, D.K. and J.P. Spillane (1992), "Policy and practice: The relations between governance and instruction", *Review of Research in Education,* 18(3).

Colyvas, J.A. (2012), "Performance metrics as formal structures and through the lens of social mechanisms: When do they work and how do they influence?" *American Journal of Education, 118*(2), 167-197.

Copland, M.A. (2003), "Leadership of inquiry: Building and sustaining capacity for school improvement", *Educational Evaluation and Policy Analysis, 25*(4), 375-395.

Cuban, L. (1988), *The Managerial Imperative and the Practice of Leadership in Schools*, SUNY (State University of New York) Press, Albany, NY.

Drake, C., J.P. Spillane and K. Hufferd-Ackles (2001), "Storied identities: Teacher learning and subject-matter context", *Journal of Curriculum Studies,* 33(1), 1-13.

Feldman, M. S. and B.T. Pentland (2003). "Reconceptualizing organizational routines as a source of flexibility and change", *Administrative Science Quarterly,* 48(1), 94-118.

Feldman, M.S. and A. Rafaeli (2002), "Organizational routines as sources of connections and understandings", *Journal of Management Studies,* 39(3), 309-331.

Fiedler, F.E. (1967), *A Theory of Leadership Effectiveness* (Vol. III), McGraw-Hill, New York.

Floden, R.E. et al. (1988), "Instructional leadership at the district level: A closer look at autonomy and control", *Educational Administration Quarterly,* 24(2), 96-124.

Gronn, P. (2002), "Distributed leadership as a unit of analysis", *The Leadership Quarterly,* 13(4), 423-451.

Gronn, P. (2000), "Distributed properties: A new architecture for leadership", *Educational Management Administration Leadership,* 28(3), 317-338.

Grossman, P. L. and S.S. Stodolsky (1995), "Content as context: The role of school subjects in secondary school teaching", *Educational Researcher,* 24(8), 5-23.

Grossman, P.L. and S.S. Stodolsky (1994), "Considerations of content and the circumstances of secondary school teaching", in L. Darling-Hammond (ed.), *Review of Research in Education* (Vol. 20), American Educational Research Association, Washingon, DC, 179-222.

Hallinger, P. (2005), "Instructional leadership and the school principal: A passing fancy that refuses to fade away", *Leadership and Policy in Schools,* 4(3), 221-239.

Hallinger, P. and R.H. Heck (1996a), "Reassessing the principal's role in school effectiveness: A review of empirical research, 1980-1995", *Educational Administration Quarterly,* 32(1), 5-44.

Hallinger, P. and R.H. Heck (1996b), "The principal's role in school effectiveness: A review of methodological issues", in K.A. Leithwood (ed.), *The International Handbook of Educational Leadership and Administration,* Kluwer, Dordrecht, Netherlands.

Harris, A. (2005), "Leading or misleading? Distributed leadership and school improvement", *Journal of Curriculum Studies*, 37(3), 255-265.

Harris, A. (2002), "Effective leadership in schools facing challenging contexts", *School Leadership and Management*, 22(1), 15-26.

Hayton, P. and J.P. Spillane (2005), *Professional Community or Communities? School Subject Matter and Elementary School Teachers' Work Environments*, IPR Working Paper Series, Institute for Policy Research, Evanston, IL.

Heck, R.H. and P. Hallinger (1999), "Next generation methods for the study of leadership and school improvement" in J. Murphy and K. S. Louis (eds.), *Handbook of Research on Educational Administration*, Jossey-Bass, San Francisco.

Heck, R.H., T.J. Larsen and G.A. Marcoulides (1990), "Instructional leadership and school achievement: Validation of a causal model", *Educational Administration Quarterly*, 26(2), 94-125.

Heller, M.F. and W.A. Firestone (1995), "Who's in charge here? Sources of leadership for change in eight schools", *Elementary School Journal*, 96(1), 65-86.

Hemphill, J.K. (1949), "The leader and his group", *Educational Research Bulletin*, 28(9), 225-229.

Hutchins, E. (1995), *Cognition in the Wild*, MIT Press, Cambridge, MA.

Leithwood, K.A. et al. (2007), "Distributing leadership to make schools smarter: Taking the ego out of the system", *Leadership and Policy in Schools*, 6(1), 37-67.

Lieberman, A., B. Falk and L. Alexander (1994), *A Culture in the Making: Leadership in Learner-Centered Schools*, National Center for Restructuring Education, School, and Teaching, New York.

Little, J.W. (1993), "Teachers' professional development in a climate of educational reform", *Educational Evaluation and Policy Analysis*, 15(2), 129-151.

Louis, K.S. and S.D. Kruse (1995), *Professionalism and Community: Perspectives on Reforming Urban Schools*, Corwin Press, Newbury Park, CA.

McLaughlin, M.W. and J.E. Talbert (1993), "How the world of students and teachers challenges policy coherence", in S. Fuhrman (ed.), *Designing Coherent Education Policy: Improving the System*, Jossey-Bass, San Francisco.

Meyer, J.W. and B. Rowan (1977), "Institutionalized organizations: Formal structure as myth and ceremony", *American Journal of Sociology*, 83(2), 340-363.

Norman, D.A. (1988), *The Psychology of Everyday Things,* Basic Books, New York.

Ogawa, R.T. and S.T. Bossert (1995), "Leadership as an organizational quality", *Educational Administration Quarterly*, 31(2), 224-243.

Pitner, N. (1988), "The study of administrator effects and effectiveness", in N. Boyan (ed.), *Handbook of Research in Educational Administration,* Longman, New York, 99-122.

Portin, B., P. Schneider, M. DeArmond and L. Gundlach (2003), *Making Sense of Leading Schools: A Study of the School Principalship*, Center on Reinventing Public Education, Washington University, Seattle, WA.

Robinson, V.M.J., C.A. Lloyd and K.J. Rowe. (2008), "The impact of leadership on student outcomes: An analysis of the differential effects of leadership types",*Educational Administration Quarterly*, 44(5), 635-674.

Rosenholtz, S.J. (1989), "Workplace conditions that affect teacher quality and commitment: Implications for teacher induction programs", *The Elementary School Journal*, 89(4), 421-439.

Rowan, B. (2002), "Teachers' work and instructional management, Part I: Alternative views of the task of teaching", in W.K. Hoy and C.G. Miskel (eds.), *Theory and research in educational administration,* Information Age Publishing, Charlotte, NC.

Rowan, B. (1990), "Commitment and control: Alternative strategies for the organizational design of schools", *Review of Research in Education*, 16, 353-389.

Sauder, M. and W.N. Espeland (2009), "The discipline of rankings: Tight coupling and organizational change", *American Sociological Review*, 74(20), 63-82.

Sherer, J.Z. and J.P. Spillane (2010), "Constancy and change in school work practice: Exploring the role of organizational routines", *Teachers College Record*, 113(3).

Siskin, L.S. (1994), *Realms of Knowledge: Academic Departments in Secondary Schools,* Routledge and Falmer, Washington, DC.

Siskin, L.S. (1991), "Departments as different worlds: Subject subcultures in secondary schools", *Educational Administration Quarterly,* 27(2), 134-160.

Spillane, J.P. (2006), *Distributed Leadership,* Jossey-Bass, San Francisco.

Spillane, J.P. (2005), "Primary school leadership practice: How the subject matters", *School Leadership and Management*, 25(4), 383-397.

Spillane, J.P. (2000). A fifth-grade teacher's reconstruction of mathematics and literacy teaching: Exploring interactions among identity, learning, and subject matter. *The Elementary School Journal, 100*(4), 307-330.

Spillane, J.P. and L.M. Anderson (under review), "Policy, practice, and professionalism: Negotiating policy meanings in practice in a shifting institutional environment", *Sociology of Education*.

Spillane, J.P. and P. Burch (2006), "The institutional environment and instructional practice: Changing patterns of guidance and control in public education", in H.-D. Meyer and B. Rowan (eds.), *The New Institutionalism in Education*, SUNY Press, Albany, NY.

Spillane, J.P. and A.F. Coldren (2011), *Diagnosis and Design for School Improvement: Using a Distributed Perspective to Lead and Manage Change,* Teachers College Press, New York.

Spillane, J.P. and J.B. Diamond (2007), *Distributed Leadership in Practice,* Teachers College Press, New York.

Spillane, J.P., R. Halverson and J.B. Diamond (2001), "Investigating school leadership practice: A distributed perspective", *Educational Researcher,* 30(3), 23-28.

Spillane, J.P., R. Halverson and J.B. Diamond (1999), *Distributed Leadership: Toward a Theory of School Leadership Practice*, Institute for Policy Research, Evanston, IL.

Spillane, J.P. and K. Healey (2010), "Conceptualizing school leadership and management from a distributed perspective", *The Elementary School Journal*, 111(2), 253-281.

Spillane, J.P., K. Healey and C.M. Kim (2010), "Leading and managing instruction: Using social network analysis to explore formal and informal aspects of the elementary school organization", in A.J. Daly (ed.), *Social Network Theory and Educational Change*, Harvard Education Press, Cambridge, MA, 129-156.

Spillane, J.P., C.M. Kim and K.A. Frank (in press), "Instructional advice and information seeking behavior in elementary schools: Exploring tie formation as a building block in social capital development", *American Educational Research Journal*.

Spillane, J.P., L.M. Parise and J.Z. Sherer (2011), "Organizational routines as coupling mechanisms: policy, school administration, and the technical core", *American Educational Research Journal*, 48(3), 586-620.

Star, S. (1998), "Working together: Symbolic interactionism, activity theory, and information systems", in Y. Engeström and D.S. Middleton (eds.), *Cognition and Communication at Work*, Cambridge University Press, New York, 296-318.

Stinchcombe, A.L. (2001), *When Formality Works: Authority and Abstraction in Law and Organizations,* University of Chicago Press, Chicago.

Stodolsky, S.S. (1988), *The Subject Matters: Classroom Activity in Math and Social Studies,* Univeristy of Chicago Press, Chicago.

Timperley, H.S. (2005), "Distributed leadership: Developing theory from practice", *Journal of Curriculum Studies*, 37(4), 395-420.

Weick, K.E. (1979), "Cognitive processes in organizations", *Research in Organizational Behavior*, 1, 41-74.

Weick, K.E. (1976), "Educational organizations as loosely coupled systems", *Administrative Science Quarterly*, 21(1), 1-19.

Weiss, J.A. (1990), "Control in school organizations: Theoretical perspectives", in W. Clune and J. Witte (eds.), *Choice and Control in American Education,* Volume 1, The Falmer Press, Bristol, PA, 91-134.

Yukl, G. (1999), "An evaluation of conceptual weaknesses in transformational and charistmatic leadership theories", *The Leadership Quarterly*, 10(2), 285-305.

Chapter 3

Leading learning in a world of change

John MacBeath[1]
University of Cambridge, UK

This chapter by John MacBeath examines the character of leadership in both a descriptive and ethical sense. Leading learning entails the constant endeavour to stimulate the desire to learn and sustain teachers' engagement, and requires quality of insight and "connoisseurship". Five principles for learning leadership are presented: 1) a focus on learning; 2) creating conditions favourable to learning; 3) dialogue; 4) sharing leadership through structures and procedures supporting participation; and 5) a shared sense of accountability. There is discussion about the leadership challenges of creating communities of learning, self-evaluation and inducting new teachers. The final section turns to learning leadership in non-formal settings and hybrids of formal and non-formal. These forms of learning environment are very promising for the future and have, par excellence, *given more leadership to young people. But they represent significant challenges to professional practice and its understanding, dominated in the literature by "the place called school".*

Introduction

This chapter examines the character of leadership in both a descriptive and ethical sense. "Leading" and "learning" are open to a variety of interpretations and are, in many policy contexts, devalued by too facile an association with principalship on the one hand, and attainment measures on the other. Leading learning relies on willingness and courage to return to first principles – to see both leadership and learning anew, examining ways in which schools may enhance or constrain the potential which children bring them. Leading learning entails a constant effort not only to keep alive children's inherent desire to learn but also implies a sustaining of teachers' idealism in the face of relentless pressures including competitive targets. It requires a quality of insight which grasps the nature of the force field that pushes teachers, students and parents back to the comfort zone of convention and conventional wisdom. Leading learning opens to question the locus for change and what it means to be a learning community. It defines the character and resilience which helps leaders and teachers to fly below the policy radar. The final section of this chapter turns to how learning has been led in exemplary ways both within and beyond schools, working across boundaries, entering the "dilemma space" in which certainty, consistency and conformity are exchanged for spontaneity, risk and autonomy.

The character of leadership

The term "leadership" is so embedded in the common sense of everyday discourse that is difficult to perceive it anew, as it were for the first time. Our most common reference point is the individual at the apex of the organisational pyramid with a vested authority and mandate to act on behalf of others, with conviction and with benevolent intent. His or her warrant rests on the trust to act on behalf of those they lead, to do the right thing and to do things right.

So the character of leadership may be approached from two different directions. On the one hand, it is a descriptive term to refer to the characteristics of the role – "what leaders do when they accomplish well what is formally expected of them". On the other hand, we understand "character" as having a strong ethical resonance. In a school context, it has been described as the conscience, or moral compass, of the community – doing what is right, just and equitable.

Leadership may be made plainly visible in the hierarchy of the school or, alternatively, may not be easy to perceive because it is dispersed, less invested in institutional authority than in shared endeavour, enacted spontaneously by those who singly or in concert take responsibility for their fellow beings. These two forms of leadership, explicit and implicit, often exist in tension, defined by the structural order or expressed in the flow of activity in which members of the school community are engaged.

The questions "who are the learners?" and "who are the leaders?" may simply receive a default answer in the explicit structures of schools, made apparent in the everyday conduct of school life, in the arrangements of classrooms, and in the hierarchies of access and privilege. It needs no conversation for the new pupil, or the new graduate student, the new teacher or the visiting parent to know who learns, who leads, and who follows. Where there is failure to discern those explicit conventions, an apparent absence of clear demarcations between the leaders and the learners, it is likely to be a disturbing, but nonetheless an enlightening, experience.

The distinguishing character of those who lead well, whether with institutional or with personal authority, is connoisseurship – the ability to perceive what is salient amid the complexity and simultaneity of school and classroom life. As educational connoisseurs they have learned how to suspend preconception and judgment, knowing what they see rather than seeing what they already know. They have a deep understanding of the nature of learning – student, teacher, organisational and system learning – and they grasp the vital nature of their interconnections.

"Insight", seeing into, as Abraham Heschel (1969: 3) describes it, is "the perception of things to come rather than the extension of things gone by". The ability to see schools and classrooms with a focus on learning, with a focus on what might be, and not simply what is, brings with it a profound understanding of why our hopes for children so often fall short. With insight, leaders grasp the nature of the force field that pushes them back to the comfort zone of convention, persuading them to rely on what they already do rather than venture too far into the risky unknown.

As Hesselbein et al. (1996: 78) have argued in relation to exemplary school leaders, their distinguishing strength is the ability of push themselves out of their comfort zone into risky territory: "They are open to people and ideas even at a time in life when they might reasonably think – because of their success – that they know everything". In situations where children know more about some things than their teachers, the latter require a measure of humility and willingness to learn from those younger, smaller and less powerful than themselves.

Seeing with a new clarity into our own practice is an uncomfortable experience because we may become too acutely aware of the gap between how things are and how we would like them to be. There are few leaders who would not like their schools to be better places for children and there are few teachers who would not like their classrooms to be more exciting places for themselves and their students. Yet we confront the paradox that success, within the limitations imposed on senior leaders and teachers, can be the enemy of change. "Nothing fails like success", wrote Peter Senge in 1990, pointing to the complacency that comes with competitive advantage, good reports, high marks and boxes ticked.

With insight comes a discriminating response to the vagaries of policy. In David Hargreaves' words, it requires the ability and the courage to "fly below the radar". A study of Scottish school leaders (MacBeath et al., 2009) identified five self-defined categories – the "dutifully compliant", the "cautiously pragmatic", the "quietly self-confident", the "bullishly self-assertive", and the self-confessed "defiant risk-takers". In these latter categories were self-confessed rule breakers, driven by their conscience and what they believed to be right, leading their schools neither with subservience nor arrogance. They were prepared to do what they deemed to be the right thing in full knowledge of the risks and consequences of defying policy mandates. Their self-confidence (in the words of one head, "you can't frighten me, I've got children") gave them the conviction to see what matters and to navigate their way around impatient policy imperatives.

At the same time, adventurous leaders are acutely aware of the accountability they owe to their paymasters as well as to those over whom they exercise authority. It is in achieving the balance between external and internal accountability that leadership confronts its acutest dilemmas – addressing the constraining parameters which threaten ambition for transformational change. This dilemma was expressed in an English context by a principal attempting both to manage and to lead, juggling external pressures to conform with a principled stance which puts students' needs first:

> I have three pistols to my head: one is the need to prepare the school for another visit from the inspectors because we are in Special Measures, another is the need to present a case to the local authority which is threatening to close the school, and another is the need to improve the attainment figures so we can be lifted out of the status of being "a school in challenging circumstances". And then there is the small matter of trying to lead and manage the school on a day-to-day basis and meet the needs of our students and the community (Frost, 2005: 76).

What students need is open to a variety of interpretations, and attempting to both define and cater to those perceived needs is an ambitious remit. "Needs" are not only complex, contradictory and contentious, but trying to meet them is also bounded by caution and compromise. However strong the impulse to put learning first, there can be a seemingly relentless tide pushing leaders back to the known and familiar, mediating aspiration, reminding them of the costs that come with daring to be different.

Understanding and leading learning, in its most profound sense, requires a return to first principles, or axioms, as to the nature, purposes, rhythms and contexts of learning, prompting the question: to what extent can such commitments be accommodated within the constraining influences of the institutions we call schools? It implies an ability to see the unseen, to question the unquestioned and to address the intergenerational legacy of school and of being schooled. Leadership implies not only profound personal insight, but an ability to help others share those insights and to be alive to insights which others bring.

Five principles of leadership for learning

Leadership for learning was the common theme in a collaborative study (MacBeath and Dempster, 2008) to which seven countries signed up in 2002 (Australia, Austria, Denmark, Greece, Norway, the United Kingdom and the United States). Over a three-year period, five common principles took shape. Reframed in theoretical discussion and tested in school and classroom practice, these five principles proved to have powerful application, making the connections among learning and leading at individual, collective, organisational and policy levels.

The first of the five principles holds the key to the rest. A focus on learning is economic and powerful, challenging in its simplicity but far-reaching in its implications. Focusing on learning means putting learning at the centre of everything. This refers not simply to students but to every member of a school that aspires to be a learning community.

Where there is a focus on learning, a second principle follows naturally – creating conditions favourable to learning. The first principle presupposes a culture able to nurture learning for everyone, affording opportunities to reflect on the nature, skills and processes of learning and to vouchsafe the physical and the social spaces that stimulate and celebrate learning. Safe and secure environments enable everyone to take risks, to cope with failure and respond positively to challenges, equipped with tools and strategies to enhance thinking about learning and the practice of teaching.

The third principle, dialogue, is premised on the first two. A focus on, and a culture of, learning are generated and sustained by a quality of discourse in which Leadership for Learning practice is made explicit, discussable and transferable. Its impact is measured by active collegial inquiry in which a commonality of purpose is achieved through the sharing of values, understandings, and practices.

As a school develops as a community of learners it also becomes a community of leaders. So the fourth principle states that "leadership for learning practice involves the sharing of leadership in which organisational structures and procedures support participation". Shared leadership is symbolised in the day-to-day flow of activities in the school. Everyone is encouraged to take the lead as appropriate to task and context. The experience and expertise of staff, students and parents are drawn upon as a valued and dynamic resource. Collaborative patterns of work and activity across boundaries of subject, role and status are valued and promoted.

In such a collaborative climate there is a shared sense of accountability – principle five. Internal, reciprocal accountability is a precursor and precondition of accountability to external agencies, and national policies are interpreted, adopted or adapted to the extent that they accord with the school's core values. The school chooses how to tell its own story, taking account of political realities with a continuing focus on sustainability, succession and leaving a legacy.

Embedding the five principles in a learning community

It is a fortunate beginning teacher who joins a genuine learning community, one in which the five key principles are embedded in the day-to-day realities of practice. In such a culture, a teacher's own learning trajectory is recognised and supported, drawing energy and inspiration from an ethos in which learning is modelled and celebrated but also problematised and subjected to continuing inquiry. Newly-qualified teachers need, and benefit, from a quality of support which is able to enter into their intellectual and emotional frame of reference and is able to help extend the borders within which their experience is conceived.

As McLaughlin and Talbert's 2001 study reported, in such a community teachers tend to feel more empowered and see their work as meaningful. They testify to their affiliation with the school and have higher job satisfaction than teachers working in weak professional communities. There is ample evidence internationally to show that without the collegial support, without leadership able to foster conditions for professional learning, without a strong sense of reciprocal accountability, there are higher rates of stress, disaffection and attrition. Working together with a shared sense of learning purpose, teachers can more effectively rise to the challenges they face, while students experience at first hand the character of healthy interpersonal relationships when school staff are engaged in "a cohesive, co-operative organisational climate" (Ingersoll, 2003: 194).

The challenge for leadership is to help teachers to model for their charges what it means to be a learner, keeping alive the exploratory and creative instinct which children bring with them. Such leaders recognise that nurturing the resilience and optimism of children relies on teachers themselves also having a reservoir of human and social capital on which to draw. They are also keenly aware that not all teachers have an equal capacity to sustain frustrated aims. Not all teachers are able to maintain a high level of energy over time, or to resurrect day after day the passion to deal with setback and disappointment. With awareness as to staff's needs as well as those of students, creating the balance of differentiated support and challenge assumes high priority and makes the case for distributed, collegial expressions of leadership.

While on entering the profession there is commitment and openness to becoming more skilled and effective, without the stimulus and reinvigoration of new challenges and new horizons it is easy for teachers to become resigned to business as usual and, with external pressure for compliance, to submit to the seemingly inevitable. It is in this respect that induction into the profession requires radical reappraisal as O'Connell Rust has argued, claiming that pre-service education tends to be ineffective in disturbing inert ideas. He argues that neophyte teachers "most probably leave our programmes with their deeply-held beliefs intact, ready to teach as they learned during their apprenticeships of observation" (1994: 215). The perennial problem is that these neophyte teachers are "insiders" (Hoy and Murphy, 2001), their views of teaching shaped by their own experience, so that they return to the places of their past, complete with memories and preconceptions often unaffected by their higher education or training college experience. They may feel they have no need to "discover" the classroom or to see it with new eyes because they are already so familiar with the territory – having spent the last dozen or so years of their lives in similar places (Pajares, 1993).

The enduring challenge for those who lead is how to address the disconnect between what teachers believe and aspire to, on the one hand, and what they actually do on a day-to-day basis in their classrooms. As Joyce and Showers (2002) point out, it easy for teachers to know what they should do, harder for them to be able to do it, and most difficult of all for them to embed it into their daily practice. This is characterised by Mary Kennedy (1999) as "the problem of enactment" – the difficulty teachers face in translating into effective practice and coherent action the ideas they may have embraced yet struggle to make the connection between what seems to be right in principle and what is right in the circumstances. The disconnect is likely to remain without it being recognised, understood and addressed, unless teachers feel themselves to be part of a learning community in which these issues are made explicit and open to debate.

How then do leaders create a "community", a climate in which these issues can be explored? How can they bring to the surface the tensions and implicit theories that are not simply relevant for new teachers but may be even more deeply ingrained among long-serving staff who have done their time and for whom the "urgency to learn" has dissipated? How can the idealism that brought them into teaching be sustained or, for others, re-ignited, engaging them in tasks that challenge and that extend their repertoire, and provide collegial support and inspiration? Many of those who come fresh to teaching are mid-career entrants with a background outside education, accustomed to working in teams and finding difficulty with the social isolation which so often cuts teachers off from the vital sources of support – their colleagues. When teachers shut their classroom doors and deny entry to their colleagues they close themselves off from their own learning and from their own professional enrichment. They close themselves off from sources and opportunities which have been found to be powerful in country contexts as diverse as Japan, New Zealand and Singapore.

As the National Commission on Teaching and America's Future (NCTAF, 2003) reported a decade ago, where there is a culture which creates opportunities for reflection, together with colleagues and with the support of skilled mentoring, teachers are more likely to stay in the profession, more likely to continue to learn during a critical transition time (during their first year when they are expected to take theories about teaching and learning and turn them into classroom practice), and will be more effective in helping students learn.

In Sweden, Birgitte Malm's descriptions of competences and qualities necessary for future teachers were taken as a starting point for a wider discussion on the crucial role of beliefs and emotions in being and becoming a teacher (2009). The six emerging competences she described as:

- developing teachers' capacities for creative and reflective thought

- enhancing critical thinking

- heightening teachers' philosophical and pedagogical awareness

- emphasising the cognitive as well as emotional aspects of teaching

- training teachers' capacities for empathy and interpersonal collaboration

- developing a personal understanding of the implications of teaching perceived as a moral and ethical profession.

This raises the question of leadership which is able to foster the quality of collegiality most likely to achieve these six aims. It prompts the question as to how teachers are, in the first instance, inducted into a profession and what measures leaders take to sustain their professionalism over time. Without opportunities to address the emotional intelligence of teaching, without opportunities for reflection and critical re-appraisal of conventional wisdom, teachers will simply replicate the *status quo*, or even more worrisome, regress to the didactics of a mythical golden age when supposedly standards were high, when teachers taught and children learned.

The critical and contentious issues for leaders is, in Hampden-Turner's terminology, to understand, and to manage, the "dilemma space" which occurs between the rock and the whirlpool, between the push of the known and familiar, on the one hand, and the pull of an uncertain future, on the other (2007). The rock values – consistency, reliability, performance, competition and transparency – he counterpoints with the whirlpool values of choice, diversity, dynamism, spontaneity and autonomy. Failure to address the tensions between certainty and uncertainty, between individuality and collectivity, the comfort of the past and the risk of the future is, he argues, a failure of forward-looking leadership.

If inert ideas are to be confounded, insight cultivated, and energy and commitment revitalised, it will be in schools rich in opportunities for self-evaluation, reflection and celebration in which learning dispositions and behaviour are modelled, made visible and internalised. It is through a culture of inquiry and self-evaluation deeply embedded in the daily routines of classroom life, that schools gain the strength of conviction to expose what constrains authentic learning and, with an enhanced sense of agency, are able to show how things can be different (Aguerrondo and Vezub, 2011).

Self-evaluation: a hallmark of the learning community

The term "self-evaluation" has acquired so many different meanings, and been co-opted by so many political interests, that it rarely captures the depth of reflection and dialogue that is promised by such a powerful idea. In the best of practice, self-evaluation refers to the process by which leaders work to create a climate in which teachers and schools are enabled to make their intellectual and moral journey, measuring the distance they have travelled, not in the currency of summative measures that say little about deep learning. The tools of authentic, professionally-driven self-evaluation, by contrast, are set in a social context. They focus on learning and the conditions which promote it. They encourage dialogue. They enable critical reflection on the nature of leadership and accountability.

In countries where self-evaluation has taken root, it is by virtue of prescient leadership, in schools in which teachers feel safe to venture, confident in risk-taking and equipped with self-evaluation tools which serve a primarily formative purpose. Teachers are willing to adopt and adapt tools which they see as going to the heart of learning and teaching – congenial, flexible and adaptable to new situations and to emerging challenges. These tools are, however, not limited to what happens in classrooms nor only to students' learning. They apply to teacher, organisational and leadership learning. They measure how teachers are progressing in their thinking and practice and how the school is developing as a community of learners. Accountability is no longer something to be feared, but rather relished because it is the platform for telling a story rooted in evidence of the most profound kind.

Self-evaluating teachers who, in Rousseau's aphorism "lose time to save it", take time out to explore with their students the nature, processes and mysteries of learning, finding that "lost" time is repaid by students' deeper grasp of how, when, where, with whom and why, they learn best. The "what" which has been the defining characteristic of learning and of teachers' subject identity, has by the inexorable impetus of social change given way to the "why" and "how" and even the "where" and "when". To ask the question "why?", which would in the past have landed the impudent student in deep trouble, is today a more legitimate and even welcome inquiry. "Because I told you so" is no longer a persuasive response.

Sometimes characterised as the "5Ws plus H", these six interrogative propositions provide a simple but highly generative framework for self-evaluation. In workshops with school leaders and teachers, asked to prioritise among the six, the "what" of learning is frequently ranked in last place. The "who" assumes perhaps the highest priority, not only referring to parents and teachers but to siblings and peers. The peer (or "compositional") effect is a well-researched phenomenon and "who you go to school with" has been repeatedly identified as a significant determinant of parental choice for their children. The "where" and "when", issues of social context, open to question the nature and constraints of classroom learning, the ecology of homework and the growing impact of anytime learning in the virtual world. This in turn brings into question the "how", the engagement with technology and lateral networked learning as against the prevalent transmission mode of classroom learning. And the much less frequently-asked question, but for some the most salient – why?

Exploring the "how" and the "why" questions, Geert Hofstede conducted surveys in school systems around the world to gauge the relative uses of institutional power, to measure the extent to which people in positions of leadership were open to challenge and willing to draw on both feminine and masculine aspects of their character (1991). He was interested in how different societies set the parameters of what may be asked, who may ask it, and what sanctions attend either the wrong answers or the wrong questions. A key aspect of leadership he described as "the ability to tolerate ambiguity" as against a need for the right answers. Living with uncertainty and ambiguity may be a painful experience but it can provide the impulse for self-evaluation. In the words of one school student, contrasting external inspection and self-evaluation, the latter "leads you to where the bodies are buried".

Attending to the student voice has been a growing feature of self-evaluation in a number of countries over the last two decades. In New Zealand (visited by the author as part of an OECD review, see Nusche et al., 2011), students are seen as playing a key role in evaluating the quality of their school as well as contributing to external review. "Voice" is not simply giving rein to spontaneous or untutored feedback but as having a formative intent, helping young people to express their concerns with a deeper understanding of the language of assessment, evaluation and review and giving them opportunities to articulate their views with confidence and thoughtful critique. Evidence from New Zealand schools shows that these issues have been taken seriously and that staff have equipped their students with the skills and vocabulary to talk perceptively about pedagogy, what makes for good learning, and what makes a good school. The generally positive response to self-evaluation and external review by school staff and teacher organisations in that country may be explained by its non-threatening nature, its positive focus on good practice, receptivity to divergent voices, to the school's own efforts at improvement and to the primarily formative character of self-evaluation.

In Hong Kong where, in an educational context, power distance has witnessed a progressively shrinking gap, this is owed in large part to the embedding of self-evaluation in school practice and to the honouring of student voices. A continuing process over a decade has witnessed acknowledgement of the insights which students can bring. With 360 degree self-evaluation embraced, students' feedback to their teachers and teachers' feedback to their senior leaders has produced both soul-searching and transformation of pedagogy. The best of schools are now distinguished by collaborative lesson planning, lesson study, peer evaluation supported by School Improvement Teams composed of a cross section of teachers, middle and senior managers (and sometimes students) – collegial leaders of learning. (MacBeath, 2009)

A Hong Kong principal talked to me about using his first year in post "to listen and learn, to feel and experience the culture", to engage in dialogue with a range of stakeholders, each day inviting a different group of students or teachers to conversations over lunch in his office. Only when he felt he had gained their trust, did he begin to encourage teachers "to venture forth", to learn from their colleagues and from their students. Professional development grew from an identification of what were described as the "satisfiers" and "dissatisfiers", those aspects of school and classroom life that enhanced learning and those that eroded motivation and engagement. With deeper understanding of these counteracting impulses, self-evaluation tools were developed to take account of the nesting of teachers' experience – within their own classrooms, their departments, their schools, their local neighbourhoods, local policy and national politics and the international standards agendas which touch, however invisibly, teachers' daily work.

In Pasi Sahlberg's recent book *Finnish Lessons* (2011), he points to the critical nature of the teacher collective, their receptivity to challenging their practice and the preconditions essential to pedagogic intercourse. He argues that Finland's high-performing education system is owed to adopting policies counter to those of most Western education systems built on standardisation and prescription, transfer of models of administration from the corporate world, high stakes accountability policies, and control and punitive inspection.

> As Finnish teachers were exploring the theoretical foundations of knowledge and learning and redesigning their school curricula to be congruent with them, their peers in England, Germany, France and the United States struggled with increased school inspection, controversial externally-imposed learning standards, and competition that disturbed some teachers to the point that they decided to leave their jobs (Sahlberg, 2011: 5)

Changing contexts for learning

How we view the concept of a "high-performing system" depends on what we see as the purposes of education and the expectations we have of children and teachers. As contexts for learning broaden and diversify, what counts as valued performance is bound to change. With reference to the changing contexts of learning and teaching Mayer, Pecheone and Merino write:

> Challenging curriculum expectations and more diverse learners mean that teachers have to be more sophisticated in their understanding of the effects of context and learner variability on teaching and learning. Instead of implementing set routines, teachers need to become ever more skilful in their ability to evaluate teaching situations and develop teaching responses that can be effective under different circumstances. (2012: 115)

As the information explosion accelerates and paths of entry to information become more and more accessible, the role and expertise of the teacher shifts from knowledge (or information) provider to mediator and learner. In what is referred to as "the knowledge society", the emphasis is on the skills that are needed to create new forms of understanding.

> These are skills such as problem solving, communication, collaboration, experimentation, critical thinking and creative expression. These skills become curricular goals in themselves and the objects of new assessment methods. Perhaps the most significant aim is for students to be able to create their own learning goals and plans – to establish what they already know, assess their strengths and weaknesses, design a learning plan, stay on-task, track their own progress, build on successes

and adjust to failures. These are skills that can be used throughout a lifetime to participate in a learning society. (UNESCO, 2012: 17)

"Under different circumstances" is a telling phrase because it challenges the contained setting of the classroom. It challenges the comfort zone of those who know telling those who don't know. It opens to scrutiny the nature of behaviour settings and "construction sites". The former refers to the conditioned response of human beings to the physical environment in which they find themselves. The latter refers to ways in which intelligence is "constructed" by the places and people whom we congregate with, who either constrain or enhance desire and determination.

Learning beyond schooling

Success in school does not, contended John Dewey, vouchsafe "the capacity to act intelligently in new situations". "How many students were rendered callous to ideas? How many lost the impetus to learn because of the way in which learning was experienced by them?" (1938: 7)

The most conspicuous failure of schools as we know them has been to isolate and insulate learning so that school learning stays obstinately within classrooms while learning for living is what happens outside. Dewey's prescient comment is now supported by empirical evidence as to the "special skills" that children acquire in order to navigate the peculiar territory that is school. Evidence shows that this navigational know-how is one the most significant factors in discriminating between those who succeed in school and those who fail. It was described by Gray and colleagues (1999) as "tactical learning", a surrogate for deep and meaningful learning.

In 2010 at a conference in the United Arab Emirates, the Oxford scholar Baroness Greenfield reported how eleven-year-olds spent their time: over the course of a school year, 900 hours in school are overshadowed by 1 277 hours spent out of school and 1 934 hours in the virtual world. More important perhaps than the relative amounts of time in different settings, however, is the nature of the learning activity in differing contexts. Learning in informal environments, when compared with classroom learning, reveals a primarily social, spontaneous and exploratory character. Learning to swim, ride a bicycle, play the piano, read a map, navigate unfamiliar terrain, lead a team, solve a problem, all benefit from certain common features – they are embedded in relationships, learner-centred, concerned with skills and dispositions, contextualised, enjoyable but risky, supportive but challenging, relaxed but alert, age blind.

As Gardner, Perkins, Dweck and others have shown, transfer of learning from the structured teacher-directed ethos of the classroom to an unstructured ambiguous "open field" has a very low success rate. This is due, argued David Perkins in a lecture at Strathclyde University in March, 2008 to three key factors. One, students have to be able to spot the problem. Two, they need to be motivated to want to engage with the problem. Three, they then need to have the ability to select and use the most appropriate tools to solve the problem. In his book *The Unschooled Mind* (1991), Howard Gardner reported similar findings with college students. He found that physics students could not solve the most basic problems if posed in a context slightly different from the one in which they first encountered them. Even successful students responded to problems with the same confusions and misconceptions as young children, reverting to their own implicit theories formed in childhood.

In much of the problem-solving in classrooms, it is the teachers who present the problems, and often also provide a method for solving them. Psychologist Robert Sternberg describes students who arrive in college bright, well-schooled, and examination-smart but without what he called the practical, creative and successful intelligences that really matter in life (Sternberg. 2007). Gardner, revisiting his own well-known seven intelligences, added a further eighth to the list which he calls naturalistic (or environmental) intelligence, finding your way and negotiating a path in the complex social world beyond the cloisters of the classroom.

To be truly skilful outside of school, children and young people must develop situation-specific forms of competence. In school, learning is more generalised, creating a situation whereby "very little can be transported directly from school to out-of-school use", writes Carol Dweck (1986). She makes the following contrasts:

- individual cognition in school versus shared cognition outside

- pure mentation in school versus tool manipulation outside

- symbol manipulation in school versus contextualised reasoning outside

- generalised learning in school versus situation-specific competencies outside (1986: 12).

The more we learn about the nature and processes of learning that take place out of school, the less we are justified in the pretence that schools and teachers alone can repair the impact of society and the economy on the lives of families and on children as yet unborn. As the political imperative grows to make schools more effective, more accountable and more transparent, so the burden falls more squarely on school leaders to demonstrate that it is teaching, not environment, not family, not socio-economics, not culture, not history, that makes the difference. At the same time they recognise the critical importance of cultivating opportunities for "other learning experiences".

In Hong Kong where 15% of the curriculum must now be devoted to "other learning experiences" (OLE), teachers attest to a profound impact on their knowledge and professional expertise when they work with young people in unfamiliar or less tightly structured and prescriptive contexts than the classroom, such as in community projects, visits to Macau, Singapore or mainland China. It is, as in other examples, a liberating experience not to be cast in the teacher/teller role but to be free not to know, not to be the expert or the ultimate authority. The evaluation of OLEs found that the key distinguishing feature of school leaders was the ability and insight to see "other" learning experiences not simply as an additional curricular activity, or at worst, as a tedious distraction from the real business of the school. Rather the best of leaders saw OLE as the vital spark, stimulating curiosity, invention and renewed motivation, and re-invigorating classroom learning.

> The evaluation brought to light one of the inherent paradoxes of school and out-of-school learning. Senior students in their final two years of school were asked their opinions of OLE, resulting in mainly negative comments. They were then asked to review their last school week, drawing a horizon line across the middle of a landscape A4 sheet, and writing in, above and below the line, their most engaging learning experiences as against those least engaging. In the great majority of cases the "above-the-line" entries all referred to aspects of OLE. Brought to consciousness it came as a surprise to these young people. For a minority, however, they had made the connections, attributed in large part to the quality of leadership in their schools, not only of their senior managers but by virtue of the leadership of teachers and students themselves. They also understood the concept of "deep learning" and were able to speak with confidence about their own meta-cognitive activity and about education without "containing walls".

Schools without walls

Twenty years ago, before the invention of the virtual world, the world beyond the school offered an alternative arena for lifelong learning. Parkway in Philadelphia was an iconic demonstration of a powerful alternative to desk-bound learning. Parkway, the central artery which runs through the heart of the city, offered the learning space for a whole curriculum, centred on the agencies which compose the life of a city. With no school building, the classroom was the city and the hidden resources for learning were at first hand. This not only saved millions on school buildings, textbooks, administration and all the paraphernalia that consumes the lion's share of the education budget but also was able to show that young people have a much greater capacity for initiative than schools give them credit for.

The Parkway model inspired an initiative in the 1970s in two secondary schools in Scotland. Two classes of young people enjoyed the experience of learning in and around the city of Glasgow for the third term of their third secondary school year, never touching down at school but trusted to make journeys on their own across the city to learning destinations chosen by them. These included the AA (Automobile Association), the ambulance service, hospitals, car workshops and car markets, manufacturers, shops and farms, the Scottish National Orchestra, the Glasgow University Observatory, the Royal Navy, the zoo, the Glasgow Museum, and art galleries. These sites not only hosted young people but, together with them, built coherent, structured, individualised educational programmes.

A radical extension of learning without walls is exemplified in another Scottish venture. Now in its fifteenth year, the *Learning School* brings together students from schools around the globe, provides a four-week induction in the Shetland Islands and then sends these young people off on a nine-month exploratory journey, on their own and teacher-less, around the world. Their task is to evaluate school life and learning in countries which have, over its 14-year lifespan, included Germany, Sweden, the Czech Republic, South Africa, South Korea, Hong Kong, Japan, New Zealand and the United States. In each country, these young people live with host families for a four-week period, experiencing neighbourhood and community life, shadowing their peers as they go to school and then, armed with a toolbox of evaluation strategies, compiling and presenting a report back to the school at the end of the stay.

One of products of their experience is their co-authored book "Self Evaluation in the Global Classroom" (MacBeath and Sugimime, 2003), in which they describe some of the challenges they faced in two key respects. On the one hand, critical accounts of learning and teaching told from a student's eye view could be welcome and enlightening but also discomforting for teachers to hear in feedback sessions from these acolyte researchers. Even harder to deal with was the challenge of how to deal with values and expectations of the families, which could be disturbing. For example Sophie, who lived with a black family in the South African township, recounts the shock on the first day when the daughter of her own age expressed her dislike for white people, a shock for Sophie, who had never before had to face such explicit racism. This experience was instrumental in helping Sophie reflect on her own prejudices, acknowledging her own ignorance as a root of bigotry, and coming to value harsh experience, as she later wrote, "an important lesson for life". Jolene, 16 years old, summarised her experience in these words – "I have probably learnt as much in these ten months as I did in thirteen years of school".

Who leads learning in these very diffuse and fluid contexts? One of the most profound lessons we have learned from the Learning School is the hidden capacity of young people to rise spectacularly to the challenges of leadership in the most challenging and unpredictable of circumstances. The bold architect of the programme, Stewart Hay, had a vision plus an incredible act of faith, believing that young people, entrusted with agency and ownership, would quickly learn to lead and to share leadership when faced with new and sometimes formidable obstacles. The situations they encountered and the obstacles they surmounted required them to reframe their identities, to see themselves not simply as students and the "consumers of other people's wisdom", but as leaders of their own and of other students' learning.

In every new challenge or crisis, encountered on an almost daily basis, they found their own solution in a pragmatic exercise of shared leadership. Over 14 years, involving over 150 young soon-to-be leaders of learning, as Stewart Hay testified, no one ever let him down or betrayed the trust invested in them. A 16-year-old student from Shetland wrote, in summary:

> This year has been a massive education to us all, an almost vertical learning curve. I often worried that I was not using this opportunity to learn as much as I could, but now after having stepped back indefinitely from this particular journey I can see how by watching and feeling another culture from within you cannot help but learn infinite amounts. It is the greatest educational tool ever to have at one's disposal. Teaching things schools will never be able to teach, through first-hand experience, feeding a desire to understand the world in which we live. This year has given me a real thirst to continue to test myself academically and to become more aware of different societies, cultures and people, as I am sure it has to everyone who was a part of Learning School 2. (Colin, in MacBeath and Sugimine, 2003: 36)

"Feeding a desire to understand the world" is a profound statement, a counterpoint to these young people's school experience that at best had offered a vicarious view of the world and always attended by the need to reproduce a condensed version for the benefit of examinations. A 16-year-old Korean student, speaking emotionally at a Cambridge conference at the culmination of Learning School 3, described how, for the first time, he had found his own voice after ten years of school. Preoccupation with hard work, after-hours cramming and swotting for exams, had left neither time nor incentive to think for himself, nor to question received wisdom from his teachers.

A university for children

The power of learning beyond school is nowhere better exemplified than in the Children's University (CU). Now its fourth year it describes itself on the website like this:

The Children's University aims to promote social mobility by providing high quality, exciting and innovative learning activities and experiences outside normal school hours to children aged 7 to 14 (and 5 and 6 year olds with their families) and engaging the wider communities as learning partners in the realisation of this. At the heart of its work is the ambition to raise aspirations, boost achievement and foster a love of learning, so that young people can make the most of their abilities and interests, regardless of the background into which they were born. (www.childrensuniversity.co.uk/about-us/)

The aim is for children to engage voluntarily with a variety of high quality learning activities, outside school hours. These activities, which take children into new learning sites and new experiences, are known as "Learning Destinations". These are validated by the Children's University following a national framework, *Planning for Learning,* which provides a guide to quality assurance in informal environments such as art galleries, docks, stations, airports, stately homes and gardens, DIY superstores and urban trails (MacBeath and Graus, undated). Children are in charge of their own learning and accumulate credits towards "graduation". Mick Waters, former director of the Qualifications and Curriculum Authority (QCA) in England emphasises the voluntary and active nature of learning in the CU in an unpublished interview for Bangs, MacBeath and Galton (2010) (quotation reproduced in MacBeath, 2012: 18).

Children's learning is best when they do the natural things and we help them to cross thresholds as a result. They make, do and mend, they have adventures, they produce plays and shows, play instruments, speak different languages, and they grow things, care for creatures and have collections. All of these are gateways that teachers make into turnstiles to a brighter future. The Children's University is committed to offering children a brighter future by showing them how learning can be a challenging but enjoyable way to organise time and can make the changing horizon irresistible.

By April 2012, there were 80 local CUs in the U.K., accounting for 3 000 schools and academies and over 100 000 children, with a total of just over 2 million hours of attendance. Visits to the 175 learning destinations across the country are validated by stamps on children's passports, accumulating credits for graduation which take place in universities presided over by the Vice Chancellor celebrating 30, 60, 90, or 120 hours of credits gained. These formal occasions introduce children and their parents, from disadvantaged backgrounds, to what a university is and the route to this previously undreamed of destination. The loss rate among the 250 000 passports issued is around 2%, comparing favourably with the 17% adult loss rate of their actual international passports.

An important principle of the Children's University is that participation is voluntary. It is intentionally something other than school – with a distinctive ethos, different kinds of activities, often with different staff members and peer group membership. The ultimate testament to the effectiveness of the Children's University is that young people give up their time to attend and that they begin to realise that learning can be "a satellite navigation system to better places in life". As children's participation and commitment continue to increase, they begin to play a more proactive role in generating ideas for future activities and grow greater confidence in assuming leadership. However, as long as the Children's University is seen as a contrast, a counterbalance or an alternative to school the less scope there is for systemic change. A critical measure in the evaluation of the success of the CU has to be the extent to which it feeds back into the classroom experience and helps to build the bridges between learning and leadership in and out of school.

The more the potential to learn in sites outside school is opened up, the more imaginative and unexpected the result and the greater the challenge to the nature of children's classroom experience. One of the latest additions to the repertoire of learning destinations which have fed back into classroom inquiry is a cemetery. What questions might be provoked and pursued by structured and focused explorations in a cemetery? Family histories, changing family size over the years, child mortality, changing life expectancy and advances in medical care, are just some possible examples.

Each CU site is linked to a "grown up" university which may offer its own programmes and lectures on, for example: how insects see the world, pyromania, the truth behind *Finding Nemo*, "the Mummy Project" led by a leading world expert in Egyptology which offers hands-on activities such as making a mummy, ancient Egyptian gods, writing in hieroglyphs, the Egyptian number system and Egyptian jigsaws. On Saturday mornings, a do-it-yourself superstore offers its own lectures and workshops. In communities around the country, local libraries sign up and display the *Learning Destinations* logo, crediting children's reading and peer book reviews together with engaging activities such as Eat Your Words Edible Poetry, Kid's Poetry Tea Party and Kids' Poetry Treasure Hunt, in which children hunt for individual lines of poetry and use them to create their own poem. (MacBeath, 2012: 15)

As the evaluation of the Children's University (MacBeath, 2012) shows, where there is imagination, inspiration and the revitalisation of learning it is owed to exemplary leadership, inspirational people who refuse to be captive of limiting boundaries and conventions. What the evaluation also highlights are unforeseen opportunities to complement and enrich classroom learning, proving to be life changing for teachers as well as for their pupils. Disillusion can become ambition and failure may be turned to success. The escape from the classroom allows teachers to engage with children in different environments and to listen, free from pressures of time and targets, leading to a new understanding of children's lives and learning. For parents too there are beneficial returns resulting from their children's motivation and as they gain new insights from their offspring.

A set of propositions and principles for leading learning and learning leadership arise from these various initiatives and from the national evaluation of the Children's University:

- The scope for learning without being taught complements and enriches children's learning and teachers' teaching.

- Recognising that learning is a social activity requires attention to ways in which children and young people are able to support, share and challenge one another.

- Engagement and ownership are fostered in contexts where opportunities for learning are scaffolded so as to promote inquiry and discovery.

- The potential of sites for learning ("construction sites") is still largely unexplored but have a major contribution to make in bringing learning to life.

- Classroom learning has to be seen not as the whole but as the complement to what is learned outside school, both drawing on and feeding into what is learned elsewhere.

These principles and propositions assume that school will still be with us for the foreseeable future. Schools may, however, assume less of a monopoly and play a role more as hubs or agencies, defining what schools can do best and what is best learned in other contexts and through other agencies. Herein lies a leadership challenge, looking outwards as well as inwards, loosening rather than tightening the scope of learning from the "closed" to the "open" classroom. We can say with some confidence that, with prescient leadership, learning in the captive classroom will increasingly be challenged and complemented by other pathways, sites and forms of relationship. We can assert with some confidence that the nature of teaching will be shaped and enriched by the sources and possibilities that progressively open up.

The greater the opportunities that arise to exploit learning sites beyond the classroom, the more it will demand of those who lead learning in whatever capacity they hold within a school or within associated agencies. It will require them to help teachers to extend their repertories individually and in concert. The more children and young people assume control of their own learning the greater the pedagogic insight and adaptability it will require of teachers and teacher leaders. The more children and young people become independent and interdependent learners the greater the strategic resourcefulness it will imply for those who lead and shape children's learning. The more there is a genuine sense of agency among learners, the greater is the need for an enhanced capacity on the part of teachers to steer, guide, intervene or stand back as the occasion demands. This does not preclude conventional teaching strategies – question and answer sessions, demonstrations and direct instruction, for example – but these will become a smaller and complementary part of the teacher's repertoire and rest on a fine judgment as to when, where and how to intervene in the learning process and to what end.

As young people are exposed to a range of "construction sites" there is an obvious corollary for those who teach them. Teachers who live out their entire careers within the four walls of their classroom may be deprived of the kind of wider experiences which their students enjoy, trapped within a limited and limiting version of "real life". With opportunities to move beyond the classroom, teachers may be encouraged and enabled to travel across different sectors of the economy, to experience different working environments, to learn from team working, from opportunities for individual and shared leadership, from new forms of incentives and rewards. Coming to recognise and live with change as a constant, can revitalise teaching and learning. Leaders of learning may then look forward to a new and challenging age.

Note

1.   Professor Emeritus, Faculty of Education, University of Cambridge.

References

Aguerrondo, I. and L. Vezub (2011), "Leadership for effective school improvement: Support for schools and teachers' professional development in the Latin American region", in T. Townsend and J. MacBeath (eds.), *International Handbook of Leadership for Learning,* Springer, Rotterdam.

Bangs, J., J. MacBeath and M. Galton (2010), *Reinventing Schools, Reforming Teaching: From Political Visions to Classroom Reality,* Routledge, London.

Dewey, J. (1938) *Experience and Education,* Kappa Delta Pi, New York.

Dweck, C.S. (1986), "Motivational processes affecting learning", *American Psychologist.* 41(10), 10-48.

Frost, D. (2005), "Resisting the juggernaut: Building capacity through teacher leadership in spite of it all", *Leading and Managing,* 10(2), 70-87.

Garavan, T. (1997), "The learning organization: A review and evaluation", *The Learning Organization*, 4)(1), 18-29.

Gardner, H. (1991), *The Unschooled Mind: How Children Think and How Schools Should Teach,* Basic Books, Philadelphia, PA.

Gray, J. et al. (1999), *Improving Schools: Performance and Potential*, Open University Press, Buckingham.

Hampden-Turner, C. (2007), "Keynote address", Leadership of Learning Seminar, Peterhouse College, Cambridge, April.

Heschel, A.J. (1969), *The Prophets,* Harper Rowe, New York.

Hesselbein, F., M. Goldsmith, R. Beckard and P. Drucker (1996), *The Leader of the Future*, Jossey-Bass, San Francisco.

Hofstede, G. (1991), *Culture and Organisations,* McGraw-Hill, London.

Hoy, A. and P. Murphy (2001), "Teaching educational psychology to the implicit mind", in B. Torff, and R. Sternberg (eds.), *Understanding and Teaching the Intuitive Mind: Student and Teacher Learning,* Lawrence Erlbaum Associates, Mahwah, NJ, 145-86.

Ingersoll, R.M. (2003) *Is There Really a Teacher Shortage?* Center for the Study of Teaching and Policy, University of Washington, Seattle.

Joyce, B. and B. Showers (2002), *Student Achievement through Staff Development,* 3rd edition, Longman, New York.

Kennedy, M.M. (1999), "The role of pre-service teacher education", in L. Darling-Hammond and G. Sykes (eds.), *Teaching as the Learning Profession: Handbook of Teaching and Policy,* Jossey Bass, San Francisco, 54-86.

MacBeath, J. (2012), *Evaluating Provision, Progress and Quality of Learning in the Children's University*, Fourth Report to the CU Trust, Faculty of Education, University of Cambridge, Cambridge UK.

MacBeath, J. (2009), *Impact Study on the Implementation of School Development and Accountability Framework for Enhancing School Improvement in Hong Kong,* Education Manpower Bureau, Hong Kong.

MacBeath, J. et al. (2009), *The Recruitment and Retention of Headteachers in Scotland*, Scottish Government, Edinburgh.

MacBeath, J. and N. Dempster (eds.) (2008), *Connecting Leadership and Learning: Principles for Practice*, Routledge, London.

MacBeath, J. and H. Sugimine, with Gregor Sutherland, Miki Nishimura and the students of the Learning School (2003), *Self-Evaluation in the Global Classroom,* Routledge Falmer, London.

MacBeath, J. and G. Graus (undated), *Planning for Learning; A National Framework for Validating Learning,* Children's University, Manchester.

Malm, B. (2009), "Towards a new professionalism: enhancing personal and professional development in teacher education", *Journal of Education for Teaching,* 35(1), 77–91.

Martin, P.R. (1997), *The Sickening Mind*, Flamingo, London.

Mayer, D., R. Pecheone and N. Merino (2012), "Rethinking teacher education in Australia", in L. Darling-Hammond and A. Lieberman (eds.), *Teacher Education Around the World*, New York, Routledge.

McLaughlin, M,W. and J.E. Talbert (2001), *Professional Communities and the Work of High School Teaching,* University of Chicago Press, Chicago.

NCTAF (2003), *No Dream Denied: A Pledge to America's Children*, National Commission on Teaching and America's Future, Washington, DC.

Nusche, D., D. Laveault, J. MacBeath and P. Santiago (2011), *OECD Reviews of Evaluation and Assessment in Education: New Zealand*, OECD Publishing, Paris. http://dx.doi.org/10.1787/9789264116917-en.

O'Connell Rust, F. (1994), "The first year of teaching: It's not what they expected", *Teaching and Teacher Education,* 10(2), 205-217.

Pajares, F. (1993), "Pre-service teachers' beliefs: A focus for teacher education", *Action in Education*, 15(2), 45–54.

Sahlberg, P. (2011), *Finnish Lessons: What Can the World Learn from Educational Change in Finland?* Teachers College Press, Columbia University, New York.

Senge, P. (1990), *The Fifth Discipline: The Art and Practice of the Learning Organization,* Doubleday Currency, New York.

Sternberg, R.J. (2007), *Wisdom, Intelligence, and Creativity Synthesized*, Cambridge University Press, New York.

UNESCO (2011), *UNESCO ICT Competency Framework for Teachers*, UNESCO (United Nations Educational, Scientific and Cultural Organization), Paris.

Wright, D.P., M.D. McKibbin and P.A. Walton (1987), *The Effectiveness of the Teacher Trainee Program: An Alternative Route into Teaching in California,* California Commission on Teacher Credentialing, Sacramento, CA.

Chapter 4

Leadership for 21st century learning in Singapore's high-performing schools

Clive Dimmock
University of Glasgow

Dennis Kwek
National Institute of Education, Nanyang Technological University, Singapore

Yancy Toh
National Institute of Education, Nanyang Technological University, Singapore

This chapter by Clive Dimmock, Dennis Kwek, and Yancy Toh presents a model for developing learning-centred leadership appropriate for the 21st century. The approach is the "school design model", employing a distinctive "backward mapping" or iterative methodology. It starts with "21st century knowledge and skills" covering global awareness, health literacy, creativity, financial and economic literacy, citizenship, critical thinking and problem-solving, and digital literacy. It then moves to the corresponding teaching, learning and support systems covering curriculum, teaching and pedagogy, assessment and standards, organisational structures, teacher professional development, and culture and environment. Finally, it maps leadership onto this, understood as learning-centred, *emphasising leadership of curricula, teaching and learning;* distributed *thereby empowering teachers and building capacity; and* community networked, *and so benefiting from the resources of other schools and the community. The chapter applies the model in detail to two case-study schools in Singapore that for more than a decade have practised learning-centred leadership.*

Introduction

This chapter presents a model for developing learning-centred leadership appropriate for school improvement and transformation in the 21st century. It applies the model to two schools in Singapore that for more than a decade have practised learning-centred leadership aimed at creating innovative 21st century learning environments. The approach is that of the school design model, employing a distinctive "backward mapping" or iterative methodology.

Applying the model in Singapore is significant for two main reasons. First, Singapore is generally regarded on a range of international indicators as a high-performing Asian school system adhering to traditional methods of pedagogy. Even so, there are schools that have boldly undertaken transformation for more than a decade, convinced of the need to create innovative learning environments built on contemporary notions of school design and leadership. Their motive has been to equip their students with the knowledge and skills thought to be essential for Singapore to maintain its competitive and innovative edge in the global marketplace. Second, previous applications of the school design model have been largely confined to Anglo-American contexts, in particular the USA (Dimmock, 2000), with few examples if any of cross-cultural applications, in Asia and in Singapore specifically.

The context of the Singapore school system

Singapore is a small island republic with a population that has grown from 1.8 million in 1965 to 5.1 million in 2011. It has just over 350 schools, with only about 20 of these independent. Singapore sought independence as a city state on breaking away from Malaysia in 1965, although it had ended a long period of British colonial rule in 1959. Remarkably, Singapore has risen from a third-world to a first-world economy, with a gross domestic product per capita now higher than that of the UK. Singapore's population is urbanised and densely concentrated – hence the relatively small number of schools and their large, uniform size – the average student numbers in primary and secondary schools are a high 1 500 and 1 300, respectively (Barber, Whelan and Clark, 2010). Singapore students have performed at or near the top of international achievement tests in mathematics and science for years, earning it the reputation as one of the best performing systems in the world (Mourshed, Chijoke and Barber, 2010).

The Singapore educational system remains highly centralised and regulated after three decades of reorganisation, consolidation and reform (Gopinathan, 1985; Hogan and Gopinathan, 2008). Over the last five years, there has been a significant but limited shift towards the decentralisation of administrative and pedagogical authority to individual schools. All teachers are trained at the National Institute of Education (NIE), whose policies and practices, as well as educational research agenda, are closely aligned to the Ministry of Education's (MOE) priorities and schools' needs.

The Ministry of Education's strategic policies since 1997 are indicative of top-down initiatives to create the infrastructure for school change. Such measures have sought to professionalise teachers, promote their professional development, and encourage schools and teachers to adopt more innovative teaching and learning practices. Evidence from a system-wide research programme sponsored by the MOE (Hogan et al., 2013) reveals, however, that despite the policy platform in place to promote innovative school learning environments, teachers' practices and classroom pedagogy in Singapore are still focused principally on the transmission and assessment ("reproduction") of subject-based curriculum knowledge. The research concludes that the instructional system is dominated by traditional forms of pedagogy at the expense of new pedagogies, for a number of reasons including the national high-stakes assessment. Overwhelmingly, teachers in Singapore rely on whole-class forms of lesson organisation, with whole-class lectures and question-and-answer sequences.

A 21st century leadership model

A basic tenet of the design model for schools is that they prepare students with the knowledge, skills and values to enable them to usefully contribute to future society, and to live successful and fulfilled lives. Innovative school learning environments need to reflect evolving trends in society and economy, and especially the workplaces of the future. As David Hargreaves argues, "We should examine the most impressive of today's workplaces and then re-design schools to serve as a preparation for life in the companies of tomorrow's knowledge economy. That would be radical innovation indeed." (2003:3) Transforming schools on such a scale requires more than piecemeal tinkering. It calls for courageous leadership to engineer changes in leader and teacher roles and practices, and institutional cultures and structures. It demands rethinking leadership, and learning-centred leadership in particular, in a more holistic, strategic perspective and with a strong focus on the elements that shape and support innovative 21st century learning environments. It is "strategic" in connecting broader elements that shape the design process itself (especially the aims, goals and outcomes of learning, namely, what are students learning for?) with an understanding of leadership that extends beyond established 20th century institutional models.

A strategic approach to transforming school learning environments as fit-for-purpose for the 21st century is the school design model (see Dimmock, 2000, 2012). It embraces key interconnected elements, such as curriculum aims and content, assessment systems, learning processes, and teaching practices, as well as structural and technological supports to teaching and learning. At the heart of the model is leadership and its re-conceptualisation; leadership is conceived as the main driving force, orchestrating, implementing, sustaining and scaling up the transformation process in the complex social organisations that are schools. Transformation typically demands sustained leadership over many years, and is anything but smooth and algorithmic.

The school design model has five salient characteristics. First, the model identifies the main elements of a school that are fundamental to its redesign as a 21st century learning environment. Second, it recognises interconnectivity, in that change in one element requires concomitant change in the other elements that functionally inter-relate with it. Third, it is strategic in the sense that, with many changing elements, it is imperative that the process has some order and rationale. Fourth, leadership is the key agency for securing and achieving the school redesign in its completeness, and fundamentally, it is the school design process and the nature of the new learning environments themselves that help to reconceptualise the new leadership that is presaged. Fifth, the model is underpinned by an explicit methodology, known as "backward mapping".

Backward mapping underpinning the school-design model

Redesigning the complex set of operations involved in delivering a 21st century learning environment with relevant curriculum, and high quality teaching and learning, demands the most robust of models. Such a model needs to show the interconnections between the key elements. It should predict the concomitant changes necessary in interconnected elements in responding to an initial trigger change in a particular key element; and it should generate clear strategies to justify the rationale, as well as the sequence and order in which the elements are redesigned and transformed.

Traditionally, reform strategies begin with policy makers and operate top down, so that by the time they permeate through to teachers in classrooms, the original policy aims are distorted or diffused, and practitioners feel minimal ownership. Elmore (1979-80) thus suggested that reform had more chance of maintaining its integrity if the process was reversed so that policy makers map back from the outcomes and classroom practices they want to see implemented, thinking through the implications for each set of agents at different levels up through the system. "Backward mapping", for Elmore, is more likely to achieve fidelity to the original policy intention and to win ownership of the practitioners charged with implementation since they have contributed to the policy formation. It is, in this sense, a bottom-up approach.

The principle of backward mapping meets one of Covey's dictums – namely, that successful people "begin with the end in mind" (Covey, 1989). That is, it asks what learning outcomes – knowledge, skills and values – are needed by 21st century learners. When answers to this question are clarified it is possible to rethink the nature of learning environments, beginning with the curriculum. What curriculum content and structure are most likely to achieve the knowledge, skills and values identified for 21st century learners?

Backward mapping further, the next set of questions are: what learning processes, skills and knowledge will enable students to acquire the desired outcomes? How do different student best learn? How do we enable all students to learn? And, what assessment processes are needed to gauge students' achievement of the learning outcomes, whether they be cognitive, affective, moral or physical?

Further steps in the backward-mapping progression are: what pedagogic practices are most supportive of the learning experiences? In what ways do teachers best enable all students to learn? And then, in support of the new learning and teaching arrangements, how are classrooms and organisational and structural arrangements best designed and configured to support these learning environments? Of particular importance here are the timetable, physical layouts, and the role of technology in teaching and learning.

Backward mapping a further stage, achieving many of the above changes in assessment, learning and teaching – known as the "core technology" – are predicated on furthering teachers' professional development to acquire new skills and practices.

Finally, all the foregoing backward-mapping steps implicitly involve leadership in strategising, organising, sustaining and scaling up. The key roles played by leaders centre on how they approach the transformation of their schools to create innovative learning environments, how they provide appropriate support and professional development, and use the available resources represented by society, the community and parents. It is the core technology of teaching and learning that is at the heart of the model and shapes new conceptions of leadership required to deliver it. This process of backward mapping – from learning outcomes through the key interconnected elements of learning, teaching, technology and organisational infrastructure, to leadership – is depicted in Figure 4.1.

The school design model is holistic and comprehensive and the backward-mapping methodology is logical and algorithmic, driven by the aims of achieving consistency of organisational structures and practices, and of synergy. Both the model and the methodology are by nature simplifications and abstractions. Schools undertaking transformation are unlikely to adopt such a holistic model and algorithmic methodology in its pure form as the basis of their strategy. Over many years, however, school transformations will pass through different phases which, taken together, will include most or all of the elements in the school design model. The change sequence might not be as comprehensive as backward mapping, but the model serves as a heuristic tool by which to assess and evaluate the extent to which schools achieve holistic transformation by following a robust and comprehensive strategy and methodology.

21ˢᵗ century learning outcomes for knowledge-based economies

Figure 4.1 reveals a set of specific knowledge and skills outcomes for 21ˢᵗ century knowledge-based economies. A more globally integrated yet competitive world now places a premium on students having global awareness and literacy. Nation states are concerned about growing income and wealth gaps within their frontiers and declining social mobility, both of which in a globalising world might threaten people's sense of loyalty to, and pride in, their country. These concerns lead to an emphasis on citizenship and life skills. As governments struggle to make state budgets meet growing expectations and aspirations, there is need for better financial and economic literacy, with a view to citizens becoming more financially independent of the state. Likewise, better health education not only results in a more productive labour force, but reduces the state health bill. 21ˢᵗ century workplaces increasingly require their workforces to have innovative and creative skills, critical-thinking and problem-solving capabilities, and to be highly literate in technology and communication.

Curricula and learning experiences that deliver 21ˢᵗ century learning outcomes

Backward mapping from the desired learning outcomes contributes to formulating a curriculum with learning experiences that will help to achieve those outcomes. Hence, as shown in Figure 4.1, alongside the present curriculum emphasis on core subject disciplines (mathematics, sciences, history and so on), there needs to be a greater presence of trans-disciplinary knowledge, enabling the application of knowledge to complex, real-world problems.

If greater emphasis is placed on learners acquiring the techniques of learning and developing higher-order thinking skills across disciplines in addition to disciplinary learning, then curricula and classroom practices are needed that enable students to:

- learn how to learn and acquire meta-cognitive and thinking skills
- learn co-operatively in teams
- seek and create new knowledge

- cope with ambiguous situations and unpredictable problems
- communicate verbally – the spoken and written word
- be creative, innovative and entrepreneurial
- learn trans-disciplinary as well as disciplinary knowledge.

Two aspects deserve particular emphasis: the importance of holistic education, since it incorporates many of the so-called soft skills essential to 21st century learners (e.g. leadership, team work and citizenship), and the key role of technology as a catalyst (rather than an end in itself) for realising the learning skills listed above, as well as driving changes in pedagogy.

Figure 4.1. **The school design model: a framework for 21st century learning leadership**

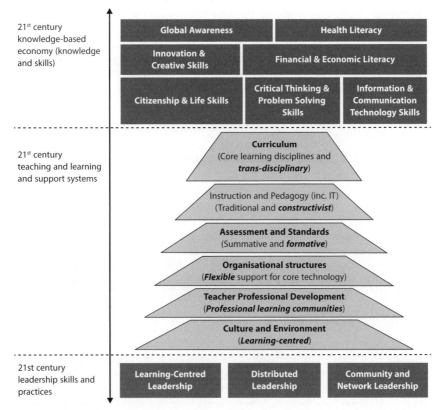

Source: Dimmock, C. and J.W.P Goh (2011).

Such interdisciplinary, integrated and project-based activities provide opportunities for students to experience: *1)* independent learning; *2)* collaborative work as well as interpersonal communication – oral and written; *3)* the integration of knowledge and skills from various disciplines; and *4)* the presentation of their views and learning through different modes of communication such as online discussion boards and student weblogs – all of which are essential skills in the twenty-first century. These practices need to be school-wide (across all departments and domains) and school-deep (adopted by all teachers).

Delivering learning experiences and outcomes

If teachers, leaders and organisational structures are to support students to learn in the ways described above, then school-wide and school-deep transformation is required. Teachers and leaders need to model the knowledge, skills and dispositions their students are to acquire (Hargreaves, 2003). While not rejecting traditional forms of teaching altogether as they can be highly effective in certain situations, teachers are challenged to broaden their repertoire of instructional strategies and methods. Not only must they make pedagogical judgments as to which methods to use and when, but they need the knowledge and skills to use such methods effectively (see Dimmock, 2000).

In broadening their pedagogic strategies, teachers embrace student-focused as well as teacher-focused pedagogies, constructivist as well as didactic methods, and forms of individual and group learning as well as whole-class learning. While still experts in their own discipline, they demonstrate epistemological understanding of how their subject connects across domains and with other disciplines. In creating trans-disciplinary and integrated curricula and classroom learning opportunities, teachers need a flexible cognitive capacity that enables them to adopt interdisciplinary practices. Knowledge is seen as more complex and problematic, requiring problem-based learning (PBL) and inquiry-based learning (IBL) approaches. To enable all students to experience successful learning experiences, more individualised approaches are needed.

Technology and 21st century learning environments

Information technology (IT) occupies an increasingly important place in shaping the innovative learning environments of 21st century schools, and it fulfils diverse roles. It enables students of all abilities to acquire knowledge when and where they need it. It also enables them to gain higher-order skills, such as independent learning, team work and problem-solving. In another way, however, it is a powerful tool for teachers, enabling them to adopt a broader range of teaching methods, facilitating student-focused learning, and extending the boundaries of teaching and learning beyond the classroom. In particular, the use of mobile technologies represent profound technological influences that promise to redefine the ways – when, where and how – in which teaching and learning take place.

For more than a decade, critics of technology in schools have voiced concerns about three main issues: *1)* the take-up of IT by teachers who range from enthusiastic adopters to IT illiterates; *2)* differential access by students whereby wealthier groups are advantaged; and *3)* variable degrees of "embeddedness" across the curriculum as some subjects adopt it whole-heartedly and other subjects less so. While these concerns still exist, considerable progress has been made. Few teachers nowadays can afford to be cynics. The widespread adoption of mobile devices by students (and teachers and society at large), driven by affordability, has led many teachers to keep up to the mark. More especially, any school that denies its students exposure to learning opportunities through IT would be seriously disadvantaging them. IT should still be serving the larger interests of the curriculum, teaching and learning – that is, as a means to an end rather than an end in itself – but its growing influence in the 21st century knowledge-based economy means it has to be understood as a powerful force in its own right.

Wider forms of assessment

Biggs (1999) argues that "constructive alignment" is necessary between the curriculum, pedagogy and assessment. Changes to the curriculum and pedagogy are less likely to be accepted by teachers without concomitant changes to assessment. Teachers need to be convinced that assessment will accurately measure the new curriculum knowledge, skills and values. Many of the 21st century skills are not readily quantifiable through traditional examinations. Hence, new formative and non-quantitative methods of assessment are needed alongside traditional examinations as a gauge of student learning.

Organisational structures for the 21st century

Many past school reforms have foundered on the rigidity of school structures, including the timetable, teachers who are organised into subject departments and guard their independence, and the uniform physical layout of classrooms. The step-wise process of backward mapping through learning outcomes, then the curriculum and pedagogic practices depicted in Figure 4.1 carries instead a strong assumption of flexible organisational structures to enable successful implementation. New curricular, learning and pedagogical practices are presaged on sympathetic changes to organisational structures, especially to teacher grouping, the timetable and classroom layout (including use of physical space, technology and equipment).

Collaborative cross-disciplinary teams

New forms of collaboration involving teachers from different but related disciplines are required for trans-disciplinary curriculum planning and delivery. Teachers thus engage in the same cognitive processes as their students. Collaborative interdisciplinary teaching teams facilitate problem-based learning and the delivery of integrated curricula. Grouping teachers into core teams of four, say, means that such teams may assume responsibility for delivering the whole curriculum to a cohort of students, moving with their cohort through the school and enabling them to develop a close understanding of their students' learning strengths and weaknesses. Specialist teachers for, say, languages, music and physical education can be brought in by each team.

Greater flexibility in time use

An important pre-requisite for innovation in the school design model is greater timetable flexibility. Problem-based learning and trans-disciplinary study, for example, cannot be undertaken in standard 40-minute lessons. Hence, flexibility of learning time is necessary to free up blocks of curricular time (Dimmock, 2000). Blocked timetabling leaves teachers with curricular discretion, as long as each subject area receives its overall allocated share of time over, say, a month or a term.

Schools could also adopt more flexibility in regard to the school year and school day. In some systems, schools are open for little more than half the days of the year, and typically between the hours of 8.30 and 16.00. There is scope for them to open more days of the year, and extend the school day into the evening, with supervised homework classes, and allowing access to facilities such as the gymnasium and library for extended hours, including weekends.

Reconfiguring the classroom

Embedding innovatory classroom practices will often require reconfiguring the physical layout and use of classroom space. Flexible classroom furniture, for example, affords teachers the ability to change the patterns and clusters of desks which, with wireless technology, enables a range of different classroom settings and an array of teaching methods to be adopted, from whole-class teaching, through group work to individual problem solving. Moving the teacher's desk away from the front symbolises a more student-centred learning approach. Mobile desks with computer nodes or wireless network connections enable group and individual work to take place with easy access to the Internet for all students. Redesigning and planning classroom physical space is thus essential in promoting a multi-faceted learning environment. Foldable partitions allow for the reconfiguration of space, as does locating flexi-pods near learning courtyards and eco-trails. These and similar conditions pertaining to flexibility and ease of access to technology, equipment and use of space all interconnect to enable new forms of teaching and learning.

All of the above elements in the school design model are, however, dependent on new configurations of teacher professional development, and new forms of leadership for their school-wide and school-deep adoption. Without a concerted effort towards purposeful teacher professional development, and bold and innovative leadership, the direction, goals and alignment of effort required to build sustainable innovative learning environments will fail to materialise (Hargreaves, 2003).

Developing leaders to deliver the new core technology

In schools successfully undertaking transformation journeys – a process often taking a decade or more – the contribution made by outstanding leadership is critical, especially, but not exclusively, by principals. High-performing leaders use their time more effectively to change the important elements of school design to impact student learning outcomes. They are less mired in administration. The leadership required to transform school learning environments can be deduced by backward mapping through the elements of the school design model. Leadership for transforming schools into 21st century learning environments can thus be characterised as: **learning-centred**, emphasising leadership of curricula, teaching and learning; **distributed**, so that leadership empowers teachers and builds the capacity of available human capital; and **community networked**, thereby benefiting from the resources of other schools and the community. (Dimmock, 2000, 2012)

Learning-centred leaders place teaching and learning – and hence teachers and students – at the heart of their leadership of the school. The creation of learning-centred schools requires leadership which is itself a continuing process of learning (MacBeath and Dempster, 2008). Learning-centred leaders possess the knowledge, skills and dispositions to lead their teachers in adopting innovative curricular, pedagogical and assessment practices. They possess the technical and professional knowledge to engage in close professional relationships and influential dialogue and communication with their teacher colleagues. Such leadership focuses on the strategic vision and goals to improve the learning outcomes of the school, as well as the orchestration and organisational operations to implement the transformation process.

While building 21st century learning environments requires learning-centred leadership, it also necessitates a reconfiguration away from principal-centred to distributed leadership (Heck and Hallinger, 2009; Spillane and Diamond, 2007). Schools need to maximise their use of resources through capacity building – including the empowerment of leaders at all levels – flatter structures and more democratic processes. In short, leadership is nurtured among less experienced teacher colleagues by senior leaders, and leadership itself is dispersed and shared at middle and senior levels. Distributing leadership places even greater onus on senior school leaders, especially principals, to orchestrate and secure alignment, consistency and coherence of policy and leadership practices across the school. Flatter structures bring principals and senior leaders into closer functional relationships with classroom teachers.

The third element of contemporary leadership – community networked – is to engage in networking and sharing of resources with other schools and the community. In creating the vision, strategy and practice to underpin the transformation trajectory, leaders need to garner ideas and resources from multiple sources. Such sources may be other schools which have begun their transformation. They may be research literature and case studies to suggest models and frameworks for an evidence-based approach. Or, they may be through the accumulated tacit knowledge of staff experiences of what they have found to work (Guile, 2006). Principals especially need their communities to see the need for whole-school transformation in preparing students for 21st century workplaces. Parents and community members often oppose departures from tradition, especially in relation to teaching, high stakes assessment and discipline. Yet harnessing parental support is a strategic imperative for any principal intent on transforming the school as a learning environment.

All three forms of leadership – learning-centred, distributed and networked – are involved in developing the school's most important resource of all: its own staff. The building of innovative learning environments is dependent on the quality of professional development, and that in turn is reliant on the quality of leadership.

Promoting teacher professional development

Leaders have an important responsibility for teacher professional development that provides the skills, knowledge and values for 21st century classrooms. Transforming curriculum, pedagogy and assessment school-wide and school-deep renders traditional forms of teacher professional development, such as individual teacher attendance on short courses external to the school, largely ineffectual. Professional development is thus re-conceptualised around schools as professional learning communities (PLCs) (Wenger, 1998; Hord, 2008). School leaders, and especially principals, are instrumental in promoting, sustaining and evaluating PLCs as vehicles for teachers to own and implement the innovations required (Bolam et al., 2005; Louis and Kruse, 1995). In PLCs, all teachers take responsibility for their own professional learning and must engage in peer learning and collaboration. Leaders take responsibility for overseeing the effectiveness of the PLC teams, ensuring that: teacher learning is relevant to the curricular and teaching goals; all teachers are researching and evaluating their practices; all are sharing ideas and working together to research and collect evidence on new improved teaching practices and their implementation; and synergies of adopting new practices are achieved across the school. Primacy is given to promoting shared teacher decision making for adopting evidence-informed practices, whether they are based on peer learning from tacit knowledge or academic research.

Enabling teachers to fully participate in PLC activities requires leaders to invest resources in developing teachers' research and evaluation skills, non-contact time, and provision of tools and templates to make their tasks more manageable. School-wide PLCs are powerful agents for creating learning cultures among teachers. They can also be a key source for leaders' own professional development, in fostering their ability to understand the elements of the school design model and their functional interrelationships, and their capacity to strategise the organisational structures and leadership necessary to deliver new curricula and pedagogies. PLCs offer the opportunity for leadership preparation and development to be more closely aligned with teacher professional development and to be conducted within the school and its network (DuFour and Eaker, 1998).

Leadership *per se* assumes a central role in the development of the intellectual and social capital of the school, and in the deployment of high-leverage strategies to achieve the best learning outcomes. Such leadership activities are vital in building and sustaining a learning-centred school culture.

Case studies of transformation in two schools

The previous section sketched a perspective of learning-centred leadership that derives from a holistic model of school design, the purpose of which is to transform schools into innovative 21st century learning environments. It offers a useful heuristic tool in helping explain and analyse how whole-school transformation takes place in practice; it is applied in this section to two Singapore school case studies.

Case study 1: Fortitude Primary School

Fortitude Primary School (FPS) was founded in the 1940s by a Chinese clan association to provide basic education for the children of immigrants from China. FPS is a government-aided primary school, receiving partial funding from the government and supplementary funding from private sources. It is typically large, with around 1 900 students and 130 teachers. It has a reputation as a high-performing neighbourhood school.

Evidence of success

FPS has received recognition for its innovative use of technology in changing pedagogical practices from a teacher-centred to a student-centred orientation. It has earned a string of accolades over its decade-long use of technology in education, including as a "Microsoft Worldwide Mentor School" and by the Singapore MOE as a centre of excellence for information technology. Earmarked as one of the 15 "Future Schools" by the government, the school serves as an exemplar for integrating the use of information and communications technology (ICT) into its curriculum, pedagogy and assessment across all levels. Unlike many schools, however, technology has increasingly become a catalyst for driving whole-school transformation rather than propagating piecemeal innovations.

School redesign efforts

FPS has redesigned its learning and teaching through a technology-enhanced curriculum since 2002. The whole-school transformation was a gradual process and continued to gain momentum when the new principal came on board in 2007. The redesign effort predicated on the use of technology and incorporated two aspects of the 21st century school-design model: 1) learning leadership skills and practices, and 2) embedding of teaching and learning skills and support systems. This case study is based on qualitative data emerging from interviews, observations of lessons and meetings, and document analysis (Toh, 2013).

21st century leadership skills and practices

Both the former and current principals have played a vital role in shaping the direction of FPS's development. Both envisioned ICT as the catalyst to improve the quality of teaching and learning. They saw its value in fostering participatory learning and connecting students to the larger body of knowledge beyond the classroom. They envisioned that by harnessing technology, students would be well-prepared to become future "knowledge workers". Pedagogically, both principals saw technology as a catalyst for changing teaching practices and transforming classrooms to become student-centred and fundamentally compatible with 21st century learning needs.

A strategic decision was established in 2005 to encourage collective accountability. Decision-making authority was increasingly distributed through different layers of the hierarchy, especially in terms of deciding on which ICT programmes to embark and scale up. This resulted in the effective empowerment of teachers and middle-level leaders, with wider and greater advocacy of the initiatives, and enhanced the organisation's professional capital to make informed choices. Together with the middle-level leaders and teachers, the principal re-examined the priorities for learning and developed an educational framework that strove to balance students' learning of content knowledge and their acquisition of 21st century competencies and values. Three key elements exemplify the latter – developing students' media literacy skills, fostering social-emotional behaviours and competencies, and building capacity for curriculum leadership. Technology was seen as the nexus to bring all three areas together.

Concomitantly, the senior leadership provided an overarching curriculum framework for the use of ICT that was purposefully aligned with the key thrusts of national educational policies. In 2010 – some 10 years after initial ICT reforms had begun – the principal decided that the school would adopt the "Teaching for Understanding" (TfU) framework of Blythe and Perkins (1998). The framework was seen as a way to distil students' depth of understanding as well as to promote collaborative and self-directed learning, both of which were 21st century skills emphasised by the Ministry of Education. A further framework from literature was adopted to guide staff on teaching strategy, namely, Saphier and Gower's (1997), "Skilful Teacher" model, incorporating the philosophy that technology could cater to the different needs of students.

Over time, capacity-building strategies became increasingly structured and multi-pronged, and discernible in: *1)* developing teachers as researchers by leveraging NIE expertise; *2)* deepening the innovation culture by promoting learning circles; *3)* identifying teachers' professional development needs and devising corresponding plans; and *4)* providing mechanisms for reflection through multiple sharing platforms and feedback sessions.

The complexity of ICT-related reform necessitated a concerted effort to change culture, pedagogy, curriculum and assessment. The school could "not walk the journey alone" and so the leadership cemented partnerships with industry and institutes of higher learning. These partners were carefully selected to ensure they added value to the teaching fraternity. For example, in 2009, the school partnered with NIE to set up an in-house research centre. Microsoft Singapore and Microsoft Research Asia joined the alliance in June 2012 to further provide technical expertise. A network of overseas consultants helped to secure additional sponsorship for students' learning tools.

However, as the number of agents and projects increased, so did systemic tensions. These emanated from: *1)* research-practice gaps, most apparent in the divergence between espoused and actual use of ICT; *2)* ideological chasms, such as whether technology should be used as an essential and routine tool in classrooms; and *3)* school-industry-research incompatibilities between bureaucratic and commercial interests, resulting in frustrating delays and additional development costs. These tensions were collectively debated by the senior- and middle-level leadership. The way ahead was seen in establishing a climate of openness and spirit of innovation; a unifying agenda around the key goals of learning and teaching; alignment of resources (financial, structural, professional, time) to support transformation; opportunities for dialogue sessions with key stakeholders, such as parents, teachers, researchers and the clan association around the rationale and outcomes of the interventions; and the prudent spread of innovations where projects that had obtained proof-of-concept were scaled up systematically, leading to a whole-school programme of transformation.

Learning-centred leadership: juxtaposing this approach against the framework for the 21st-century school-design model outlined earlier in the chapter, both principals can be seen to have displayed learning-centred leadership by prioritising student-centred principles when rationalising the use of technology and setting up mechanisms for teacher reflexivity. The new principal after 2008 declared his strong support for the unifying curriculum and pedagogical framework that underpinned all ICT projects, thus giving continuity and sustainability to the change model under way.

Distributed leadership: leadership became increasingly distributed from early on in the change agenda, evident from the fact that the cognition embodied in the decision-making process was spread throughout the hierarchy and driven by the belief that distributed leadership is the key to the sustainability of innovations.

Community and network leadership: the third element of leadership became increasingly sophisticated through the period of actively establishing strategic partnerships to expand the social capital of the school in congruence with the school-design model. Both principals scanned the environment to understand socio-political trends in order to align the school change agenda with trends in system policy making, assessed the school's contextual readiness for transformation, expended energy to mitigate systemic tensions between stakeholders, and explored sources of funding for scaling up technology-related innovations. All of these required nuanced political acumen and navigation, so emphasising the "political skills" element that is fundamental to community and network leadership encapsulated by the school design model.

Embedding 21ˢᵗ century teaching and learning skills and support systems

School leaders saw the importance of the interconnectedness of innovatory processes of teaching, learning skills and support systems in the successful embedding of new practices. The time element is emphasised in the frequent references to, and celebrations of, the transformation journey, thereby building "institutional memory" as a form of social capital. FPS has achieved an evolutionary growth trajectory.

Curriculum: recognising that many of the initial ICT projects were ad hoc and of limited impact, FPS started a more integrated mobile learning trail programme in 2005 and has since scaled it up across all levels in the school. Correspondingly, the curriculum advanced from piecemeal projects to whole-school programmes, and these were anchored more in pedagogical research. Further projects with proof of concepts were incorporated into departmental schemes of work; more cross-departmental collaborations sprang up.

Instruction and pedagogy: departing from the predominant use of electronic worksheets in the earlier years, teachers came to a broad consensus on the purpose and place of ICT within a broader student-centred learning approach. Although there was some incongruence between what was espoused and what was actually enacted, a growing majority of teachers were able to adopt constructivist practices in applying ICT.

Assessment and standards: assessment and standards proved especially unresponsive to change. Along with the curriculum and pedagogical frameworks which were established in 2008, emergent attempts were introduced to make formative assessment more varied and just-in-time, and summative assessment more open-ended and aligned with higher order-thinking skills.

Organisational structures: as FPS accelerated its efforts in scaling up successful innovations from 2009, the demand for organisational restructuring became more pronounced. Teacher grouping was reconfigured based on common interests, or facilitated through centralised flagship projects. An additional three periods were created on a fortnightly basis for science. Teachers also utilised the weekly block timetabling of one and a half hours to discuss projects. The infrastructure in computer laboratories was also reconfigured to facilitate collaborative learning, and classrooms were rewired so that students could charge their equipment when needed.

Professional development: over time, teacher professional development became less technically driven by ICT and more broad based to realise the potential of technology in generating new methods of teaching and learning. Abundant opportunities for professional development were provided, with the focus shifting to capacity building through small, customised programmes. Professional development shifted to the wider ramifications of ICT for developing curriculum innovation, implementation issues, instructional strategies, expert views and mentoring strategies.

Culture and environment: a re-culturing process has permeated the entire process of FPS's evolutionary trajectory. Back in 2001, learning circles were established, which were widened and deepened over time. Every staff member was involved in at least one learning circle. A safe and risk-accepting environment was created with a school ethos of tolerance towards "failure", and where no teacher was penalised for lagging behind.

FPS's transformation was based on emergent and iterative feedback along the way. Neither principal had a very precise view of what the transformation would or should be to begin with and instead the trajectory was shaped along the way by multi-level influences and actors. Both principals were guided by the belief that technology, while acting as a powerful catalyst for school transformation, should not supersede pedagogy, and that learning goals should coalesce around the needs of 21st century learners. Through exercising their leadership skills, FPS leaders provided a range of support systems which eventually became better defined through the collective effort of the school community.

Case study 2: Singapore Girls Secondary School

Singapore Girls Secondary School (SGSS) is an independent all-girls secondary school with a highly selective intake. It enjoys greater autonomy than government schools in staff deployment, salaries, finance, management and curriculum. It has a student enrolment of 1 800, mostly from middle and upper income groups, and a teaching staff of 160. In 2004, the school shifted from preparing students for the General Certificate of Education (GCE) O Level examinations to the government-initiated "Integrated Programme" (IP) that provides a seamless six-year education. It is designed to be more flexible, with broader learning experiences and outcomes.

Evidence of success

SGSS is a top-performing school as measured by conventional indicators such as GCE A Level results and has established itself as a leading future-oriented and progressive school by teachers, parents, students and policy makers. In 2012, the school was awarded numerous school excellence and best practice awards.

An NIE evaluation of the school's IP curriculum showed that whole-school reform to enact IP had been successful. Teaching had shifted from a focus on curriculum coverage to student-centred learning, with high levels of student engagement, personalised learning, dialogic teaching, strong disciplinary practices, meta-cognitive skills, and cognitive and epistemic flexibility. Open-ended, loosely-structured, authentic performance tasks were integrating learning across subjects and engaging students in creative problem-solving. Across a range of pedagogical indicators, SGSS outperformed most secondary schools in Singapore.

21st century leadership skills and practices

Prior to the IP, SGSS was producing academically outstanding students through a traditional focus on examination preparation. In 2001, the principal led the process to rethink its fundamental aims. Discussions around the nature of teaching and learning, disciplines and student identities resulted in an educational vision to develop students who would be "persons, thinkers, leaders and pioneers". Embedded in this vision was an explicit focus on core 21st century knowledge and skills including global awareness, leadership skills, innovation and entrepreneurship, creative critical thinking, and problem-solving skills.

The principal introduced the other leaders in the school to the "Understanding by Design" (UbD) framework (Wiggins and McTighe, 2005) to help teachers design curriculum maps. By 2004, the leadership team was well prepared to implement an IP design that embedded key vision outcomes. The team recognised that the UbD-driven curriculum had shifted the scale of reform from a piecemeal, department-level innovation to a high-stakes whole-of-school transformation process. The new vision required radical changes to assessment and instructional practices, teacher capacities and school culture in order to teach 21st century knowledge and skills. With the vision as an anchor, the principal guided the school through strategic stages of transformation towards student-centred learning.

The whole-school transition to the IP from 2004 onwards was far-reaching and risky. Many stakeholders, including teachers, were uncertain of the changes. To ensure staff commitment to change and to minimise staff attrition, the principal frequently reassured staff, shared the new vision and stressed that the transformation was crucial for the future of the students. She provided substantial professional and financial support to help staff build their capacities. Leadership capacities were further distributed to empower staff and improve their buy-in. The principal introduced a layer of leaders to manage the transformation process. These "directors" held key organisational responsibilities, with the resulting leadership eventually spread across the principal, deputy principals, directors and department heads. Even so, the principal maintained oversight and control of implementation up to 2008, regarding this as necessary to ensure a continuous, progressive and focused whole-school transformation. It was only after the major transformational processes were completed that more bottom-up opportunities for innovation and leadership were fostered.

To ensure alignment with the new vision and school objectives, the leadership team held numerous conversations with parents, students and alumni. Strong community involvement was established to justify and demonstrate new student-centred teaching and learning to parents and students. Throughout the implementation, continuous feedback was sought from parents and students. Leadership meetings with other schools shared transformation experiences. Communication and feedback channels were introduced to allow leaders to react to issues, and to adjust the pace and direction of change accordingly. Partnerships with businesses were established to help increase financial revenue and support, and collaborations with research centres helped to boost the research capacities of the school and teachers.

Like the architect overseeing a new building, the principal not only maintained the school vision, but ensured that the transformation trajectory was progressively directed towards achieving that vision. In relation to the school design model, the principal's leadership was aligned to the three forms of leadership.

Learning-centred leadership: the principal drew on research-based resources to help plan and drive forward the transformation. She used her professional, technical and pedagogical knowledge to form close collegial relationships with staff across all levels, encouraged them to become learners through role modelling, and aligned financial, organisational and professional resources to support the school as a learning organisation. Mechanisms for reflection, including platforms for formative feedback, allowed the leadership team to respond rapidly to issues and adjust the pace and direction of change.

Distributed leadership: the principal held the strong belief that top-down leadership was required during key stages of transformation, even as she established new positions to help steer and manage the transformation processes. It was only after the main transformations were completed that she encouraged bottom-up initiatives from those to whom leadership was increasingly distributed.

Community-network leadership: as one of the IP pioneers, the school was unable to depend on the resources and experiences of other schools. Nevertheless, strong engagement and dialogue with stakeholders allowed the sharing of vision and student-centred teaching and learning practices. The school subsequently shared their transformation experiences with other schools, researchers and policy-makers. Partnerships with businesses and research institutes helped to boost the financial and research capacities of the school.

The leaders exhibited an additional leadership role that was arguably essential in the SGSS transformation – a "risk leadership" that helped to manage the uncertainty inherent in the transformation process (Hancock, 2012). They guided the change process intentionally, while adapting to challenges and opportunities. They acted as buffers against uncertainty (especially from stakeholders), constantly focusing on vision-guided outcomes, trying to ensure that the benefits of the transformation outweighed the risks.

Embedding 21st century teaching and learning skills and support systems

SGSS's trajectory of whole-school transformation demonstrates the value of long-term commitment to teleological visions of 21st century knowledge and skills. School leaders recognised that this future orientation should come from a radical transformation of teaching and learning skills and support systems.

Curriculum: curriculum redesign began with intensive study of the UbD framework. The principal hired international consultants to help leaders and teachers understand the new curriculum designs. This was done simultaneously across all departments, with changes led and monitored by department heads. While the curriculum redesign efforts were not uniform across all departments, by 2008 all departments were beginning to move towards interdisciplinary designs and greater curriculum differentiation.

Instruction and pedagogy: as the IP curriculum required student-centred pedagogy and instructional practices, student-centred principles were applied throughout the whole school, with intensive in-house teacher training to enhance pedagogical capacity. Teachers became pedagogical learners in the transformation and by 2008, most teachers employed student-centred pedagogy with a strong emphasis on 21st century skills, knowledge and dispositions. Recently, the school has embarked on 1:1 computing (a laptop for each student) with associated pedagogical innovation.

Assessment and standards: assessment redesign was the second major transformation after curriculum redesign. The leaders recognised that the UbD framework required authentic performance tasks and alternative assessment practices. These were introduced into all departments, again with advice from international consultants. Such practices, tasks and standards were aligned to student-centred learning and the curriculum, with a director having oversight of task designs and curriculum alignment to 21st century knowledge and skills.

Organisational structures: the design and implementation of authentic performance tasks required trans-disciplinary collaboration between departments. There was mandated collaboration time to allow teachers to work across departments to design and align assessment and practices. The school timetable shifted to a two-week schedule to allow longer and more intensive lessons across all subjects. Yet, because the school was in an old building with limited space, flexibility in classroom configurations was restricted (the school is moving to a new campus in a few years' time).

Teacher professional development: multiple professional learning communities (PLCs) were formed to encourage innovative teacher learning. Staff across the school hierarchy worked together to design the curriculum, share practices, and guide whole-school transformation. The principal was involved in numerous PLCs and workshops. An in-house teachers' academy was formed to provide a compulsory three-year professional development programme for new teachers. Professional growth was encouraged through attachment to other institutions, scholarships, research activities and graduate studies. In 2010, an in-house centre was established in collaboration with NIE to generate school-based research, develop teachers' research capacities, share knowledge with other schools, and continue the commitment to developing and empowering teachers as professionals.

Culture and environment: new organisational capacities and structures contributed to developing the learning culture. The principal felt it was crucial for a learning culture to exist to handle the transformation. The learning culture was increasingly refined to handle insights and understandings gained from school change. Common meta-languages and platforms were developed to make sense of the changes and document new understandings about curriculum, assessment and pedagogy.

In sum, embedding 21st century teaching and learning practices, skills and support systems took place recursively across the sub-systems described above. It was non-linear and networked, with these sub-systems – particularly curriculum, assessment, pedagogy and teacher professional development – constantly referencing the school vision of 21st century knowledge and skills. The learning skills and support systems were driven by the school leaders, especially exercising learning-centred and distributed leadership. The redesign process took over eight years, and was conducted in stages initially – curriculum first, assessment next, pedagogy after – with subsequent systems developing concurrently. Under the second principal, the transformation process has continued as the school constantly seeks innovative ways to equip students with a growing range of 21st century knowledge, skills and dispositions.

Comparing transformation trajectories and leadership

Despite one being a primary school in the government system and the other a secondary school with greater independence, the case studies share similarities in their transformations. First, both embraced and committed to long-term visions of future schooling to benefit their students and society at large. They recognised that the *status quo* with its traditional transmission model, although useful in achieving narrow academic high-stakes outcomes, is no longer tenable for educating and preparing students for the 21st century. Second, both schools centred their redesign trajectories on curriculum, assessment and teaching strategies for personalised, student-centred learning through technological and pedagogical innovations. Third, each school recognised the necessity of distributing leadership, albeit through different routes: with SGSS it evolved cautiously, top-down from the principal; in

FPS, it was more bottom-up and organic. Fourth, leadership in both schools recognised the dependence of transformation on teacher buy-in and enhanced professionalism and professional development. Enhanced professional practice was driven in both schools by a model of teacher-driven research and learning. Fifth, both schools displayed a willingness to communicate with and involve key stakeholders, and to seek ideas and resources, as well as share them with other schools.

There are also important differences between the schools. Each had different drivers of change, and in the pace and scaling of joined-up innovation. Transformation in SGSS was driven by the decision to introduce the new IP curriculum, requiring more radical and joined-up rethinking of learning, teaching and assessment. Transformation in FPS, on the other hand, was largely driven by the desire to harness new technology for teaching and learning. Connectivity between the broader elements of the school design model – such as teacher professional development and whole-curricular change – have been achieved more recently.

Distributed leadership in FPS was more hybrid from the start, being a mix of top-down and bottom-up approaches, while leadership in SGSS was more top-down especially initially, moving more slowly towards a top-down/bottom-up mix.

FPS leveraged social and corporate contacts to build its organisational capital to become a technology-rich environment, while this was less a feature for SGSS, possibly because of its greater financial independence.

Teacher professional learning communities (PLCs) in SGSS were initiated by the principal, who was directly involved to ensure direction, continuity and accountability. Professional learning communities were more emergent and informal in FPS, even in the early years of transformation when teachers were encouraged to form their own learning circles, and have latterly become more decentralised and customised to meet teachers' wishes for professional development in smaller, "hands-on" sessions.

While curricular change in both schools was about 21st century knowledge and skills, SGSS focused on innovation and creative skills, citizenship and life skills, critical thinking, problem-solving skills and global awareness, while the cornerstone for FPS was using communication technology skills as levers to achieve new learning goals.

Leadership of the change process in both cases can be summarised by referencing the school design model. The SGSS principal demonstrated awareness of the multiple interconnected elements, but the process evolved in response to the challenges of innovation and transformation with each new opportunity for change that arose. As the change gathered momentum, many of the elements began to change concurrently rather than in sequence.

The principal adjusted her focus and energy to particular areas of change as circumstances dictated, according to what she thought was imperative in order to initiate, sustain and scale up the innovation. Leadership of FPS, in contrast, demonstrated no prior master plan or strategy: early innovations tended to be discrete and small scale, but with time became more comprehensive and connected. By 2010, with a new principal in place, a coherent overall vision had evolved, with large stakeholder involvement forming a "collective intelligence". Throughout, however, the change process was governed by two core ideas – student welfare at the heart of all reform, and technology harnessed to improve teaching and learning.

Conclusion

Using the school design model and understanding the transformational journeys of the two Singapore case-study schools enables us to draw the following conclusions. First, the onus for school transformation lies primarily with the individual school and its leadership, particularly the principal. This is apparent even in traditionally centralised systems of control such as Singapore, where the MOE policy framework supports school-level initiatives aimed at creating 21st century learning environments. More generally across the globe, there is an increasing recognition of the need for school leadership to be reforming and a corresponding discouragement of principals to be over-dependent on central administrations. Second, it is not the case that only poorly performing schools look to transform themselves into 21st century learning environments as a means of regeneration. Indeed the two Singapore schools are in their different ways both highly successful according to traditional indicators such as public examination and test results. Rather, it is their unwillingness to be complacent that has propelled them to keep ahead of the competition and of the "education game". Third, with the school design model offering comprehensiveness in its elements, including leadership, and a methodology, which together provide the essential components of transformation towards innovative learning environments, the model is generic in accommodating and embracing the different and unique reform paths of individual schools.

One of us (Dimmock, 2000) has elsewhere argued that the basic tenets or principles of school redesign are generic. Any school undertaking transformation of its learning environment must inevitably give consideration to the same common elements covered by the school design model. Successful transformation implies:

- Identifying and maximising the main drivers for change.
- Recognising the elements (captured in the school design model) and their interdependence, with leadership ensuring strong strategic alignment and functional interrelationship between them.

- Sequencing the implementation of redesigned elements in ways that achieve alignment, coherence and synergy – as reflected in backward and iterative mapping.

An obvious starting point is the envisioning of the learning outcomes (knowledge, skills, and values) and the types of graduates aimed at, together with the motivations for so doing. Other key elements concern the processes considered most likely to achieve the outcomes, such as new configurations of curriculum, pedagogy, assessment and technology, supporting structures such as timetable, student and teacher grouping, and finally, leadership that is learner-centred, distributed and networked. Transformation that is "school-wide" and "school-deep" involves all of these elements and sees them as functionally interconnected, thus achieving embeddedness, sustainability and scalability. In reality, many schools undergoing reform will be on a trajectory that is as yet incomplete and partial in terms of the school design model. They may be working to a generic model similar or akin to the school design model, but have only reached an intermediate stage of redesigning some of the elements. Or, more problematical still, they may periodically implement separate piecemeal innovations without a design model to engineer synergistic, operational and logical connections between the key elements.

Leadership is an integral and main component of the school design model. Three salient aspects of leadership that come to the fore emanate from the very characteristics of 21st century learning environments. That is, through backward and iterative mapping, the question implicitly posed is: given the requirements and features of a 21st century learning environment, what forms of leadership are necessary? This turns upside down the conventional thinking which first asks, "What type of leadership is needed going forward?" and then, "What teaching and learning methods will leaders promote?" The three forms of leadership derived from the backward-mapping/iterative methodology – learning-centred, distributed, and community networked – are not meant to be exclusive, but they are highlighted as the three mainstays of leadership for whole-school transformation. As the two Singaporean case-study schools reveal, a premium is also placed on capacity to strategise, political acumen, risk-taking and boldness – all are invaluable characteristics for transforming 21st century schools.

The pace and sequence in which the elements are transformed, the emphases given to particular elements, and the styles and patterns of leadership, will all differ as each transforming school follows its own trajectory. Activating the model necessarily introduces the uniqueness of each school and every system, reflecting their own cultural norms, patterns of governance and leadership; school type, aims, size and intake; resource availability; degree of teacher professionalism; and, not least, the starting point from which each school and system takes off. It will also reflect the main drivers of the transformation. Cultural norms in particular will shape variance in patterns and styles of leadership in the transformation process: "distributed leadership", for example, will normally assume different configurations in Asian hierarchical societies than in Anglo-Saxon social organisations (Dimmock, 2012).

Hence, schools will engineer their transformations towards 21st century learning environments in diverse ways in the decades to come, in line with greater school discretion over implementation and increasingly professionalised teachers and leaders. This leads to the conclusion that the model *per se* is transferable and has high validity, even though the drivers, processes, and emphases involved in operationalising it will vary according to the particular contexts of each school system. This is all to the good – the last thing needed from transformed 21st century education systems is standardisation, conformity and convergence.

References

Barber M., F. Whelan and M. Clark (2010), *Capturing the Leadership Premium: How the World's Top School Systems are Building Leadership Capacity for the Future*, McKinsey & Company, www.mckinsey.com/clientservice/ Social_Sector/our_practices/Education/Knowledge_Highlights/~/media/ Reports/SSO/schoolleadership_final.ashx (accessed 29 December 2011).

Biggs, J. (1999), *Teaching for Quality Learning at University,* Open University Press, Buckingham.

Bolam, R. et al. (2005), *Creating and Sustaining Effective Professional Learning Communities.* Research Report No. 637,Department for Education and Skills, UK.

Blythe, T. and D. Perkins (1998), "Understanding understanding", in T. Blythe (ed.), *The Teaching for Understanding Guide* Jossey-Bass, San Francisco, 9-16.

Covey, S.R. (1989), *The Seven Habits of Highly Effective People,* Free Press, New York.

Dimmock, C. (2012), *Leadership, Capacity Building and School Improvement: Concepts, Themes and Impact,* Routledge, London.

Dimmock, C. (2000), *Designing the Learning-Centred School: A Cross-Cultural Perspective*, The Falmer Press, London.

Dimmock, C. and J.W.P Goh (2011), *Transformative pedagogy, leadership and school organisation for the 21st century knowledge-based economy: the case of Singapore, School Leadership and Management*, vol. 31. 3, 215-234.

DuFour, R. and R. Eaker (1998), *Professional Learning Communities at Work: Best Practices for Enhancing Student Achievement,* Solution Tree, Bloomington, IN.

Elmore, R.F. (1979-80), "Backward mapping: Implementation research and policy decisions", *Political Science Quarterly,* 94(4), 601-616.

Gopinathan, S. (1985), "Education in Singapore: Progress and prospect". In J.S.T. Quah, H.C. Chan, and C.M. Seah (eds.), *Government and Politics of Singapore,* Oxford University Press, Singapore, 197-232.

Guile, D. (2006), "What is distinctive about the knowledge economy? Implications for education", in H. Lauder, P. Brown, J.A. Dillabough and A.H. Halsey (eds.), *Education, Globalization, and Social Change,* Oxford University Press, Oxford, 355-366.

Hancock, D. (2012), "The case for risk leadership", *Strategic Risk*, November 2012, at www.strategic-risk-global.com/the-case-for-risk-leadership/1399431.article (accessed 14 May 2013).

Hargreaves, D.H. (2003), "From improvement to transformation", Keynote lecture at International Congress for School Effectiveness and Improvement, Schooling in the Knowledge Society. Sydney, Australia, 5 January 2003.

Heck, R. and P. Hallinger (2009), "Assessing the contribution of distributed leadership to school improvement and growth in math achievement", *American Educational Research Journal*, 46(3), 659-689.

Hogan, D. et al. (2013), "Assessment and the logic of instructional practices in Secondary 3 English and mathematics classrooms in Singapore", *Review of Education,* 1(1), 57-106.

Hogan, D. and S. Gopinathan (2008), "Knowledge management, sustainable innovation, and pre-service teacher education in Singapore", *Teachers and Teaching*, 14 (4), 369-384.

Hord, S.M. (2008), "Evolution of the professional learning community", *Journal of Staff Development*, 29(3), 10-13.

Louis, K. and S. Kruse (1995), *Professionalism and Community: Perspectives on Reforming Urban Schools,* Corwin Press, Newbury Park, CA.

MacBeath, J. and N. Dempster (eds.) (2008), *Connecting Leadership and Learning: Principles for Practice,* Routledge, London.

Mourshed, M., C. Chijioke and M. Barber (2010), *How the World's Most Improved School Systems Keep Getting Better,* McKinsey & Company, https://mckinseyonsociety.com/downloads/reports/Education/How-the-Worlds-Most-Improved-School-Systems-Keep-Getting-Better_Download-version_Final.pdf (accessed 6 June 2011).

Saphier, J. and R. Gower (1997), *The Skilful Teacher: Building your Teaching Skills*, 5th edition, Research for Better Teaching, Acton, MA.

Spillane, J. P. and J.B. Diamond (eds.) (2007), *Distributed Leadership in Practice,* Teachers College Press, New York.

Toh, Y. (2013), "Sustaining the use of ICT for student-centred learning: A case study of technology leadership in a Singapore ICT-enriched primary school", unpublished doctoral dissertation, University of Leicester, https://lra.le.ac.uk/handle/2381/27830.

Wenger, E. (1998). *Communities of Practice: Learning, Meaning and Identity,*, Cambridge University Press, Cambridge, UK.

Wiggins, G. and J. McTighe (2005), *Understanding by Design,* 2nd edition, ASCD (Association for Supervision and Curriculum Development), Alexandria, VA.

Chapter 5

Approaches to learning leadership development in different school systems

Tanja Westfall-Greiter
University of Innsbruck

Judy Halbert and Linda Kaser
Vancouver Island University, British Columbia, Canada

Roser Salavert[1]
Fordham Graduate School of Education, New York City

Lone Lønne Christiansen and Per Tronsmo
Norwegian Directorate for Education and Training

Susanne Owen[2]
Department for Education and Child Development (DECD),
Strategic and Performance, South Australia

Dorit Tubin
Department of Education, Ben-Gurion University of the Negev, Israel

*This chapter presents a selection of the leadership initiatives and analyses gathered through the Innovative Learning Environments project. Tanja Westfall-Greiter describes the strategy of creating teacher learning leaders (*lerndesigners*) in the current Austrian reform (*Neue Mittelschule *or* NMS*). Judy Halbert and Linda Kaser discuss a leadership programme in British Columbia, Canada that engages leaders together in a "spiral of inquiry" about learning in their own school and networked activity across sites. The New York City examples described by Roser Salavert cover Professional Learning Communities, coaching, teacher teams, and student "voice". Lone Christiansen and Per Tronsmo present Norwegian approaches to leadership, and national programmes for school leadership professional development and the Advisory Team programme for mentoring principals and local providers. The South Australian and Israeli examples presented by Susanne Owen and Dorit Tubin feature the work of particular sections of the education ministries looking to drive innovative learning and provide conditions to support it.*

Introduction

Leadership naturally features in the strategies and initiatives brought together as part of the Innovative Learning Environments project. This chapter presents a selection of these. They are diverse and operate at different levels. They complement the conceptual and research-based discussion of the foregoing chapters by presenting diverse applications and learning leadership developments in different systems covering a range of educational traditions: Austria; British Columbia, Canada; New York City; Norway; South Australia; and Israel.

The teacher learning leaders (*lerndesigners*) that have been created in the current Austrian *Neue Mittelschule* (NMS) reform represent an excellent example of a strategy that is operating at once at the micro, meso and macro levels. It is working on innovating learning in individual schools through change agents, creating conditions for them to network together, and is aimed at helping to drive the system-wide innovation reform. The leadership programme in British Columbia, Canada (Certificate in Innovative Educational Leadership, CIEL) is a year-long graduate programme for practising formal and informal leaders. It is highly focused on innovative learning, it engages the leaders together in a "spiral of inquiry" about the nature of learning in their own school or learning environment, and it networks these different leaders after completing the programme.

The examples of learning leadership strategies and initiatives from New York City represent a range of approaches and levels of action. They cover innovation through professional learning communities, coaching aimed at developing distributive leadership, facilitating inquiry through collaborative teacher teams, and strategies for recognising and promoting student "voice". The Norwegian examples are systemic in being created as part of broader school reform and implemented by a national agency under the ministry in a system that is highly decentralised in its governance arrangements. The two initiatives presented are a national programme for school leadership professional development and the Advisory Team programme for mentoring principals and local providers to develop quality learning.

The South Australian and Israeli examples feature the work of particular sections of the education ministries looking to drive innovative learning and provide conditions to support it. The team in the South Australian Department for Education and Child Development operates in diverse ways, including conferences and workshops, an innovations website, part-time advisory support from an innovation principal, practitioner research grants with academic support, and innovation newsletters. Particular attention is paid to the Innovation "Community of Practice". The Israeli Experiments and Entrepreneurship Division aims to encourage the motivation and practice of learning innovation, alternative teaching and learning methods, and the design of innovative learning environments. The discussion is founded on an analysis of the conditions for system-level learning leadership.

A network of change agents: *Lerndesigners* as teacher leaders in Austria
(Tanja Westfall-Greiter)

The Austrian school reform initiative *Neue Mittelschule* (NMS) began in 2008 in 67 pilot schools and has since led to a mandated school reform that will be completed in phases by 2018. National guidelines for pilot schools were released by the Ministry for Education, Arts and Culture in 2007, based on which each state province (*Bundesland*) developed its own pilot guidelines and requirements. This federalist approach to the pilot created nine broad pilot regions defined by provincial boundaries. Participating schools opted in by submitting a pilot concept for their site that was in line with requirements of both their *Bundesland* and the ministry. Applications were formally approved by a review board at the ministry level. Although the NMS is now a mandate, this opting-in process is still in place, enabling at least some dynamic of ownership for those schools which are implementing rather than piloting.

The *NMS-Entwicklungsbegleitung* (NMS-EB), an external consultancy team, was hired by the Ministry to guide system development during the pilot. The NMS-EB created networking events, engaged system players on all system levels and initiated a new role, "*Lerndesigner*". *Lerndesigners* are teacher leaders with specific expertise in areas of curriculum and instructional development related to the reform goals of equity and excellence. Each NMS site designates a teacher to be the *Lerndesigner,* to attend national and regional "*Lernateliers*" as well as local networking events. Ideally they act as change agents in a shared leadership dynamic with school principals and other teacher leaders (subject co-ordinators, school development teams, etc.). The rationale for creating, qualifying and networking change agents was clear and focused: transformation at all system levels occurs when change agents are networked and establish communities of practice.

The reform pilot came to an end in September 2012 and along with it the NMS-EB external consultancy. To sustain positive change and foster learning environments which are equitable and challenging for all pupils at NMS sites, the ministry established the National Centre for Learning Schools (CLS) in 2012. Co-directed by members of the original NMS-EB team, two central objectives of the CLS were, first, to sustain and foster school networks and communities of practice, and, second, to support *Lerndesigners* as change agents through qualification programmes, symposia and networking.

The Lerndesigner *network*

The fundamental aim of the *Lerndesigner* network is to foster the development of effective learning environments at each school, driven by the principle of school-specific reform (Marzano, 2003) and focused on the goals of equity and excellence. The strategy lies in qualifying teachers to become teacher leaders, thereby enabling them and their schools to realise effective shared leadership. DuFour (2002) argues that the central task of school leaders is to foster the disposition and structure of professional learning communities. More than ever before, school leadership needs to focus on student achievement and foster a culture of learning throughout the school.

Barth (2000: v) points out, however, just how complex and demanding the concept of "learning schools" is:

> "Our school is a community of learners!" How many times do we see and hear this assertion, now so common in public schools? This is an ambitious promissory note, indeed. The promise, is, first, that the school is a "community," a place full of adults and youngsters who care about, look after, and root for one another and who work together for the good of the whole – in times of need as well as times of celebration. I find that precious few schools live up to this mantle of "community." Many more are simply organisations or institutions. As if "community" were not enough to promise, a "community of learners" is much more. Such a school is a community whose defining, underlying culture is one of learning. A community of learners is a community whose most important condition for membership is that one be a learner – whether one is called a student, teacher, principal, parent, support staff, or certified staff. Everyone. A tall order to fill. And one to which all too few schools aspire, and even fewer attain.

Typically Austrian schools have a flat hierarchy and school culture is dominated by the "autonomy-parity" pattern in which individual teachers enjoy equal freedom to control what goes on inside their own classrooms (Lortie, 1975) – a far cry from the "ambitious promissory note" of learning schools as vibrant communities (Schratz and Westfall-Greiter, 2010). Not surprisingly, the *Lerndesigner* role was and is a powerful system intervention. Because an official function for teacher leaders as *Lerndesigners* does not yet exist in school legislation and salary structures, each *Lerndesigner* creates his or her own role in the context of the school through processes of role-taking and role-making.

The *Lerndesigners* are also not alone. As a result of educational reform efforts throughout the system, several new teacher leadership roles have emerged since 2008 which have had an impact on schools' social architecture. In the NMS, these include contact persons or co-ordinators with specific agendas required by the ministry (eLearning, gender issues, culture and arts programming, standards and school quality), school development team members and co-ordinators created at the school level as part of their school-specific model and roles required in the *Bundesland*-level guidelines, such as the "learning coaches" in Vienna. Of these teacher leaders, *Lerndesigners* are the most visible, in part due to their two-year qualification programme including national face-to-face events, but also due to their name. "*Lerndesign*", as the catch-all term for the new teaching and learning culture promoted through the NMS, was a new coinage that received some media attention early on and has become part of everyday vocabulary at all system levels.

The effectiveness of *Lerndesigners* as change agents in a teacher leadership role depends to a significant degree on the culture and leadership in their schools. An informal survey of Generation 2 and 3 *Lerndesigners* (those who began in the 2nd and 3rd year of NMS) in mid-2010 revealed how the role was developing (Westfall-Greiter and Hofbauer, 2010). These second and third generation *Lerndesigners* were asked to write a one-minute essay on the question, "What does a *Lerndesigner* do?" Responses were clustered and revealed their roles as that of teacher leaders acting in shared leadership with school principals as well as that of change agents:

Figure 5.1. **What does a *Lerndesigner* do?**

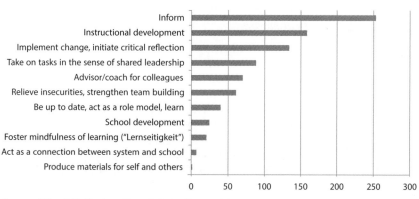

Source: Westfall-Greiter, T. and C. Hofbauer (2010).

As one *Lerndesigner* put it, "The *Lerndesigner* prepares the soil upon which the seeds of the new learning culture and assessment are planted." At the same time, the newness of the role brought with it uncertainty. By the end of the second pilot year, *Lerndesigners* had become important partners in school for asking questions and solving problems. As a *Lerndesigner* in

Generation 3 advised: "Listen when colleagues come with problems. Try to find solutions. Don't give up or get tired of asking questions. (Has something changed for the better? If not, why? How can that work?)" Nonetheless, the new role was not easy for some, as one teacher indicated: "The *Lerndesigner* is a difficult role at my school. I see my role in being a good example. Slowly the term is no longer being laughed at. Slowly the colleagues see that I do things differently. Slowly even questions are being asked – 'How do you do that…?'" (Westfall-Greiter and Hofbauer, 2010).

Beyond face-to-face events, communication and feedback occur online, a strategy which has been developed closely with a company contracted by the ministry to provide digital infrastructure and system development initiatives in the field of eLearning, digital media and digital competence. The NMS development is supported by an online platform comprising some 200 eduMoodle courses which is operated by the National Centre for Virtual Teacher Education (Onlinecampus VPH) in co-operation with the National Centre for Learning Schools. In addition, the NMS Online Library was implemented in autumn 2012 and serves as a portal for NMS-related resources, including dissemination of the newest resources for curriculum and instructional developed by CLS, a bi-weekly newsletter for school principals and insights into the NMS experience through personal anecdotes and a series of online events and publications called "NMS Insights" conducted by Onlinecampus VPH.

The qualification programme

The two-year national qualification programme for *Lerndesigners* contributes significantly to their profile. The programme enables them to gain theoretical and practical insights in areas of expertise related to instructional quality, to develop with one another the knowledge and skills necessary for them to be effective in their own schools as teachers and teacher leaders, and to network with other *Lerndesigners*. Developed and refined over three years in response to pilot schools' needs, the qualification comprises six development areas represented in the so-called "NMS-House" deemed essential for fostering change in the learning culture realised in each subject in each lesson of the NMS (Figure 5.2).

- mindfulness of learning (Schratz, 2009)
- diversity
- competence orientation
- "backwards design" curriculum development (Wiggins and McTighe, 2005; Tomlinson and McTighe, 2006)

- differentiated instruction (Tomlinson, 2003; Tomlinson and Imbeau, 2010)

- assessment (Earl, 2013; Wiggins, 1998).

Figure 5.2. **The "NMS House"**

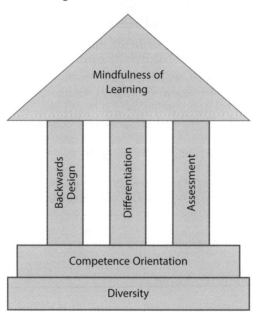

Lerndesigners earn a certificate worth 12 college credits relevant for further study programmes towards a master degree. The programme design consists of national and regional *Lernateliers* for networking and qualification purposes as well as a self-study component which is co-ordinated online and includes practice-based tasks for exploration in school-based professional learning communities (PLCs). The "Meta-Course", the virtual networking and learning space for all *Lerndesigners,* is located on the NMS platform. This space is closed to visitors so that *Lerndesigners* can safely exchange ideas and receive feedback on their development work. The goals with this designated digital space are to:

- connect *Lerndesigners* across generations

- promote exchange, learning and development

- foster identity

- provide a location for materials
- enable direct communication between the national development team and *Lerndesigners*
- provide up-to-date information
- conduct intra-school PLC work.

The advantages of the Meta-Course for *Lerndesigners* were already clear in the pilot phase. It enables communication, exchange, regular contact, access to expertise and support as well as relationship-building.

As of 2012/13, Generation 5, this programme is a joint effort between the National Centre for Learning Schools at the national level and the *Pädagogische Hochschulen* (PHs), which is responsible for compulsory school teacher education as well as continuing education programmes and school development measures. This new structure called for prototyping at several levels. To foster the evolution of the programme and support the transition to the PHs, the Ministry provided financial start-up incentives for programme development. Five PHs agreed to participate in the prototyping phase. Programme directors and their trainer teams meet with the National Centre for Learning Schools twice a year. The curriculum, which had been defined with system partners in 2011/12, is the common basis for programme development.

Key strategies

Because the qualification occurs parallel to the implementation of the new school reform at their school sites, the qualification programme for *Lerndesigners* is the key national strategy for guiding school development at each NMS site. To foster transformation, school principals were also invited to national network meetings each semester in which they could address their own leadership issues. These network meetings for school principals have since been replaced by joint national *Lernateliers* for *Lerndesigners* and principals. Participants' feedback was very positive and this "dynamic development duo", as it has come to be called, has been recognised as key for the *Lerndesigners* to become effective change agents.

In addition, a strategy for maintaining the NMS network at the national level with Generation 1 and 2 schools whose qualification programmes had already concluded was first piloted in early 2012 in the form of two symposia. Dynamic development duos from schools no longer in the national programme were invited to a two-day symposium in which they could update their information and attend workshops related to NMS goals and development issues. The participants' feedback was overwhelmingly positive so that three regional symposia were offered in December 2012 for Generations 1-3 and four are planned in January 2014 for Generations 1-4.

The main leadership of the *Lerndesigner* Network was the Minister of Education, Claudia Schmied, who initiated the NMS school reform, and Under-Secretary Helmut Bachmann, the NMS project leader. In addition to the already-mentioned partner institutions, the National Centre for Learning Schools is also networked with other national centres belonging to the Ministry, including the National Centre for Gifted and Talented Education, the National Centre for Multilingual Education, and the National Centre for Personal Development and Social Learning. The NMS project is also carefully linked with other ministerial education initiatives in Austria, including the implementation of standards (BiSt) and school quality for compulsory schools (SQA) as well as diversity and equity measures in various areas including gender, integration and special needs. Regular communication and a yearly retreat with key persons in the ministry ensure that the National Centre for Learning Schools development is coherent with these key initiatives.

Because the NMS-EB culture and those responsible at the ministry have focused especially on building relationships, individuals from NMS schools, local school authorities and PHs are in direct contact via email with members of the National Centre for Learning Schools and the NMS Project Team at the ministry when questions or problems arise. This is at once a strength and a weakness. Personal relationships enable targeted support, but a lack of staff makes it difficult to manage, particularly in phases where new information and requirements lead to a wave of individual questions. National meetings with school authorities, regional development teams and PH programme developers also take place biannually. Co-operation with directors and staff of the qualification programme for *Lerndesigners* is sustained with biannual work meetings and online exchange.

Evidence-informed development requires data. BIFIE (*Bildungsforschung, Innovation and Entwicklung des österreichischen Schulwesens*), Austria's testing and assessment institution, has conducted qualitative studies each year of the NMS pilot in co-operation with the Evaluation Committee (*Evaluationsverbund*) comprising representatives from local school authorities in all state provinces. The studies are conceptualised with the committee so that they can be oriented to their development questions and provide desired data. A qualitative survey of *Lerndesigners* in spring 2012 indicated the need for a formalised function in the system and otherwise confirmed the analysis conducted in 2010 by Westfall-Greiter and Hofbauer. The work in professional learning communities seems to have established itself well in the majority of schools, which was somewhat surprising because it was merely a recommendation during the pilot phase. Offering protocols and questions for PLC work seems to have contributed to this positive development.

In addition, a study of *Lerndesigners'* learning in the *Lernateliers* based on vignette methodology was conducted in 2011/12 (Kahlhammer, 2012), to gain key insights into such adult learning, and the National Centre for Learning Schools is also closely linked with the University of Innsbruck's Centre for Learning Research. Learning research conducted in NMS Generation 2 schools has been integrated into the qualification programme for *Lerndesigners* and methods for working with so-called "vignettes" were developed within the *Lernateliers* and published as protocols for professional learning communities (Schratz, Schwarz and Westfall-Greiter, 2012).

Further, the curriculum developed for the *Lerndesigner* qualification programme has been recognised by the Development Board of Teacher Education (*Entwicklungsrat zur PädagogInnenbildung,* NEU) and has influenced the new Master's degree programmes and the new curriculum guidelines for lower secondary teacher education. The recognition and integration of the six qualification areas of the NMS House in these broader contexts has led to synergetic strengthening in all reform efforts. In the same spirit, connections and synergies among the three primary reform initiatives for lower secondary mentioned above – standards, school quality and NMS – are communicated to all actors in the system to enhance effectiveness and impact.

Reform in lower secondary education has a long political history in Austria, driven by the issue of equity in the school system, and has also been the focus of recommendations from the OECD and the European Commission. The political commitment of the Minister of Education has certainly been a key factor in the success of the project, but the success factors of the reform pilot are very difficult to identify. In part, the time was ripe for many teachers and school principals at the lower secondary level. The minister also travelled to each state province for dialogue events with system players, which had a positive integrative impact and served to strengthen the determination to reform the lower secondary sector. In addition, the parents' network which emerged after a survey of parents in 2009/10 has been strengthened through newsletters and an online platform as well as a hotline service run by the NMS Project Team.

The power of national networking and change agents are generally seen as keys to the success, but these claims have yet to be supported by data. The NMS-EB focused on networking on all system levels, so that by the second pilot year the reform gained significant momentum and by the third year it became clear that the reform spirit could not be dampened. This is probably one reason why the school reform was mandated earlier than planned.

Factors related to the success of the *Lerndesigner* network are more easily identifiable:

- The online platform for *Lerndesigners* enables easy communication and exchange of ideas and innovations.

- Regular networking events in which the qualification is embedded build identity, professionalism and confidence.

- Personal relationships, support and easy access to expertise build trust.

There were many challenges to the successful introduction of the *Lerndesigner* role, in particular the acceptance by, and co-operation of, system partners at all levels. The form and establishment of shared leadership is a voluntary matter: if schools chose not to participate, nothing could be done because the external consultancy had no formal authority. The partnerships and support of the local school authorities have been invaluable in this regard; their strong recommendation and in some cases mandating of participation within the scope of their local competence led to a high participation rate on the part of the schools. Trust on the personal level has had a clear impact on this aspect of success. Other success factors for the development and implementation of the *Lerndesigner* role as well as the creation of a strong school network include the financial commitment of the ministry to enable national network meetings and qualification programmes as well as the co-operation and commitment of key players in the ministry to ensure the linking of development strategies with other initiatives and institutions.

The lack of security in salary schemes and school legislation for *Lerndesigners* means that a role exists, but a function does not. While all but one of the nine local school authorities have reached consensus regarding the importance of the *Lerndesigners* and advocate connecting the function to the qualification programme, until such a function exists they can only strongly recommend that schools comply. Other reforms, most notably in teacher education (*PädagogInnenbildung NEU*), are expected to strengthen the role and lead to the creation of the function in the long term. Agreements with trade unions regarding labour regulations for teachers will also have an impact on the long-term feasibility and effectiveness of all teacher leadership roles in Austria. The *Lerndesigners* are on the agenda of current negotiations with trade unions; proposals include additional salary as well as reduced teaching hours to compensate them for their work.

Education in Austria is highly politicised. While political will and support is generally strong in the ministry, this varies significantly at the local level, further exacerbated by the strong federalism which marks Austrian politics and decision making. A rigorous orientation to quality issues focused on school effectiveness and the academic achievement of learners is essential.

Innovative learning environments: Developing leadership in British Columbia (Judy Halbert and Linda Kaser)

British Columbia (BC) is by most measures a high-performing system in terms of both quality and equity. Yet, significant inequities exist and the political educational context is challenging. Tensions between the teacher association and the government have sometimes made it difficult for sustained progress at the system-wide level to take place. It is partly for this reason that for several years the authors have sought to establish "third spaces" outside the rhetoric of conflict where educators can engage in inquiry, experience new learning and try out new practices that will benefit their learners. The networks of inquiry and innovation (www.noii.ca) connecting schools across the province through focused inquiry is one of these "spaces". The CIEL (Certificate in Innovative Educational Leadership) graduate programme at Vancouver Island University represents another such space.

The CIEL programme is a year-long graduate programme for formal and informal leaders interested in transforming their schools to higher levels of quality and equity through inquiry and innovative practice. Both Canadian and international perspectives are central to the curriculum and a strong emphasis on indigenous ways of knowing makes this programme particularly relevant in the BC context.

The programme is designed to immerse participants first in the research knowledge about learning and leadership through an intensive face-to-face summer institute and then to take informed action during the school year. Working with a disciplined framework for inquiry, each participant identifies a key challenge for learners in their setting and designs new approaches during the school year. Regular reflections on the process of their inquiry as well as responses to a range of readings and online resources take place as part of an online community. In addition, participants are asked to explore the case studies from the Innovative Learning Environment project, identify an international case that is of particular interest – either because of its similarities to or contrast with their own setting – do additional research on the case, and then demonstrate how they will apply ideas from the case to their own context. Each participant works in a learning partnership with a colleague from their own setting and as part of an interdependent team with members of their cohort. Completion of the certificate programme leads to a unique design for completing a Master programme – with an emphasis on collaborative practices and problem-based learning.

A key aspect of the CIEL programme is that graduates have the opportunity to continue to extend their learning and deepen their connections upon completion through ongoing involvement in the networks of inquiry and innovation. This layering of networked learning opportunities helps to sustain and extend their leadership influence.

CIEL builds on the previous experience of the authors in designing and leading a graduate leadership programme at the University of Victoria which was designed around seven key leadership mind-sets (Kaser and Halbert, 2009) identified from international research and substantiated by case studies in British Columbia. Both CIEL and the earlier programme have been informed by international research on school leadership development, in particular the work of Stefan Huber and Viviane Robinson. Huber's (2010) research on school leadership development indicated a number of characteristics evident in CIEL. These include:

- Leadership programmes need a clear and explicitly stated set of aims, using the core moral purpose of school as a focus.

- Programmes must be based on a set of values and educational beliefs.

- Development must be viewed as a continuous process.

- There is a need to shift from fixed bodies of knowledge towards the development of conditional and procedural knowledge, conceptual literacy and knowledge management.

- There needs to be an intelligent balance between theory and practice.

- The programme must have a strong orientation to the individual and actual needs of the participants.

- Inspiring collegial learning and intensive collaboration are key elements.

- Problem-based learning and learning opportunities at the workplace are central.

- Dual focus on the personal and professional development needs of the participants as well as a focus on transforming their schools is required.

Robinson's (2011) findings on the leadership behaviours that are directly connected to improved student outcomes underscore the importance of promoting, supporting and participating in professional learning. This is a key expectation for CIEL participants and is central to their individual inquiry initiatives.

With these overall design considerations, there are three aspects of the CIEL programme that are especially relevant to the OECD focus on innovative learning environments. The first is the use of *The Nature of Learning*: *Using Research to Inspire Practice* (Dumont, Istance and Benavides, 2010) as a basis for in-depth study connected to the seven key transversals identified in the final chapter of this resource. Second, is the intense exploration of case studies from the OECD/ILE "Inventory" of innovative learning environments (see OECD, 2013, Annex A) as a way to prompt new thinking and action based on experiences in other parts of the world. Third, is the use of a disciplined spiral of inquiry focused on creating more innovative and engaging learning environments.

Learning principles as a core framework

The seven concluding learning principles from *The Nature of Learning* act as a set of cognitive tools in the leadership programme. CIEL participants study the research, explore each principle individually, enact inquiries to actualise the seven principles in their contexts, and present the results of their inquiries to their colleagues in a final presentation.

In addition – and this is extremely important to transforming leadership practices – participants experience all seven of the learning principles as a deliberate part of their own learning in the programme. Participants are immersed in problem-based learning and have regular opportunities for developing more self-regulated practices. All assessment is formative, with a significant emphasis on descriptive feedback. Social and emotional learning are strengthened and integrated with their colleagues through teamwork and collaborative inquiry. There is a strong emphasis on experiential and blended forms of learning. The setting for the face-to-face parts of the programme is purposefully in non-traditional learning environments. Getting the right degree of challenge without overload is especially important for graduate students who are fully engaged with their work responsibilities and active family lives in addition to their formal studies. The inclusion of community leaders from outside education as well as the expectation that participants connect across their settings helps to develop horizontal connectedness.

Currently we are working with the CIEL participants to develop a rubric based on the seven OECD/ILE principles for educators to use both as a diagnostic for their own settings and as a prompt for new action to deepen learning experiences for their learners.

Innovative cases to prompt action

The use of case studies from the "Inventory" of the OECD innovative learning environments has been highly useful in opening up thinking about new local possibilities based on the experiences in a wide range of vastly diverse settings. The case studies have served as existence proofs of innovation and deeper forms of learning. Chief Dan George, a wise elder from British Columbia said many years ago, "What we cannot see we cannot respect." He was talking about the need for people of different cultures to be open to other ways of being. We have seen the same response from educators who can be heard sometimes to say: "That (new practice, new programme, new approach) will never work here."

By delving into the case studies, CIEL participants are asked to look beyond the apparent context differences to gain a deeper understanding of the case they have selected and then to consider ways they might apply what they have learned in their own setting. They are encouraged to go beyond the confines of the case study itself, to contact the school directly and to examine other resources readily available on the web.

As a result, a small rural school in British Columbia is drawing on the work of a nature school in Israel to shape and sharpen their focus on environmental sustainability. The BC school is now working as part of a small network of nature-based schools throughout the province to transform their settings. Another CIEL participant, a principal of Aboriginal ancestry in a remote community, is using the case study from Vilna, Finland as a model for creating a school with high levels of self-regulation and appreciation for the natural world. A middle school principal has transformed the practices and plans in her school by studying the staffing models and more flexible timetables of a school in South Australia.

The response to these evidence proofs from other settings has been extremely positive and is prompting actions in ways that were unanticipated. "Seeing" in this part of the CIEL programme is leading to deeper respect and to new possibilities.

The "spiral of inquiry" as a framework for transformation

Educators across the world are bombarded with seemingly incompatible ideas about system direction and desirable models of reform. The call for disruptive innovation of education systems where schools, as we have known them, cease to exist has a certain appeal for those frustrated with the seeming snail's pace of system change. Others urge systems to focus intensely and consistently on improving the quality of teaching and learning with a few strong and carefully constructed goals. From this perspective, a focus on transformation and innovation is just one more system distraction. A third approach, usually advocated by politicians, is to make systems more accountable for learner performance guided by a belief that somehow someone will work out how to do this.

Although reformers may like to argue the relative merits of improvement, innovation and accountability, these distinctions are not particularly helpful for practitioners struggling to make learning more engaging and relevant in this moment in their particular context. The stance underlying the CIEL programme is that new approaches to learning *are* necessary and new designs for learning *are* required. Educators in the CIEL programme engage in a disciplined approach to collaborative inquiry designed to assist them to gain the confidence, the insights and the mindsets required to design new and powerful learning environments – indeed to transform their schools and their systems.

The spiral of inquiry is the result of collaboration with Professor Helen Timperely from the University of Auckland and evolved from inquiry work in British Columbia and New Zealand. Central to the spiral is the attention at every phase to the experience of the learners framed by three key questions: "What's going on for our learners?" "How do we know?" and "Why does this matter?" Our recent publication – *Spirals of Inquiry: For Quality and Equity* (Halbert and Kaser, 2013) – includes a full description of this approach, illustrated with examples from BC schools. What distinguishes the inquiry spiral from other forms of action research is the relentless focus on the experiences of the learners to frame and inform the process.

Figure 5.3. **The spiral of inquiry**

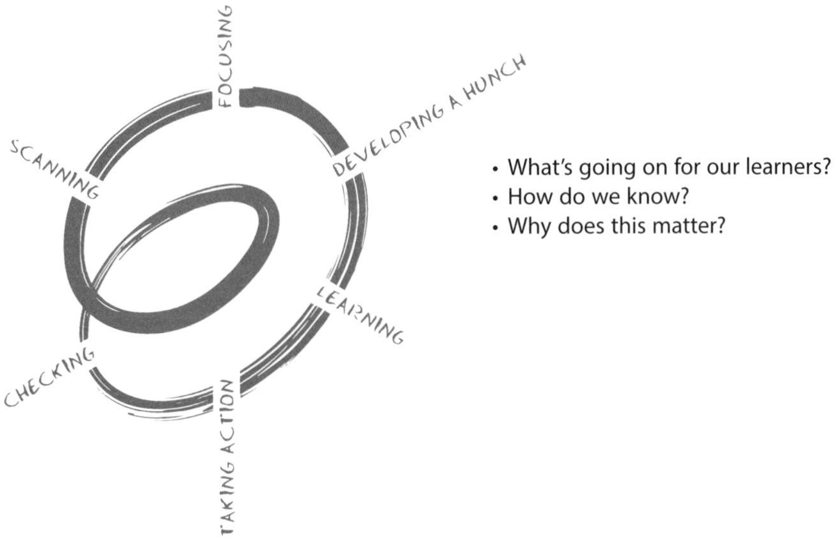

- What's going on for our learners?
- How do we know?
- Why does this matter?

Source: Halbert, J. and L. Kaser (2013).

The process begins by scanning the learning environment to gain a deeper understanding of the experience of the learners. The scanning process goes far beyond a simple look at available achievement data or results from satisfaction surveys. Scanning also involves asking questions related to the seven key learning principles, for example:

- Do learners see and understand themselves as learners? Are they self-regulated? Are they becoming increasingly meta-cognitive?

- Do learners see and understand the connections across content areas?

- Are learning professionals tuned into the emotions of learners – and the connection between emotions and motivation?

- Do learners receive high-quality focused feedback that provides clear directions for improvement?

- Are learners confident and comfortable in both giving and receiving feedback with their peers based on co-constructed criteria?

- Are all learners stretched through demanding, engaging and challenging work?

- Are learners engaged in high-quality, well-organised co-operative learning on a regular basis?

- Is the prior knowledge that learners bring to the setting respected and valued?

- Are learners at the centre of every decision made in the school?

Scanning typically raises lots of issues, but there is a limit to how many initiatives any one setting can take on simultaneously. So, inquiry teams now sharpen the focus on an area for change that has high leverage while at the same time being manageable. The next phase involves developing hunches about the ways in which the learning professionals themselves are contributing to this situation. This "hunching" stage leads to discussion about what needs to be learned and how that learning will occur. Changing practice involves new learning and designing new adult learning is the critical next step. New learning leads to new actions and the final phase involves checking to determine how much of a difference has been made.

Engaging in a spiral of inquiry throughout the CIEL programme provides participants with the experience of leading change in their own settings. Working as a collaborative team with the other members of their cohort builds confidence and allows them to learn quickly from each other's experiences. The findings from OECD/ILE report on *The Nature of Learning* provide a strong conceptual basis to inform and shape the design of new learning experiences in their settings. And, exploring and applying ideas from the international case studies in the *Innovative Learning Environments* initiative, opens up new possibilities and connections on many levels. The CIEL programme provides a third space for learning – and change – to take hold.

Developing and nurturing leadership for learning in New York City
(Roser Salavert)

In an effort to improve the education of all its students, the New York City Public Schools system has adopted a learning-centred vision, and empowered school principals with greater latitude and discretion regarding organisational, management and instructional decisions. This reorganisation started a decade ago in 2002/03, the school year when the author was appointed superintendent of schools for District 3, a post held to 2010. The New York City Public School system is the largest in the United States and serves over 1.1 million students. The schools are organised into 32 districts, each led by a schools superintendent. District 3 in the West Side and Harlem section of Manhattan includes 35 schools and serves approximately 14 000 students. This text reflects on my experience as a change agent and direct observer of transformation, especially on key strategies that support, nurture and develop the leadership of teachers and administrators that enabled this to take place.

Strategy 1: collaboration and innovation through professional learning communities

Until 2002, school principals were instructional leaders responsible for the implementation of the curriculum and other initiatives driven by the school superintendent's office. As principals gained greater autonomy and acquired additional responsibilities they became learning leaders in a truer sense. The new structures, based on principles similar to those described by Dimmock et al. in Chapter 4, transformed the role of the principals, which in turn impacted on the entire school system.

One major organisational breakthrough was the requirement that principals had to join a network of their choice. The networks follow the principles of a professional learning community (PLC) (DeFour and Eaker, 1998); they have made possible the development of a common language around learning, and have fostered ongoing collaboration and exchange of best practices among schools from the city's markedly diverse economic, linguistic and cultural communities.

Networks operate at a "meso" level; the network leader and his/her team function as consultants and advisors and provide school organisation and management support to content area instruction and job-embedded professional development. This has enabled a seamless connection between cutting-edge research and best practices, always with a clear focus on developing and nurturing the leadership of principals, teachers and students to sustain learning environments. Members of the New York City Department of Education lead some networks, but the structure also includes a group of private sector networks called Partnership Support Organizations (PSO). Unusually in

Fordham PSO (to which this author contributes), the university extends its academic expertise and programmes to the schools in the network including opportunities for postgraduate and doctoral degrees.

Strategy 2: coaching to develop distributive leadership

Leadership coaching is a feature of today's most accomplished organisations (Whitmore, 2009). It is becoming a key tool for principals who face complex decisions and ever-increasing responsibilities. Research on educational reform has provided the field with tremendous resources and well-documented, research-based practices, but there is a general disconnect between theory and practice, between what researchers say works and how principals and schools apply it (Berliner, 2008; Istance, Benavides and Dumont, 2008). At times, and with the latitude provided by their autonomy, schools may interpret the research so as to accommodate or justify well-established practices; at other times, schools with the best intentions may apply research practices and recommendations too literally, resulting in understandable frustration.

Take the case of an inner-city school in Harlem I observed in which coaching helped to bridge this gap. The principal had taken over the school previously managed by a top-down administrator. The principal had attended several sessions on distributive leadership and was well read on the subject, but she was discouraged by a lack of progress when attempting to translate this new knowledge into an effective school-wide practice. The complexity of the organisation and a traditional school culture that placed the highest premium on the implementation of the curriculum presented real and difficult challenges. In partnership with the coach, the principal guided her staff in the development of a shared vision, established the conditions for a rigorous and collaborative culture, and effectively implemented distributive leadership. This continues to help the school improve their practice and has increased student achievement.

Strategy 3: facilitating inquiry through collaborative teacher teams

Whereas networks operate at the "meso" level, school principals should be encouraged to facilitate the collaboration among teachers within their own school. The purpose of some of my work at this micro level was to foster the understanding of the interrelationships between professional growth and students' achievement, particularly the academic success of students new to the country with no English language skills and limited or no formal education in their native language. Based on my background in data analysis, and to foster cross-fertilisation of experiences, I provided support to one of the networks with schools that were not under my direct supervision as schools superintendent.

The Collaborative Teacher Team inquiry model that is implemented in the New York City public schools is an adaptation of the Scaffolded Apprenticeship Model (SAM) of School Improvement through Leadership Development (Talbert and Scharff, 2008). The theory of change behind this model postulates that to extend the sphere of student success in a complex organisation, one must "stay small". That is, teacher teams work systematically and creatively to improve the outcomes of a targeted group of students. These teachers learn to analyse and triangulate data from different sources as they look closely at instructional practices and their alignment to the needs of the target students. Together, they drive the implementation of strategies that can work for their particular students and evaluate their impact towards achieving ambitious end-of-year learning goals. The outcomes of these teams then inform the teaching and/or organisational practices of the school thus creating the conditions for an innovating learning environment, and a school culture that promotes evidence-based student achievement. This process is best illustrated by the example below (Figures 5.4 and 5.5).

Figure 5.4. **Instructional inquiry cycle**

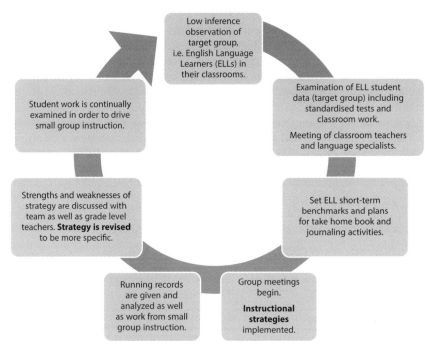

Figure 5.5. **School-wide inquiry cycle**

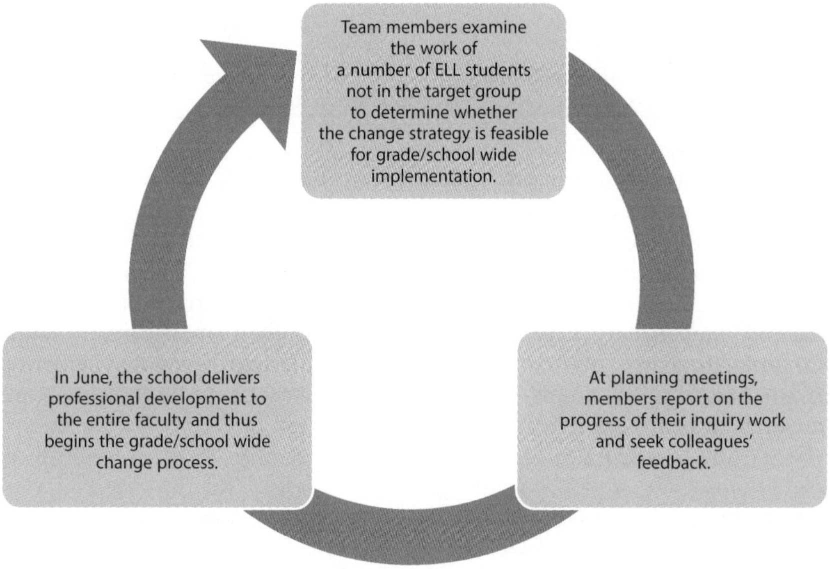

In one of the schools located in the Bronx, the principal showed some hesitation towards this small-target approach because the number of students who were under-performing was significantly high. With some trepidation, the school formed a Collaborative Inquiry Team. As teachers began documenting their observations and the progress of the target students, the principal noticed a change in the teachers' attitudes and an improvement in their practice. By the end of the year, most target students reached their academic goals. In addition, the team had identified and documented the specific strategies that had led to the desired student outcomes. The principal not only congratulated the work and accomplishments of the team, but also encouraged these teachers to share their results with the entire faculty. As a result, some of the strategies researched and implemented by the Collaborative Inquiry Team are now practices that have been implemented throughout the school.

This example shows the power of the SAM model by "staying small". An important key to substantial change is the ability to understand the interrelationships that influence behaviour over time and their impact on student learning. In the example presented, one of these critical interrelationships, and one that influenced student achievement, was the degree of collaboration among teachers. The success of the collaboration among the teachers in the Inquiry Team inspired the principal to reorganise teachers' planning time and support the learning research of the entire faculty, which resulted in the establishment of 14 Collaborative Inquiry Teams.

Strategy 4: listening to students and giving them a voice in their learning

A school that focuses on learning seeks the involvement of all its constituencies, including its students (Leithwood et al., 2004). This involvement is fundamental to developing their independence as learners, which is also the purpose of the academic competences (NYSED, 2011).

The impact of students in a formal role should not be underestimated, and a goal that I have pursued as leadership coach or superintendent has been to guide principals in the establishment of academic advisories, as well as student councils, or other forms of student governance. When principals seek the active participation of students as a strategy towards improving learning, they foster students' responsibility for their own learning while demonstrating their ability to enable sustainable and innovative learning environments. For example, in a K-8 (kindergarten to grade 8) school, the principal had adopted writing as an important part of a school-wide change strategy, and invited the Student Council to organise monthly publishing celebrations. The students would post the activities for the day and visit classrooms to facilitate the readings of compositions, including to introduce the writing process to their classmates. The efficacy of the Student Council reached a turning point when the students decided to interview classmates and teachers about writing genres to create a video, the success of which was marked when the faculty suggested that the video be uploaded and shared with the community via the school's website.

Collaboration and action: a broader shared vision

The strategies described above illustrate some of the benefits of bridging educational research and practice, and underscore its importance in educational reform. My experience also suggests that a school community needs to establish first and foremost a climate of trust and respect among its constituencies. This environment enables leadership for learning. That is, it makes possible the conditions for a collaborative culture that encourages teachers to continuously reflect upon their practices to improve and sustain student achievement.

Developing learning leadership in Norway (Lone Lønne Christiansen and Per Tronsmo)

The Norwegian PISA shock

When the first Programme for International Student Assessment (PISA) findings were published in 2001, our poor results surprised most people in Norway. We have always had big ambitions. We have had many initiatives, reforms and plans, a great degree of political agreement and will, deeply committed teachers and school administrators, and also more resources than most countries. But there was a big gap between the ambitions, on the one hand, and actual practices in the schools, on the other. The challenge was one of implementation and change.

In 2006 the government passed a major school reform ("The Knowledge Promotion Reform"), with new curricula and increased local responsibility for primary education. In addition to the students' increased learning outcomes, the reform states in the basic principles for education that the school and apprenticeship-training enterprise shall be learning organisations that make it possible for teachers to learn from each other through co-operation on planning, implementing and assessing their teaching.

The responsibility for the implementation of the reform was given to the Directorate for Education and Training, a subordinate agency of the Ministry of Education and Research. Two of the most important initiatives were a national programme for school leadership and the Advisory Team programme, which are discussed below.

The importance of leadership

Traditionally, the public sector has used legislation and budgetary instruments to drive change, often with very modest effect. In Norway we now emphasise more empowering strategies, partly because they are more effective, partly because they suit the Scandinavian model better. Empowering is about giving people new authority and responsibilities, and helping them to be more powerful by giving help and support. It is about introducing recognition, feedback and reward systems that inspire, promote optimism and build self-confidence, including the non-punitive use of data. It is about encouraging risk-taking and non-traditional ideas and activities.

A key factor in this strategy is leadership, at all levels. In all kinds of organisations there is a strong need for leadership to focus on the core business. In a school the core business is learning. There are different expressions for this focus: "learning-centred leadership", "leadership for learning", "leadership of learning organisations", "leadership of learning processes", "instructional leadership", "leading to learn" and, as here, "learning leadership". In many countries, there is a perception that there is too much focus on administration and too little focus on processes for student learning. (OECD, 2008) An expanded role which combines administration with instructional leadership focuses strongly on the principal's management of teachers and their teaching.

Leadership can have an enormous influence on learning environments and outcomes. The Norwegian school system is highly decentralised, which calls for responsible leaders who are powerful, loyal, competent and courageous; they need to have the "right" role, with enough focus on learning leadership and with legitimacy from the teachers. In most sectors the importance of leadership is obvious, but in the education sector this has not always been the case. A great deal of resistance to leadership can be found among teachers, and schools have little tradition for the leader to directly influence the work done by the teacher. But things are changing, and many good initiatives have been taken during the last ten years to improve leadership in the education sector (OECD, 2008).

Leadership will probably be even more important in the future. School autonomy and local freedom demand more from leaders. Leading change processes will be more common and more challenging. Important societal changes will influence schools, such as migration and mobility, the digital world, a more diverse society, individualisation, boys' under-achievement, smaller households, budgetary challenges, growing income inequality, increasing pressure from social expenditure (OECD, 2010, 2013b).

A school principal equipped to meet these challenges is one who is secure in the leadership role, having courage and strength to lead and manage, and the personal and professional strength to stand up and take on leadership and the identity of a leader. Leadership means taking responsibility for achieving good results. A leader is also responsible for those results being achieved in a good way, that colleagues enjoy a good working environment, and that these might continue to produce good results in the future. A school leader therefore has a social responsibility in addition to taking care of the day-to-day leadership and management of the individual school. By definition, a leader is responsible for everything that happens within his or her own unit, and in this sense the leader also has an employer's role.

Obviously, having responsibility does not mean that leaders must do everything themselves. Leadership is primarily exercised through others. A leader delegates tasks and authority, but the responsibility itself cannot be delegated. This does not mean that colleagues have no responsibility but a leader is never relieved of his or her responsibilities. Leadership is exercised by many, not just by those who occupy formal leadership or management positions. In this respect, leadership is a function to be attended to, or a set of leadership tasks to be performed. At the same time, the organisation is made up of people, with their own roles, relationships and abilities. Formal responsibility for results is linked to specific persons in formal positions.

Leadership, management and knowledge organisations

The OECD's Teaching and Learning International Survey (TALIS: OECD, 2009) describes the role of school leaders and examines the support they give to their teachers. It found that a number of countries have a relatively weak evaluation structure and do not benefit from school evaluations and teacher appraisal and feedback. The principal's role is summarised as two main management styles – instructional leadership and administrative leadership – in which Norway scores lower on instructional leadership than most of the other countries, and higher on administration than most of the other countries. The two styles are not mutually exclusive, even though they are sometimes portrayed as such in the research literature. We want stronger focus on student learning, but at the same time we know that effective leadership also involves administrative accountability and a workable bureaucracy.

It has been fashionable to distinguish leaders from managers. Mintzberg (2009: 9) rejects the facile distinction: "By putting leadership on a pedestal separated from management, we turn a social process into a personal one ... I want to put managing ahead, seeing it together with leadership as naturally embedded in what can be called *communityship"*. He sees management as neither a science nor a profession; it is a practice, learned primarily through experience and rooted in context. Leadership practice has to be learned on the job, through apprenticeship, mentorship and direct experience. A challenge for leadership education, training and development, in Mintzberg's view, is that too often it is individualised and participant-focused rather than rooted in the organisation and workplace (Mintzberg, 2011).

There is a large body of research and literature about so-called "knowledge organisations" (hospitals, universities, law offices, consulting firms, schools, etc.) and their leadership challenges. Three main such challenges are: *1)* tension between professionals and leaders; *2)* too much focus on steering and control; and *3)* problems of legitimacy for the leaders. A school is a knowledge organisation with strict professional requirements and strong focus on professional questions at all levels. The ability to lead learning processes is crucial in order to be both a good leader and sufficiently skilled academically to make one's own professional assessments and make the best use of internal and external human resources. Leading knowledge organisations is often more difficult than leading other organisations, because those working in them tend to be independent, vigorous, competent and, first and foremost, professionally oriented.

Leadership challenges and development in Norway

According to Geert Hofstede (2001), there is a distinctive leadership profile of Scandinavian countries which combines very short "power distance" and a very "feminine culture". A study from Norway (Grenness, 2006) confirms this distinctiveness in more detail, characterising Scandinavian leadership as having high ethical standards; proximity to employees, team orientation, and preference for good working relations; striving for consensus; high gender equality; strong focus on process; conflict avoidance; low results-orientation; slow decision making; fuzzy control mechanisms; and lack of "warrior" attitudes. It could be said that the Scandinavian leadership style is particularly suited for a post-industrial knowledge economy where success is dependent on collaboration across the value chain, networks and partnerships and the ability to innovate in an environment of high levels of ambiguity and change. There are of course both positive and negative aspects of this "Scandinavian leadership model".

The Norwegian school system is decentralised, with nearly 450 municipalities responsible for the schools. There are big differences between the quality of municipalities, between schools and between school leaders. But the problems confronted overall in Norway are:

- Insufficiently strong leadership, at all levels.

- Insufficient expertise and strength among school owners.

- Fragmentation in the school sector, meaning that there is insufficient focus on the sector as a system.

- Fragmented schools, so that there is insufficient focus on schools as organisations.

The national policy is to give leaders more support, help and professional training, and to support schools and municipalities in their organisational and systems development work. These are described in the next two sections, with particular emphasis on the latter.

Leadership development in Norway

The national framework describes the requirements and expectations that can reasonably be set for a school principal, and forms the basis for the national programme for leadership training and development for principals in Norway (Norwegian Directorate for Education and Training, 2008). It involves the following main areas:

1. the pupils' learning outcomes and learning environment

2. management and administration

3. collaboration and organisation development; the guidance of teachers

4. development and change.

The most important of these four areas is the first one, which is associated with learning leadership. The principal is responsible for the pupils' learning outcomes and learning environment, and the principal's ability to lead the learning process and guide teachers in this is crucial. A school is a knowledge organisation with strict professional requirements. The principal must therefore have sufficient academic competence and legitimacy to make good professional assessments and make the best use of internal and external human resources.

There is another area of leadership development which is of another kind as it has to do with the personal side of leadership – the leadership role. This is about developing leaders who are clear about their own role as leader, able to define and redefine, and if necessary negotiate and renegotiate, their leadership role and their conditions for exercising good leadership.

The national management training programme for principals, which was established in 2008, is for all newly employed head teachers in primary and secondary education. It has been set up to be an answer to the challenges of the school system, with a strong emphasis on being well managed and goal oriented and based in a practical way on the experienced needs of school managers and others.

The leadership training programme has been evaluated by highly-respected research institutions. To now they have finished two out of four reports and concluded in very positive terms (Hybertsen et al., 2012a, 2012b). There are also other indications that the programme is leading to good results. One is its popularity, with an increasing number of applicants every year. Another is the positive evaluation made by the providers. There seems to be a shift in attitudes with leadership and leaders increasingly recognised as important for school improvement, including attitudes expressed by different stakeholders (unions, politicians, school owners, universities, etc.). Added to this, there are signs of improvement in student performance.

The Advisory Team programme

In Norway, most schools are public, with a large number of small municipalities, and school management and leadership development is a local responsibility. School owners often lack the competence and capacity to meet the challenges involved and hence the government started the Advisory Team programme. It is aimed to help school owners and school leaders who are facing special challenges in core areas for quality, such as students lacking reading and mathematics skills, learning environments that do not promote learning, and students and apprentices who do not complete upper secondary education or do not pass their exams in upper secondary education and training. The aim is to enable school owners and schools to implement national goals through local development strategies by strengthening the school as an organisation, using proven tools and methods.

The programme is led by the Directorate of Education and Training, and the main national partners are the Norwegian Association of Local and Regional Authorities (KS), county governors (the national education offices at county level), the university/college sector, consulting groups, and practitioners.

The school development work itself takes place locally. The political and administrative school owner is involved, principals participate, and other local support groups are also involved, depending on the guidance topic in question.

The Advisory Team was piloted in two counties in 2009-10, and the first regular portfolio of the Advisory Team was started 2011. During the next 3 years, the Advisory Team's activities will cover 18 counties and 429 municipalities, the whole country except for Oslo. About 30 municipalities have 80-100 schools in each portfolio, receiving guidance for 18 months. By the end of 2013, all municipalities in the country will have been offered guidance from the Advisory Team for the first time.

There has been a research-based evaluation of the system of the Advisory Team. The first interim report (Norwegian Directorate for Education and Training, 2013) is a study covering the feedback of advisors and those who have received guidance and the next report will be available in December 2013, containing an evaluation of the results and impacts.

The advisors in the Advisory Team are recruited from among school managers and municipal educational administrations from all over the country. The team of advisors is national and governmental, but has no formal authority and so it is up to the municipality whether it will accept this support. The advisors are grouped in smaller teams responsible for two or three municipalities and their schools. The teams work with the schools and their owners on an individual basis during the process. School owners are gathered at the beginning and the end of the guidance process for joint competence development and sharing of experiences and planning. The aim is to enable the schools and their owners to continue their quality development work on their own. Development work is a continuous process, comprising identification of needs, option evaluation leading to solutions, the implementation of these measures and evaluating them. The guidance takes the form of a coach/mentor relationship, and focuses on the first phases of the municipalities' quality development that can be achieved in 18 months.

The phases that the Advisory Team takes part in are:

- *Identify developmental needs*: the advisors actively deploy analytical tools so that the school identifies areas for development and at the same time the advisors identify the school's counselling needs.

- *Planning the development project*: the guidance is given according to revealed needs, and complementary external assessments of the school's potential and developmental needs are also offered.

- *Implementation*: the guidance is based on local need and on knowledge of learning organisations and change management, backed up by meetings and seminars.

The tools used are for mapping, reflecting and analysing the current situation – the Quality Status tool and the Organisational Analysis tool[3] – together with an external assessment methodology for starting and anchoring development work at the school level.

The guidance is supportive, aimed to help schools and their owners start their local development work. The Advisory Team gives no guarantees, but can contribute to schools' and their owners' successful development work. A prerequisite for success is the active and responsible participation from all parties. Acceptance of the offer of guidance is an indication of the will for development, a basic prerequisite for change. The guidance considers the school and its owner as an overall organisation, and considers how it works and how it can be improved. The advisors contribute with knowledge, experience and counselling (Schein, 1998), enabling the school to better meet the challenges coming to the surface during implementation and pedagogical changes. Some schools may additionally need competence development related to basic skills, evaluation or other core tasks. The Advisory Team can contribute to finding the relevant competence groups, but does not offer guidance on these fields and the Advisory Team itself never assumes responsibility for the development processes.

Guidance, practised as national support for local development work through the Advisory Team, is a tool that the Directorate of Education and Training and the public authorities in Norway have had no tradition in using hitherto. Since Norway traditionally has had little control, access to and evaluation of schools, the Advisory Team was seen as controversial, and efforts were made to reduce the risk of resistance in the education sector.

This resistance was handled through a deliberate emphasis on its voluntary nature (Schein, 2009), and emphasising that school owners seeking counselling were not "losers", but instead were showing courage and flexibility. The university and college sector and the public administration also resisted the measure. For the public administration, the resistance was to the state interfering in a local authority, while higher education resisted the Advisory Team as a professional competitor. This resistance has now turned to support, based on good results in terms of satisfied school owners and advisors. Both the public administration and the higher education sector have been involved in the Advisory Team in such a way that the activity has become professionally and organisationally anchored and in both sectors a change of attitude has taken place.

The result to date is of satisfied school owners having received counselling, as well as the advisors being satisfied in seeing the guided municipalities making progress and earning important experience and development competence in their own municipalities and schools (Norwegian Directorate for Education and Training, 2013). The Advisory Team has been an effective foundation for disseminating the Directorate of Education and Training's web-based quality development tools and the external school evaluation methodology. These tools seem to be very useful, especially for the schools and school owners that have no previous experience or confidence with quality evaluation.

An important success factor has been the centralised, tight management of the programme, and the strategy was thoroughly worked through and was familiar to the different actors and stakeholders. The Directorate has defined the competency requirements for the advisors, carefully selected them, established an obligatory training programme, and do not re-engage advisors who were not adequate. The focus for the Advisory Team is the school owner and the school as a unit, and there are strong conditions for the participating school owners in terms of active engagement. It is thus both a top-down and a bottom-up approach.

Learning leadership in South Australia (Susanne Owen)

Background and context

During 2011, seven South Australian Department for Education and Child Development (DECD) schools, preschools and early learning centres were accepted into the OECD Innovative Learning Environment (ILE) project, having met the criteria for significant innovation. An additional 8 sites have since been identified by the department as being significantly innovative; with all 15 now being recognised and operating within the state-wide Innovation Community of Practice and with others also joining the group as emerging contexts for innovation. These sites, which range from birth to year 12 levels of schooling and care, represent "grassroots" innovation, having developed innovative approaches over various timeframes to meet the needs of their children and students, and their different learning and community contexts.

While the innovations are highly specific, they are generally characterised by features that are consistent with the OECD Innovative Learning Environment project in relation to the key elements and dynamics related to teachers, learners, content, resources, and organisation and pedagogy. Innovative aspects include learners being within multi-age groupings (such as reception to year 7 "Magpie" groupings and year 10-12 tutor groups) and content being about big picture or fertile questions which provide opportunities for interdisciplinary and deep learning experiences. Individual student learning plans are a key feature in all sites and there are sometimes purpose-built facilities or traditional physical spaces that have been renovated and transformed into "campfires" for targeted master classes and specialist skill building, or "cave spaces" for quiet reflection. Professional learning teams meet regularly and typically engage in co-planning, co-teaching and co-assessing, while also considering data and other evidence about individual student progress. A key characteristic of these innovative sites is the nurturing of leadership skills for all members of these professional learning teams, supported by the school/preschool leader through the provision of time and/or funding for professional learning.

These innovative schools and preschools operate with some degree of autonomy within a centralised public education system that is currently undergoing significant change to achieve the state government's vision of a fully integrated child development, education and child protection system. Currently (2013), the department is being restructured across its birth to year 12 education and care contexts, with the incorporation of some former Health and also Families and Communities services. The redesign strategy – *Brighter Futures* (DECD, 2013) – is focusing on changing culture, service delivery practices, processes, roles and systems to ensure higher achievement standards, improved health and well-being outcomes, better family-carer support, stronger community-led engagement in determining local provisions, and greater emphasis on student voice in shaping policies and practices. The principles guiding this work include "creating sustainable growth and continuous improvement", and "building a culture characterised by positivity, finding solutions, creativity and innovation". Establishing networks of preschools and schools with a focus on local community is highlighted as a key feature of the state-wide *Brighter Futures* initiative.

Networks and communities of practice and professional learning communities are therefore a significant aspect of the department's future direction. Individual innovation sites are already strongly committed to using teacher professional learning communities focused on a particular group of students or involving action research. Planning, teaching and assessing in teams is an ongoing professional learning approach to support teachers in changing their role to that of being learning facilitators, teacher "engagers" and co-learners with students.

Leadership approach

In examining professional learning at an individual site level, it is apparent that teacher learning in the most innovative DECD schools reflects the professional learning community characteristics generally identified in the literature (Haar, 2003; Vescio, Ross and Adams, 2008; Darling-Hammond and Richardson, 2009; Scott, Clarkson and McDonough, 2011). Indeed, in South Australian case study research conducted recently on innovation and professional learning communities, the key themes identified were: shared values and vision, on-going collaboration, commitment to joint practical activities and student learning outcomes, supportive and shared leadership, and teacher inquiry and learning together (Owen, 2012). Collegial and on-going professional learning to build respect and trust and to share the vision and language are also viewed as a critical aspect of this process, as indicated in one representative leader comment:

> We're talking about whole school innovation, change, focused on improvement. You can't do that unless you've got people who are speaking the same language, sharing the same vision … they're trusting and respecting of each other, constantly looking at ways of changing … You can't do that by yourself. It's incredibly isolating, threatening … [It involves] structuring the whole approach to the professional learning, to the professional learning community as a baseline (Owen, 2012: Leader Interview 1).

The leadership and communities of practice diagrammatic model for innovation which has been used within some of the DECD leading innovation workshops and which captures this approach is set out in Figure 5.6.

In the South Australian innovative sites case study research (Owen, 2012), professional learning team members and principals both emphasised the importance of contributive leadership which is about true "grassroots"

Figure 5.6. **DECD educational innovation**

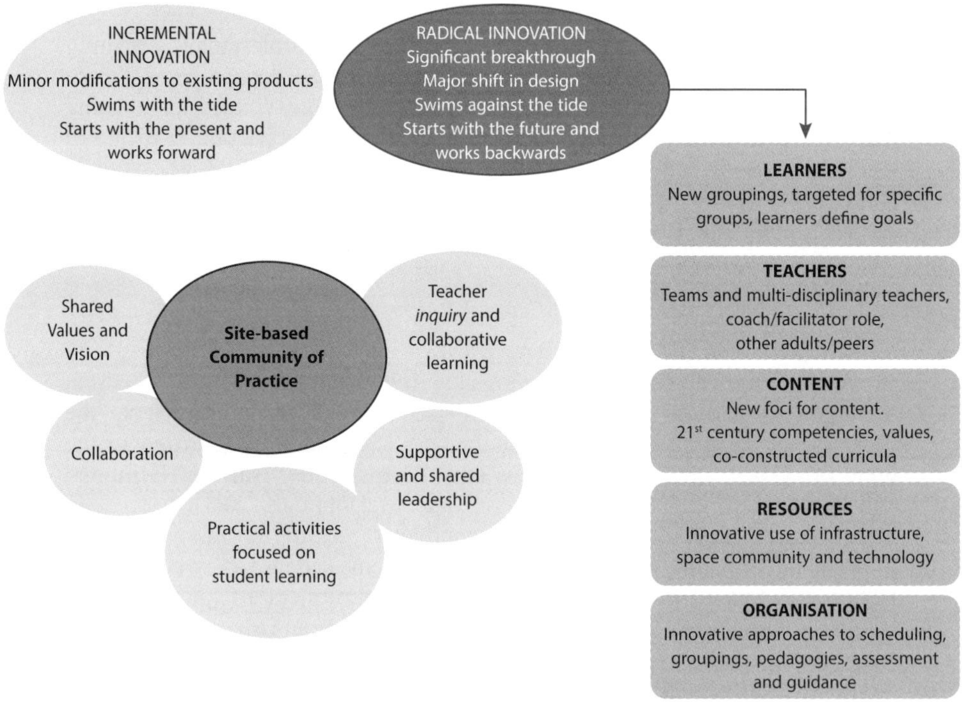

INCREMENTAL INNOVATION
Minor modifications to existing products
Swims with the tide
Starts with the present and works forward

RADICAL INNOVATION
Significant breakthrough
Major shift in design
Swims against the tide
Starts with the future and works backwards

LEARNERS
New groupings, targeted for specific groups, learners define goals

Shared Values and Vision

Site-based Community of Practice

Teacher *inquiry* and collaborative learning

TEACHERS
Teams and multi-disciplinary teachers, coach/facilitator role, other adults/peers

Collaboration

Supportive and shared leadership

CONTENT
New foci for content.
21st century competencies, values, co-constructed curricula

Practical activities focused on student learning

RESOURCES
Innovative use of infrastructure, space community and technology

ORGANISATION
Innovative approaches to scheduling, groupings, pedagogies, assessment and guidance

valuing of staff ideas in driving change agendas. This is reflected in the following school documentation:

> There is a strong ownership as a staff for the curriculum and pedagogical practices. ... This ownership is due to the staff creating them as a team and continuing to develop them. ... We have collectively developed a culture of change, high expectations and commitment to the school's philosoph ... Shared leadership reinforces the ownership that staff have for the success of the school in achieving improved outcomes for student ... Having all staff leading gives an appreciation for the role, which has increased the sense of trust in one another, so initiatives can progress more efficiently and with great support (OECD, 2012; School B, supplementary information: 8).

The school leader's role in supporting professional learning teams cannot be overestimated. Teachers working together in teams, focusing on particular student groups and sharing leadership and responsibility for the learning of others, need to be supported by leaders who not only provide time and funding for professional learning to occur, but who support the establishment of teams as "deliberate structures where people can challenge each other about the level at which they do that work" (Owen, 2012: Leader Interview 3). Many examples of this type of supportive leadership are provided by participants within the South Australian innovation case study research.

Leading innovation through a community of practice

Beyond innovation in individual schools and preschools and the professional learning communities being nurtured and operating within them, the work of the innovative schools across the South Australian public education system has been supported through a small team operating in the department's central office. The focus of this co-ordinated work has been to "build the momentum" for innovation more widely across schools and preschools. Various strategies are involved, including conferences and workshops, an innovations website, part-time advisory support from an innovation principal, practitioner research grants with academic support, and innovation newsletters.

Much of the co-ordinated systems work operates through the DECD Innovation Community of Practice (CoP) which has involved about 30 people from across the 15 identified innovation sites (but which has been expanding during 2013 as more sites were included). Participants regularly attend face-to-face meetings which are held once each term to share practices, information and ideas; discuss emerging issues or opportunities; and collaborate in planning future work or events. They also provide advice and recommend policy directions in relation to innovation for wider dissemination and possible system uptake. Due to distance factors, participation is also facilitated through emails and other communications. Meetings are rotated among innovation sites, with all having the opportunity to host a visit where a tour is provided and members are updated about the site's innovation philosophy. During 2011-12, the CoP collaborated to facilitate a series of one-day state-wide innovation events for other schools with up to 400 people attending some of them. The sites also undertook practitioner research about aspects of their innovative work, with academic support and collaboratively developed and contributed research reports and other materials to the project website (www.innovations. sa.edu.au) and to innovation newsletters.

The community of practice and wider activities of conferences, newsletters, and websites closely reflects the "nested communities of practice, engagement and interest" model of diffusion outlined in the Global Education Leaders' Program (GELP) publication, *Redesigning Education* (2013). In this approach, the early adopters work together in a "structured, supported and facilitated" community of practice, "share research and knowledge, work together to use disciplined innovation methods, draw on the expertise of relevant partners", and "learn from each other about overcoming obstacles and barriers". The nested communities of practice model is clearly evident in the DECD CoP, surrounded as it is by "communities of interest", that are populated by individuals and organisations interested in the case for change and wanting to be kept informed of developments with newsletters, websites, conferences and workshops all useful. Furthermore, as the GELP publication indicates, the "community of interest" are ready recipients to the work underway in the community of practice; the nested model being most efficient when the "the innovators have been authorised or legitimated to act on behalf of the system as a whole" (2013: 97-98).

A particular focus which began in mid-2013 is a specially-designed Exploring Innovation programme of visits to a number of the highly innovative schools. This programme has been planned by the CoP members, using their own practitioner action research findings to provide evidence of the impact of the innovations. The Exploring Innovation visits and the practitioner action research project are activities which have been co-ordinated by the department's innovation team (with the practitioner researchers also supported by a small grant and university academic mentors). In the "Exploring Innovation" visits, leaders and teachers from other schools and preschools are encouraged to visit in teams. The diffusion of innovative practices will be examined through tracking attendees at the visits and monitoring the uptake of innovative practices at their own sites, from the time of registering for the visit and then again at six-monthly intervals. This will enable data to be gathered and shared about their own perspectives and experiences, and about the progress of innovation in their individual contexts.

Further systems building of the innovation culture occurs through provision of a small funding grant for practitioner research to another 10-12 emerging innovation sites, including one newly operating network cluster. Grants are available to sites across the DECD public schooling system and for all levels of schooling and care. In a partnership arrangement with a university over a 12-month time frame, these emerging innovative sites are being supported through initial research training and support in developing their research proposal, access to an academic critical friend, or to purchase additional academic time for particular aspects of the research process. Presentations at various events and progress reports are required and there is the option of final report formats including longer reports, posters and power-point presentations, although certain basic research report features must be covered (background to research, research methods, findings, conclusion and references). These schools and preschools have also joined the existing innovation community of practice as active members.

A key issue which emerged through the Innovation Community of Practice review discussions, and confirmed by materials from the Center for Creative Leadership (CCL, 2009), is that leadership of innovation goes beyond the usual traditional approaches to thinking, strategic change and management that are focused on logic, deductive reasoning and right/wrong results. Leadership models need to be focused on leading for multiple perspectives, considering personal experiences to gain fresh perspectives, paying attention and perceiving deeply, being involved in serious play and generating insights through experimentation. Collaboration and embracing diverse viewpoints are key aspects.

Participants in the CoP have identified as key benefits of membership of the community to be working together beyond their own establishments, contributing to changing the nature of schooling at a systems level, learning from each other's large school/small school situations, and affirming work underway in their own contexts.

The state-wide Innovation Community of Practice is important in helping other leaders to gain the confidence to "have a go" and establish grassroots innovation appropriate to their context. The CoP is also seen as an acknowledgement that innovation has a place within the education system. As one CoP member indicated in a review discussion: "This group exists and we want to ensure it continues to exist… [we] want it to be leading edge". While many of the schools and preschools involved had previously established themselves at a grassroots level as significantly innovative, being part of a systems approach within a community of practice has benefits and the importance of connection to the innovation work of the OECD is acknowledged.

Another benefit of the DECD Innovation Community of Practice operating at the state-wide level is that individual innovation leaders can be legitimately involved in "rule bending" or experimenting with disciplined innovation within their local schools and preschools. In a larger programme of system restructure and redesign, these innovative schools are able to provide evidence about the impacts on student learning and well-being of innovative approaches they have been trialling, thereby supporting the whole system to move forward.

Given the current South Australian context, and considering the DECD *Brighter Futures* directions with its focus on creating sustainable growth and continuous improvement while building a positive culture characterised by finding solutions, creativity and innovation, there is certainly a role for the Innovation Community of Practice to influence the various projects that are being established as part of the department's overall redesign. There is a need to ensure that innovation is captured somewhere, particularly as old structures and processes are replaced and new networks, relationships and connections are created. Through an on-going and expanded Innovation Community of Practice, individual site leaders and their communities are able to use their experience and influence to work collaboratively to shape those future directions and ensure that the new department has innovation as a predominant aspect of its work.

Learning leadership for innovation at the system level: Israel
(Dorit Tubin)

Conditions for successful learning leadership at the system level

Learning leadership can usefully be understood as the ability to influence others to accomplish common goals of improving the learning environment(s) within and beyond the classroom. This definition contains four elements that represent the conditions for learning leadership to flourish at scale: *1)* social position; *2)* the ability to choose a common goal and develop a vision; *3)* the capacity to influence others and create a structure; and *4)* the ability to evaluate and provide feedback.

Social position

Leading a large-scale innovative learning reform means occupying a high prestige position in a prominent social organisation. Social position may be based on formal authority (ministry of education), expertise (university), economic and social capital (private and non-profit organisations), or a combination of these.

Ministries of education thus have the necessary social position to understand values and structures and to influence change. Public education systems as bureaucracies, however, tend to have only few directors at the top and even fewer innovators. Thus, it is usually one person, sometimes together with a small leading team, who initiates and leads such reform. A high-ranking position provides the leader with the necessary understanding of the system's values and structure, and brings the power to be able to seize opportunities for innovations, and even the ability to change regulations, allocate resources, and implement the innovative learning reform.

The ability to choose a common goal and develop a vision

A common goal is necessary to justify innovative learning reform as part of the education system's broad social agenda and goals, whether this is promoting 21st century learning skills or reducing the inequality gap or fulfilling every child's potential. The common goal must present the essence and main challenge to be addressed so that it can serve as a symbol for the change that will foster legitimacy and stakeholder support for the investment of the time, money and expertise required.

The common goal should be translated into an educational vision, to offer a "road map" from the unsatisfactory present situation of learning towards a more promising future. The vision should attract partners and followers, and provide them with the motivation, suggested methods, and narratives to explain the importance of such reform for innovative learning. The vision gives meaning to such concepts as "improving", "learning" and "environment" providing the necessary context and relevance that are understood by and attractive to potential partners. The vision informs benchmarks and suggests evaluation criteria for assessing implementation measures. Without such a vision, there may well be too many routes to implementation and too much empty rhetoric, even mistrust in future reforms.

The capacity to influence others and create structure

To influence others, leadership must possess the ability to use various channels of communication (e.g. face-to-face meetings, lectures, media and internet facilities) for reaching target audiences at the right time and place. Also important is the ability to operate different methods, such as inspiring vision, extra resources, prizes and reward systems, to motivate others to change in line with the educational vision.

For the wider diffusion of innovative learning environments, the leadership has to create a particular structure or blueprint for people, roles, tasks, resources, equipment, and information and communications technology (ICT) to support the reform's goals. The leadership has to offer resources and means of obtaining the resources needed for realising such a structure in a way so that the same kind of innovative learning environment can be duplicated in different locations. It also has to establish co-operation and collaboration with a variety of stakeholders at various levels of the education system and outside it, delegate authority, and distribute leadership to create engagement across teams of professionals.

Evaluation and feedback

Sustainable innovative learning reform at scale needs to have a learning network embedded in its very structure, promoted by the learning leadership, and providing information about the learning taking place in the innovation venues among the participants system-wide. The circulation of information between the participants enables them to learn from each other, thus boosting success and reducing the repetition of failures.

The leadership should first ensure that the information is circulated in the system, and second verify that it is being used to refine the vision, establish benchmarks for evaluation, using the outcomes for accountability reports, and reconnecting performance to the goals of innovative learning. The evaluation outcomes should serve leaders at all levels (teachers, principals, high-ranking officials and stakeholders) for redesigning learning environments, providing positive feedback to the learners, and enhancing leadership abilities through self-awareness.

Self-awareness includes the ability of those in different leadership positions to understand their values, motives and effectiveness in influencing others. It enables leaders to improve their capacity for inquiry, reflection and learning from experience. Thus, reforms to spread innovative learning environments are able to serve not only the end-users – students and teachers – but also the leaders themselves. For this to happen with diffusion among as many participants as possible, different methods are required such as a professional learning community, workshops, training, conferences and academic studies.

Concrete examples

The most notable example in Israel of leading and disseminating innovative learning is the Ministry of Education Experiments and Entrepreneurship Division. This began operating in 1996 with the aim of supporting changes and initiatives originating in the education field, and providing them with backing and support within the education system. The initiatives engage with a variety of aspects of enhancing education, including learning advancement, increasing motivation, developing alternative teaching and learning methods, and designing innovative learning environments. The target audiences are learners and teachers in educational institutions from kindergarten to higher education. The central idea is to identify and develop innovative educational models adapted to the challenges of the present and the future, which will constitute inspiration for shaping Israel's education policy. In this way the Experiments and Entrepreneurship Division encourages the involvement of educators in shaping and enhancing education in Israel.

The Experiments and Entrepreneurship Division is part of the Ministry of Education. Its main partners are educational institutions throughout the Israeli education system, from kindergartens, through schools, to teacher-training centres and colleges. Any such institution interested in developing and applying an educational initiative designed to advance learning among its students is invited to approach the Division, and operate with its support during the initiative's first five years.

The Division's main activity is identifying educators with a vision that their place of work can be different, and enable them to develop it for the learners, the teachers, and the community. This is a five-year process in which the entrepreneurs are monitored during the implementation of their dreams, the suitability of the innovation for the institution is examined, and its assimilation into everyday educational processes is evaluated. The Division provides support, training, and research and development (R&D) tools for the initiatives and their assimilation while holding a continuous dialogue between the institution (in which the initiative is operated and applied), the division (which provides support and backing) and an academic adviser (who liaises between the initiative and the research in the chosen sphere).

In the course of the five-year period, the institution is required to apply the innovative initiative with ever-increasing scope within the school, with a Division supervisor and an academic adviser supporting it step by step. At the end of the five-year period, the school is required to write the experiment report in which it details the experiment theory, the process and its products. Schools demonstrating special success become dissemination centres in which their teachers teach teachers from other institutions interested in developing similar innovations. This is a process that advances and develops not only additional schools, but also the teachers who become instructors of the innovative initiative. To achieve this, the Division operates in five main spheres: it encourages R&D of innovative educational initiatives, examines proposals and requests for experiment, monitors the training and assimilation of innovation in educational institutions, encourages documentation and management of the knowledge accumulated in the course of the experiment, and disseminates the experiment's products throughout the education system.

Each year 15 new institutions join the Division, while fifteen others complete their 5-year experimental period and start functioning independently.

In any given year, 80 experimental schools are operating simultaneously under the aegis of the Division. This complex system has at its disposal the Division's director and secretaries, offices in the Ministry of Education complex, 40 annual training days whereby a number of supervisors work with the schools, and a half-time teaching post for each school joining the experiment. Additionally, the local authorities fund an academic adviser who works with the experimental institution, and they also provide the physical environment or dedicated equipment required for the experiment.

With time, the Division, together with the experimental schools, has developed in several directions. More and more schools have joined the experiment, and have streamlined the monitoring and evaluation of the experiments and initiatives. The Division has also expanded toward additional activities such as the advancement of special education schools, and community activities. Finally, both the Division's staff and its work processes are becoming increasingly specialised and professional.

The challenge for the Division is its institutionalisation, as it has always been original and innovative within the Ministry of Education and among educational institutions. Starting from a small number, in recent years the Division has reached some 150 schools.

In the field itself, the Division's success has depended on the school leadership. With few resources and a great deal of inspiration and motivation, the principals and their staff are leading their schools toward developing a more meaningful and varied learning environment. They are also writing and developing the experiment theory in experiment books, and they often establish dissemination centres, thus involving the whole community, not just themselves. Belonging to the Division is prestigious in itself and facilitates a support group that assists innovators to break out of their isolation and become a meaningful community that manages the risks of innovation in an informed way, and influences the Israeli education system.

There is much school interest in joining and developing educational initiatives, but budgetary constraints dictate the number that can be accepted each year. Success is not only to be judged in terms of adding schools, but also of improving and deepening successful initiatives. Leaving the Division after five years sometimes impacts on the experiments and sees them go backwards.

Looking at leadership at a still higher level in the system, it is important to recognise the role played the head of the Ministry of Education Experiments and Entrepreneurship Division (EEE). She managed to choose educational innovation and pedagogical experimentation as the principal goals for the future of the Israeli system, and elaborate it into a vision that sparked the imagination of stakeholders. Based on her previous experience as a successful school principal, charismatic leadership style and ability to convince the decision makers, she established the Division in 1996. Her deep acquaintance with the formal regulations and her experience with administrative requirements allowed her to create an efficient network of people, resources and organisations that experience an innovative environment under the control, support and guidance of the EEE Division. Hence, she too embodies the four conditions necessary and sufficient for system-wide ILE reform.

The four conditions for learning leadership outlined at the beginning of this chapter section have several implications. First, they can be adjusted to different contexts and levels, thus enabling cross-cultural comparison. Second, they can inform decision makers about the conditions needed for building learning leadership capacity, and initiating successful learning innovation reform. Finally, they can serve as a diagnostic tool for finding what works well, and which lacunas exist in innovation reform already underway, so that the invested efforts and resources effectively improve the participants' learning. The main lesson seems to be that where the system is concerned (at district, municipality or country level), the heads of these systems should take on the role of learning leaders. They enjoy the privileged position to embark on such initiatives and to lead towards sustainable and successful large-scale innovative learning implementation.

Notes

1. Roser Salavert Ed.D., was formerly Schools Superintendent for the NYC Public Schools, and her views are her own based on this experience. She is also closely involved as an advisor in Catalonia, Spain, and a member of the ILE Project at the Jaume Bofill Foundation (see Chapter 6).

2. Principal Officer Strategic Research and Innovation: Leader, Innovative Learning Environment (ILE) project.

3. The Quality Status tool: www.udir.no/Upload/skoleutvikling/Stastedsanalysen/Om%20st%c3%a5stedsanalysen.pdf?epslanguage=no. The Organisational Analysis tool: www.udir.no/Utvikling/Verktoy-for-skoleutvikling analyser/Organisasjonsanalysen/.

References

Barth, R.S. (2000), "Foreword", in P.J. Wald and M. Castleberry (ed.), *Educators as Learners: Establishing a Professional Learning Community in Your School*, ASCD (Association for Supervision and Curriculum Development), Alexandria, VA.

Berliner, D.C. (2008), "Research, policy, and practice: The great disconnect", in S.D. Lapan and M.T. Quartaroli (eds.), *Research Essentials: An Introduction to Designs and Practices,* Jossey-Bass, Hoboken, NJ, 295-325.

CCL (2009), *Innovation Leadership: How to Use Innovation to Lead Effectively, Work Collaboratively and Drive Results,* CCL (Center for Creative Leadership), Greensboro, NC, www.ccl.org/leadership/pdf/research/InnovationLeadership.pdf.

Darling-Hammond, L. and N. Richardson (2009), "Research review / teacher learning: What matters?", *Educational Leadership* 66(5), 46-53.

DECD (2013), *Brighter Futures,* DECD (Department for Education and Child Development), Adelaide.

DuFour, R. (2002), "The learning-centered principal", *Educational Leadership*, 59(8), 12-15.

DuFour, R. and R. Eaker (1998), *Professional Learning Communities at Work: Best Practices for Enhancing Student Achievement,* Solution Tree, Bloomington, IN.

Dumont, H., D. Istance and F. Benavides (eds.) (2010), *The Nature of Learning: Using Research to Inspire Practice,* OECD Publishing, Paris. http://dx.doi.org/10.1787/9789264086487-en.

Earl, L.M. (2013), *Assessment as Learning: Using Classroom Assessment to Maximize Student Learning*, 2nd edition, Corwin Press, Thousand Oaks, CA.

GELP (Global Education Leaders' Program) (2013), *Redesigning Education: Shaping Learning Systems Around the Globe,* Booktrope Editions, Seattle.

Grenness, T. (2012), "Will the 'Scandinavian leadership model' survive the forces of globalization?", *Magma,* 4.

Halbert, J. and L. Kaser (2013), *Spirals of Inquiry: For Quality and Equity*, BCPVPA (British Columbia Principals' and Vice-Principals' Association) Press, Vancouver.

Haar, J.M. (2003), "Providing professional development and team approaches to guidance", *Rural Educator,* 25(1), 30-35.

Hofstede, G. (2001), *Culture's Consequences: Comparing Values, Behaviors, Institutions and Organizations across Nations,* 2nd edition. Sage, Thousand Oaks, CA.

Huber, S. (Ed.) (2010), *School Leadership: International Perspectives.* Dordrecht: Springer.

Hybertsen Lysø, I. et al. (2012a), *Ledet til Ledelse* (Towards Leadership), Leadership Education Programme Evaluation Report 1, NTNU (Norwegian University of Science and Technology), Norway.

Hybertsen Lysø, I. et al. (2012b), *Ledet til Lederutvikling* (Towards Leadership Development), Leadership Education Programme, Evaluation Report 2, NTNU, Norway.

Istance, D., F. Benavides and H. Dumont (2008), "The search for innovative learning environments", in *Innovating to Learn, Learning to Innovate,* OECD Publishing, Paris. http://dx.doi.org/ 10.1787/9789264047983-3-en.

Kahlhammer, M. (2012), *Lernateliers als Professionelle Lerngemeinschaften. Die Wahrnehmungen und Einschätzungen der beteiligten Lerndesigner zur eigenen, gemeinsamen und systemischen Professionalisierung im Rahmen von Lernateliers der Entwicklungsbegleitung der Neuen Mittelschule* (Qualification programmes [Lernateliers] as professional learning communities. The perception and evaluation of all participating Learndesigners in terms of their individual, joint and systemic professionalisation in the framework of the "Lernateliers" as part of the development support for the New Middle School), Master thesis Pädagogische Hochschule St. Gallen.

Kaser, L and J. Halbert (2009), *Leadership Mindsets: Innovation and Learning in the Transformation of Schools,* Routledge, London.

Leithwood, K., K. Seashore, S. Anderson and K. Wahlstrom (2004), *How Leadership Influences Student Learning.* Center for Applied Research and Educational Improvement, Ontario Institute for Studies in Education, Toronto.

Lortie, D.C. (1975), *Schoolteacher: A Sociological Study,* University of Chicago Press, Chicago.

Marzano, R.J. (2003), *What Works in Schools: Translating Research into Action,* ASCD, Alexandria, VA.

MacBeath, J. and Y.C. Cheng (eds.) (2008), *Leadership for Learning: International Perspectives,* Sense Publishers, Rotterdam.

Mintzberg, H. (2011), "From management development to organization development with IM*pact*", *OD Practitioner,* 43(3), 25-29.

Mintzberg, H. (2009), *Managing,* FT Prentice Hall, Harlow, Essex.

Norwegian Directorate for Education and Training (2013), *Evaluation of The Advisory Team,* Norwegian Directorate for Education and Training, Oslo, www.udir.no/Upload/Rapporter/2013/veilederkorps_del. pdf?epslanguage=no.

Norwegian Directorate for Education and Training (2012), *Leadership in Schools: What is Required and Expected of a Principal,* Norwegian Directorate for Education and Training, Oslo.

Norwegian Directorate for Education and Training (2008), *Head Teacher Competence: Expectations and Demands,* Core document and point of departure for announcement of tender, Norwegian Directorate for Education and Training, Oslo.

NYSED (2011), "New York State p-12 Common Core Learning Standards for English Language, Arts & Literacy", New York State Education Department, New York.

OECD (2013a), *Innovative Learning Environments 2013,* OECD Publishing, Paris. http://dx.doi.org/10.1787/9789264203488-en.

OECD (2013b), *Trends Shaping Education 2013,* OECD Publishing, Paris. http://dx.doi.org/10.1787/trends_edu-2013-en.

OECD (2012), Universe Cases, www.oecd.org/edu/ceri/universecases.htm (accessed 6 October 2012).

OECD (2010), *Trends Shaping Education 2010,* OECD Publishing, Paris. http://dx.doi.org/10.1787/trends_edu-2010-en.

OECD (2009), *Creating Effective Teaching and Learning Environments: First Results from TALIS,* OECD Publishing, Paris. http://dx.doi.org/10.1787/9789264068780-en.

OECD (2008), *Improving School Leadership, Volume 1, Policy and Practice,* OECD Publishing, Paris. http://dx.doi.org/10.1787/9789264044715-en.

Owen, S. (2012), "'Fertile questions,' 'multi-age groupings', 'campfires' and 'master classes' for specialist skill-building: Innovative Learning Environments and support professional learning or 'teacher engagers' within South Australian and international contexts", Peer-reviewed paper presented at World Education Research Association (WERA) Focal meeting within Australian Association for Research in Education (AARE) conference, 2-6 December, University of Sydney, Australia, www.aare. edu.au/papers/2012/Susanne%20Owen%20Paper.pdf.

Robinson, V. (2011), *Student-Centered Leadership,* Jossey-Bass, San Francisco.

Schein, E.H. (2009), *Helping: How to Offer, Give and Receive Help,* Berrett-Koehler Publishers, San Francisco.

Schein, E.H. (1998), *Process Consultation Revisited,* Addison-Wesley, Reading MA.

Schratz, M. (2009). "Lernseits" von Unterricht. Alte Muster, neue Lebenswelten – was für Schulen?" (Learning beyond teaching: old patterns, new life-worlds – what kind of schools?), *Lernende Schule*, 12(46-47), 16-21.

Schratz, M, J.F. Schwarz and T. Westfall-Greiter (2012), *Lernen als bildende Erfahrung: Vignetten in der Praxisforschung* (Learning as educational experience: Vignettes in action research), Studienverlag, Innsbruck.

Schratz, M. and T. Westfall-Greiter (2010), *Schulqualität sichern und weiterentwickeln* (Safeguarding and developing school quality), Kallmeyer, Seelze.

Schrittesser, I. (2004), "Professional communities: Mögliche Beiträge der Gruppendynamik zur Entwicklung professionalisierten Handelns" (Professional communities: Potential contributions of group dynamics for the development of professionalised practice), in B. Hackl and G.H. Neuweg (eds.), *Zur Professionalisierung pädagogischen Handelns* (Towards professionalising pedagogical practice), LIT-Verlag, Münster, 131-150.

Scott, A., P. Clarkson and A. McDonough (2011), "Fostering professional learning communities beyond school boundaries", *Australian Journal of Teacher Education* 36(6), http://ro.ecu.edu.au/ajte/vol36/iss6/5 (accessed 6 October, 2012).

Senge, P. (2006), *The Fifth Discipline: The Art and Practice of the Learning Organization,* 2nd edition, Doubleday, New York.

Talbert, J. and N. Scharff (2008), *The Scaffolded Apprenticeship Model of School Improvement through Leadership Development,* Center for Research on the Context of Teaching, Stanford University, California.

Teacher Leadership Exploratory Consortium (2011), *Teacher Leader Model Standards*, Teacher Leadership Exploratory Consortium, www. teacherleaderstandards.org/downloads/TLS_Brochure_sm.pdf.

Tomlinson, C.A. (2003), *Fulfilling the Promise of the Differentiated Classroom: Strategies and Tools for Responsive Teaching,* ASCD, Alexandria, VA.

Tomlinson, C.A. and M. Imbeau (2010), *Leading and Managing a Differentiated Classroom*, ASCD, Alexandria, VA.

Tomlinson, C.A. and J. McTighe (2006), *Integrating Differentiated Instruction and Understanding by Design: Connecting Content and Kids*, ASCD, Alexandria, VA.

Vescio, V., D. Ross and A. Adams (2008), "A review of research on the impact of professional learning communities on teaching practice and student learning", *Teaching and Teacher Education* 24, 80–91.

Westfall-Greiter, T. and C. Hofbauer (2010), "Shared leadership setzt teacher leaders voraus: Lerndesigner/innen im Feld der Neuen Mittelschule" (Shared leadership requires teacher leaders: Learn designers in the New Secondary School), *Journal für Schulentwicklung*, 4(10), 8-15.

Whitmore, J. (2009), *Coaching for Performance: GROWing Human Potential and Purpose – The Principles and Practice of Coaching and Leadership*, 4th edition, Nicholas Brealey Publishing, Boston.

Wiggins, G. (1998), *Educative Assessment: Designing Assessments to Inform and Improve Student Performance*, Jossey-Bass, San Francisco.

Wiggins, G. and J. McTighe (2005), *Understanding by Design*, 2nd edition, ASCD, Alexandria, VA.

Online references

Organisation chart of the Ministry for Education, Art and Culture: www. bmukk.gv.at/ministerium/organigramm.xml.

Official website of the NMS: www.neuemittelschule.at.

NMS-Platform: www.nmsvernetzung.at.

NMS-Parent-Platform: www.nmseltern.at.

Center for Learning Research at the University of Innsbruck: www.lernforschung. at, Grant-funded learning research project at NMS: www.lernforschung. at/?cont=prodetailandid=%2031.

Virtual Online Campus: www.virtuelle-ph.at/.

Chapter 6

Promoting learning leadership in Catalonia and beyond[1]

Anna Jolonch
Jaume Bofill Foundation, Barcelona

Màrius Martínez
Autonomous University of Barcelona

Joan Badia
Vic University (UVic), and Open University of Catalonia

This chapter by Anna Jolonch, Màrius Martínez, and Joan Badia describes a research and development initiative that is both international in reach and aimed at creating the conditions for innovative leadership in Catalonia in Spain. It describes the rationale, methods and lessons learnt in the collaboration between the Jaume Bofill Foundation and the OECD's ILE project, and how that has resulted in cross-fertilisation and sharing benefits across the different local, regional, national and international arenas. Within Catalonia, an important aspect of the work has been a research study, clarifying concepts and conducting fieldwork in six sites which are exemplary and innovative in their learning leadership yet with typical school profiles. The research examined a set of key dimensions, including: the origins and role of identifiable innovation projects, professionals' attitudes, the role of the management team, teacher leadership, learner leadership, family and community participation, and reshaping the curriculum. It discusses the use of the research in context.

Internationalising educational innovation in Catalonia

Catalonia has a strong tradition of educational innovation. Its history features highly significant educational reform projects and important educators and teachers who have built its school system. Over the last two decades, however, schools have often lagged behind the rapid cultural, social, technological and economic changes. The arrival of a large number of immigrants and their great cultural diversity is one of the most significant changes which has forced the school system to "reinvent itself" in order to meet the pressing challenges it faces. The role of schools is crucial to the social cohesion of Catalan society, which is now multilingual and multicultural. Many of the answers, innovations, discoveries and proposals for renewal have come out of these very schools, responding to hitherto unknown challenges. However, the rates of school failure and early drop out, along with poor diagnostic test results, indicate the severity of the structural problems facing our schools today.

There is a great deal of confusion in the world of education in Catalonia as elsewhere. In times of great uncertainty and with the enormous problems posed by the crisis and cuts in the education budget, the commitment of teachers and the educational community is crucial and it becomes even more important to pay special attention to emerging forms of educational innovation. The fact that we now live in a knowledge and information society means that we are also in a learning society. School-age learning is fundamental and will remain so throughout people's lives. At a time when young people need skills and education more than ever, there are worrying signs that too many of them are drifting away from schools.

The crucial role of learning leadership: implementing change

It is for these reasons that the Jaume Bofill Foundation has been working closely over the last two years with the OECD's Innovative Learning Environments (ILE) project in its Centre for Educational Research and Innovation, precisely because it is a project that aims to put learning at the heart of the education debate. The urgent need to rethink what is going on in schools, how learning is organised and what should be the most suitable research to guide processes of change are some of the common problems in education in OECD countries.

The Foundation's interest in the analysis of the key issues in education means that we have turned to international experience and expertise. This interest exactly coincides with the concerns of the OECD's ILE project, which has led us to undertake exciting work, to join forces and build a shared reflection that may be crucial for the future of education. As part of its "Implementation and Change" strand, the project that we have carried out has focused on learning leadership as an important area requiring in-depth analysis when answering the question: "How can we implement at scale the change proposals suggested by what we know about learning and based on particular examples of innovation?"

This is the point at which learning leadership emerges as a crucial factor that affects (enhances, hinders or helps to manage) the extension of a particular innovation or an innovative environment. We had to invest time and effort to probe more deeply through theoretical reflection and the analysis of examples of leadership which have been crucial in driving forward and sustaining educational innovation in learning environments.

Our input goes beyond the importance of leadership in general, often associated with school management and administration, to gain an understanding of learning leadership that focuses the entire educational project on setting learning milestones and the strategies required to achieve them in practice. Such leadership is not individual but instead drives and distributes commitment, energy and experience through all stakeholders in the school setting. We need milestones and strategies because there is always the danger of simply generating the rhetoric of change and not building real potential for improvement. Our thinking thus addresses both theoretical and practical aspects of learning leadership capable of creating and sustaining learning environments. This means aligning learning objectives with the broader objectives of school organisation, building networks and relationships for learning while tapping the leadership of other stakeholders (including learners) in the school environment, and providing pathways for a specific policy.

The partnership between OECD/ILE and the Foundation was designed to bring benefits to Catalonia and to the broader international community. There are two sides to this collaboration, one international and one local, and we have built bridges between the two. On the international front, we established a working group of international experts which has met several times and provided its input to the educational literature by addressing an issue that hitherto had not been sufficiently explored in depth (this volume). This report has been prepared for the International Conference on "Learning Leadership in Innovative Environments" (*Lideratge per a l'aprenentatge en entorns innovadors*) in Barcelona in December 2013.

At the local level, a panel of experts came together to carry out research which is to be published by the Jaume Bofill Foundation in a report on "Learning Leadership in Catalonia" (*Lideratge per a l'aprenentatge a Catalunya*). An international seminar was held in Barcelona in November 2012 which provided a unique opportunity for exchange and dialogue between the international group and thirty major stakeholders in the Catalan educational community: head teachers, teachers, academics, researchers, union leaders and educational authority managers. At the time of writing there is a prospect that this work will continue in the future with the active involvement of the regional government. The December 2013 conference in Barcelona has been set up to make a significant contribution for all ILE participating countries but also for the educational community in Catalonia. It opens a unique avenue for theoretical analysis, insight and knowledge dissemination about learning leadership.

Hence the journey undertaken together by the OECD ILE project and the Jaume Bofill Foundation is seen as a lever for change, momentum and leadership that is taking root in Catalonia. The first part of this chapter is about this process. It describes a local example that is an original case which may inspire similar practice in other parts of the world. It shares lessons from our experience, highlighting key success factors of a process that in itself is a manifestation of learning leadership.

This process operates especially through the "meso" level via networks, clusters or communities of practice, which is the way that the Foundation usually operates. Our example exemplifies leadership that is different from school or teacher leadership; in this case, it is specifically of a foundation at the cutting edge of educational issues. In other cases, it may be an educational movement, a community, a network, education authorities (local, area, regional or general services), or other social and cultural stakeholders. In our case, it is learning leadership that involves many different stakeholders from both the local and international setting. It is an initiative that started and has grown based on shared responsibility, which is more than ever necessary in a society in which education has become one of the most significant issues in the new social, cultural, economic and political context.

The alliance between the local and international levels: distributed leadership

We would first stress the alliance that the managers of the Jaume Bofill Foundation *Learning Leadership* joint project have forged with the OECD's ILE team. The first meetings of the leaders of both sides showed they wanted to work to clarify the concept and understand their experiences. Promoting actions and research in the area of educational leadership that are circulated among teachers, head teachers, academics, researchers and policy makers is very important in Catalonia at present. With the passing of the Education Act of Catalonia in 2009, the issue of school administration and educational leadership has become a crucial factor together with the framework and background of increasing school autonomy. Prior to the project with the OECD, the Jaume Bofill Foundation had undertaken initiatives in this area including a seminar on educational leadership in 2009, which gave rise to more in-depth and still ongoing research into school administrators. The work with the OECD/ILE has helped to extend our understanding of leadership to the values, commitment, organisation and climate of schools, all geared towards learning processes and outcomes. Leadership, and specifically learning leadership, is an important factor for enhancing the model for learning and school success in Catalonia.

Introducing the concept of leadership into the world of education still comes up against a lot of resistance. Working with the OECD has provided fresh perspectives and made it possible to share other views and international experience. What has grown during these two years is a well-watered seed which may in the future become a learning leadership programme that involves a network of schools and educational innovation centres. Hence the Foundation, whose mission is to work for the improvement of education in Catalonia, seized the opportunity offered through collaboration with the OECD's ILE project. We have become part of this greater learning community, contributing the experience and know-how of a leading educational institution in Catalonia, at the time when the project's third strand on "Implementation and Change" was starting.

An understanding of distributed and collaborative leadership in educational innovation environments was introduced at the International Seminar in Barcelona in November 2012. It is leadership that empowers all stakeholders in the educational setting and brings them centre stage. Far from a vertical view, what it generates are networks for collaboration and exchange, including in the connections between local stakeholders and an international organisation such as the OECD. Some of the theoretical references about leadership in this report have been shared and tried out during this adventure together: we have implemented a particular understanding of collaborative leadership in education.

The research carried out in Catalonia has enabled us to listen to many teachers, head teachers and educators who have repeatedly emphasised the importance of the attitudes of professionals: having an open attitude to the world and being ready to interact and learn from other realities and experiences are of key importance. The attitude of lifelong learning involves setting up broader co-ordination teams, creating conditions which make it possible for new leadership, and for individual and collective education, training and development, to emerge.

If we have learned anything from learning leadership in innovative contexts it is that it is the outcome of the combination of different leaderships in a project. Having a project is to have a vision and to share it, one which is built and grows in the relationship. This achieves the most human part of educational leadership processes. Many of the successes and failures depend on how each person works and works together, and on what is done or not done. The same goes for schools, where educational success or failure has a lot to do with the ability to build a project, a project that transcends individual interests and is not just the sum of them. There is shared leadership when there is a goal that transcends the interest of each professional, each teacher, but also of each school in the same district, or transcends a secondary school by getting it to collaborate with primary schools, or that goes beyond local societal and educational stakeholders. You can also build a project and a vision shared by local and international interests. This leadership should also be present in the classroom or learning group, among teaching staff and their students.

An alliance should always be based on mutual trust and shared leadership throughout the process. Weaving personal relationships and trust, based on the human maturity of the leaders themselves, is crucial for carrying out distributed leadership projects. This is a key factor in the implementation of learning leadership processes at their micro (focusing on key aspects of learning), meso (networks and clusters), and macro (educational policy) levels.

The ILE team has encouraged the empowerment of their local partners and emphasised the mutual benefits of this joint project. The joint undertaking we have carried out aims to make a contribution to the implementation of change and set the conditions for the emergence of new leaderships. Commitment, energy, relationships, trust and shared values are the basis of what we have built.

Research and observation: drivers of change

We noted above that Catalonia has been and continues to be a place of educational innovation but this tradition and the resulting good educational practices have not always been accepted or maintained, either by the government, academic and university authorities, or by the community in a broad sense. Hence, it is common that these practices have fallen by the wayside, run out of steam or simply disappeared when the active support of their sponsors comes to an end. This has meant that many of our innovations were "innovations on the ground" rather than "innovations on paper". What is more, often when they have turned into "innovations on paper" they have ceased to be innovative and become bureaucratic and thus lost their thrust for meaningful change. Studying and analysing our own experience, connecting it with innovations from other countries, and placing it in the theoretical and practical context of the OECD innovation project has started a fruitful line of work for both the international community and education in Catalonia in a field that is highly relevant to the future of education.

The Jaume Bofill Foundation, with its strong tradition of research, has assembled a panel of Catalan experts formed by lecturers and practising teachers in primary and secondary schools who are at the chalk face every day, and has implemented one of the characteristic guiding principles of the ILE project: dialogue between research and practice. That is because one of the most valuable inputs made by the project is to reach the micro level of schools and learning environments – where learning really takes place, levels which are as critical as they are too often forgotten – and how they can respond to the changes and new learners of the 21st century.

What is new is not so much the act of looking at and examining schools but the ultimate purpose of this examination. Instead of continuing to identify what is wrong or focusing on the severity of the crisis in schools in most OECD countries, we have sought to learn from experience to generate useful knowledge (research) for solving problems (action). Without denying the difficulties faced by schools and their wider environment, we want to open doors and generate possible solutions. At a time when schools are subject to closer scrutiny and attention than ever before, the ILE project does not compare different countries but uses research to promote and foster practice, leadership and policies that promote innovative and inspiring learning experiences for 21st century pupils and young people.

The collaboration with the OECD has been enriched by the reflection and analysis carried out by people in our educational community, who have conducted research designed to look at schools from the inside in order to identify, characterise, draw conclusions, and explain the central role of leadership in educational innovation. The continuous movement between the concepts in the scientific literature and educational practice has shown that research is enriched by professional experience and vice versa. The research has been situated in the constant tension between action and reflection, doing and thinking, observation and intervention. There has been on-going movement back and forth between the logic of research (the production of new knowledge) and the logic of action (to find solutions and solve problems). The question of "what should be done", more typical of the person who acts, took us away from the question of "what is being done and how" that is characteristic of the researcher. The spiral movement between research and action has taken us away from preconceptions of the logic of action in order to focus on research.

As an example of the mutual enrichment of theory and action, one of the international experts said to teachers, educators and head teachers gathered at the 2012 seminar in Barcelona: "Some of the areas covered in my book would have been different if I could have discussed them with you beforehand". Equally, we can quote a teacher at one of the meetings of the panel of Catalan experts: "Doing research has been a privilege for me. Observation and analysis have made me experience everyday work in the school and the classroom in a very different way. I have learned a lot and I have also felt that I could contribute a lot to the group due to my background and experience as a teacher." These comments from the worlds of academia and practice stress the need to build more bridges for dialogue and meeting points to work together on research, generating shared knowledge and tackling the reality on the ground.

Visits to schools, observing classrooms, seminars with head teachers of schools: they have all brought a wealth of knowledge. In the first workshops, the local experts were immersed in the principles and theoretical framework of the ILE project and the literature of the international experts in educational leadership. In addition to the theory, however, it has been crucial to obtain the evidence from analysis of cases in the Catalan context. At the meetings of the research group, we questioned each other, we exchanged different perspectives, ideas were transformed and in their final version no longer belonged to any one person. We got to experience a way of "thinking together". The group's production has exceeded the production of each of its members and once again the whole has been greater than the sum of its parts.

The research has allowed us to appropriate a discourse and knowledge that has made us into experts because we have generated knowledge based on experience. The boundary between research and training has been blurred. The research has enabled us to say at a work meeting that we have become a learning community. In June 2013, we agreed to continue researching together with a commitment to publicising and expanding the group and inviting other schools and experts to participate and experience its research knowledge and training. This is to be done without abandoning the continuous movement back and forth between the observation and analysis of practice and the transformation of practice itself.

We have positioned ourselves in the framework of the new epistemology of practice which puts the "reflective professional" (Jolonch, 2002) centre stage and opens up approaches to professional learning and reflective practice that balance the logics of action and knowledge. It is crucial, amidst the general confusion, to focus on the concrete solutions and innovations that come out of educational practice in the classroom. We know that the schools of the 20th century are long gone, never to return, but we still do not know with any clarity what kind of schools we need for the 21st century.

It is no wonder, then, that the need to introduce research and reflection into professional practice to promote innovation is one of the conclusions we have appropriated as the definition of "learning leadership". This means a change in the teaching culture, a new training model, and a revolution in the relationship between theory and practice, between universities and the grassroots. There is still much to do in this respect in Catalonia and we would like the lessons learned from the experience set out here to inspire similar new projects.

Building synergies and networking: educational innovation

A further notable feature has been the synergies generated in this shared leadership project. We have set up a working group at the local level with researchers who come from four Catalan universities and who have worked together with government officials, head teachers, inspectors and teachers who are in the classroom every day. True to the spirit of the ILE project, which is to look at schools from the inside and in dialogue with research, we set up a working group consisting of academics and grassroots stakeholders. The experience that the Jaume Bofill Foundation has gained over the years, its legitimacy to generate debate and exchange, as well as its relational work with people and institutions, have laid the basis on which a range of stakeholders in the Catalan education community came together in the same project in on-going dialogue with international experts from the OECD's ILE project. Universities, the educational authorities, teachers and the management teams of the schools involved in the research have worked together, and we have also sought in the context of the International Conference in Barcelona, to involve the Catalan government and build on a potential interest in continuing the work on learning leadership beyond this event.

We have located ourselves at the "meso" level of leadership: forming networks. This has not been a vertical design, far from the top-down reforms which rarely come to fruition. We have woven a web of relationships that may become a driver for leadership and educational innovation in Catalonia. As a learning network we have moved forward step by step in an on-going process of mutual learning and knowledge building. We have also learned that innovation is a collective, collaborative, participatory process that is also planned in this way, with a clear opening to the learning process. It is largely the outcome of the interaction between different actors, which in this case have been universities, schools and the government, all combining the local with the international realms. The end result opens up the possibility of innovation as it gives a hybrid of knowledge and interaction among professionals who work in different environments.

The research done on learning leadership reveals that innovation in this area takes place though teams of educators working in a network who are open to learning from each other, to co-operating with families and to interacting with other schools, the local community and other countries. In the new context of change and in a reflexive society, networks have huge potential to generate learning dynamics based on openness, dialogue and co-operation. Hence innovation and reform are generated at the meso level of the community, enhancing interconnections, and spreading innovation right across the micro, meso and macro levels.

The project of the Jaume Bofill Foundation and of OECD/ILE has not operated in isolation but instead has been open to the network and has diversified and strengthened new ties. The context of uncertainty and the need to respond to the demands of new learners call for a shift in educational paradigms leading to flexible, multi-focal and smart structures and a conception of learning embodied in the knowledge society. The OECD/ILE project, the Catalan Department of Education, lecturer and teacher researchers at Catalan universities and schools, and the Jaume Bofill Foundation and its research team have all created networks and have been learning. Thus, our own experience demonstrates that learning networks make it possible to share, disseminate and distribute leadership and responsibility.

Learning Leadership – the research study

Clarifying terms of reference

The OECD's Innovative Learning Environments (ILE) project adopts a new perspective to analyse educational environments, one that has provided the focus for our study on Learning Leadership in Catalan schools. There is not a wide literature on "learning leadership", and the working group approached the project by drawing on various sources. Along with the ILE references (OECD, 2008, 2010), that gave the starting points on innovative learning environments, the new project documentation has been used such as MacBeath (earlier drafts of Chapter 3, this volume), focusing on learning, conditions for learning, dialogue, shared leadership and accountability, as well as Senge (1990), Spillane (2005, 2006), Fullan (2002, 2009), Hallinger (2011) and Leithwood et al. (2004), the reviews of MacBeath and Cheng (2008), Seashore et al. (2010) for the Wallace Foundation, and Salavert (2012).

These sources were used to delimit the concept of this new leadership that sets the conditions for learning, for both young learners (academic performance and personal development) and educators (professional development and continuing studies as members of a professional community). It is, therefore, leadership that makes educational success possible. An essential component of learning leadership can be found in the complex interrelations that form the substratum of the school and classrooms as a living, dynamic organisation that learns (Marsick, Watkins and Boswell, 2013). These interactions are not only communicative and link people, but they are also systematic. This is seen for instance in the patterned changes in pupil performance brought about by teacher expectations, or the academic rigour produced by enhanced teacher collaboration.

As the team came to realise, learning leadership does not just revolve around school directors: a successful learning environment is one in which learners develop as both learners and people. This happens when teachers create conditions that emanate warmth, respect, motivation, intellectual curiosity and support so that each learner progresses individually, while also letting the group progress and grow as a whole. A teacher's leadership is demonstrated in his or her ability to create these classroom conditions and to foster student leadership, which is demonstrated by, among other things, good study habits, an innate motivation to learn, growing autonomy, mixing and working well with others, and participation.

Learning leadership is an innovative concept and, as such, it is found in contexts of change, creating added value and breaking with the *status quo*. It results from the intersection and accumulation of several leaderships (instructional, organisational, etc.) to take them even further. This leadership continuously and sustainably teaches and creates learning, autonomy and empowerment in the learners and in the community. It aims to identify the transferable theories of change management, of shared, collaborative and team leadership strategies, and the organisations that provide learning, with the value-creation chains which can "read" and interpret the reality – of the classroom in the school, or of the school in the classroom.

A new multi-stakeholder working strategy

The leadership of the Jaume Bofill Foundation at the meso level is the first element to understand in this process, engaging a range of stakeholders (see above). The process has been importantly grounded in research in order to promote evidence-based discussions and debates. To identify the elements of learning leadership, a non-evaluative, non-judgemental research methodology has been developed for this study. It has identified and described those elements congruent with the theory and the conceptual approach to learning leadership, through the following process:

Creating a group of Catalan experts. From a small core group of four people, the Jaume Bofill Foundation invited a panel of experts from both the educational system (teachers, head teachers, inspectors, service chiefs, etc.), and the university sector (lecturer-researchers). Together, they have functioned as a work and study group.

An exploratory, intentional selection of six schools was made according to the following criteria:

- Schools should be considered typical – "normal" in their statistical profile – in order to avoid the argument that their experience does not offer reference practices for scalability or transfer.

- They should be exceptional, however, in the learning and the leadership that the school promotes – experience and leadership that facilitate greater and higher-quality learning, whether formal, curricular learning or other forms of non-formal learning.

- Each selected school site should be connected through the "meso dimension", involving groups of people, internal and external to the learning environment/project and linked by distributed leadership and collaborative teaching.

In addition, attention was also give to the size of the school, with from two to five groups per grade as a guideline. Their performance in objective tests had to be above the Catalan average or reflecting a sustained improvement over the last five years. The selection offered a balance via three infant and primary education schools and three secondary education schools, that is, schools involving children of International Standard Classification of Education (ISCED) 1 age and young people of ISCED 2 age respectively. We also sought schools that showed participation of families or other actors in the learning environment or in the project. We wanted those where the demand for places exceeds those available over the last three years (as an indicator of the school's "success" and social perception of change), and that there should be evidence of a sustained reduction in absenteeism (especially for the secondary sites) over the last five years.

Study visit to the selected schools. For each site, a planned and designed protocol for contacting, visiting and interviewing was followed, encompassing the following key stages:

- A study pair from the team members, one drawn from the academic side and one from the practitioner side, contacted the school and provided information about the project, the reasons for selecting their particular institution, and the intention to analyse, rather than evaluate or assess, its work.

- The pair visited the school on an agreed day and conducted interviews with the school management. Accompanied by a representative from the management team of the school, the pair visited a range of classes of all levels and spoke with some of the pupils. Classroom evidence was gathered and a sample was created for comment and analysis with the school management.

Seminars were held at Jaume Bofill Foundation with the school principals and the entire study team for each learning environment's project to be presented and analyse in-depth each leadership vision.

Each study pair produced a **case report** with the analysis of the evidence of learning leadership in terms of the processes, results, and other identified impacts.

Factors linked to learning leadership

The following section presents the elements identified during this work in terms of the study's focus. Each experience has revealed features that are unique, and likewise different project development stages or levels have been identified. Processes and educational results have been equally varied. The schools were selected intentionally according to the above criteria; given the newness of the topic and the lack of precedents, the study can be described as exploratory.

How the projects began

For most of the projects, the beginning of the change can be clearly identified: a milestone, a situation or a realisation of the need for change. The schools and projects analysed achieve the desire to change at a particular moment, which the collective itself is able to identify. The schools analysed arrived at that call for change via various routes; some examples include: a sustained decrease in enrolments, a change in the characteristics of the management team and its mandate, an awareness of the school's deteriorating image within the neighbourhood, a continued decline in academic results, or the creation of a new school from the division of an existing one.

These processes led to a "breaking point" or a point of change from the previous stage for the learning environment. In some cases, the change has been brought about by the entity that owns the school – the education authority or the private owners – and has entrusted its running to a person or team that has assumed responsibility for transforming the institution on the basis of improving the pupils' learning. In most cases, however, it has been the internal dynamics of the schools themselves forced by external or internal circumstances which have brought about an opportunity in which a team of people has decided to turn things around, giving a new focus by creating a space more conducive to learning or improving the conditions for learning. However, in every case it is possible to establish a "before" and an "after", a given moment when an (initially small) team of people makes the decision to change direction and starts formulating that into a new project. This beginning is also demonstrated by a new collective narrative shared by everyone at the school, one that allows for a personal interpretation of the school's past and its evolution, which leads to sharing the need for change as well.

Professionals' attitudes, especially in management

When faced with the reality of having to open up to the world and establish links and networks with other educational institutions, professionals and figures, the realisation is related to an attitude expressed by the management teams through similar statements made in the cases analysed. This attitude expresses the need to improve, to open up to the world, make connections and learn from others who have taken on difficult situations before. Visiting schools, studying reference scenarios, making study visits to countries with successful education systems, and participating in networks of schools are all found in the experiences analysed and they are justified by arguments displaying an attitude of research, inquiry, continuous learning and the incorporation of that learning into society. Examples of this include the head teacher who completed a PhD on the Finnish education system, or the school that took advantage of the improvement dynamic of an educational network (strategic planning by the network of schools).

Another behavioural element observed in the majority of cases is the sense of "agency" as opposed to the "culture of complaint": most of the management teams' explanations are focused on the awareness that the team has to be the main element of improvement and that the responsibility for resolving the school's problems is internal and collective. On the whole, they are focused on analysing the current situation in order to establish a departure point for future improvements, and not in order to legitimise opposition to change or to justify acceptance of the negative situation.

A school project

All the learning environments studied have a school-specific project expressly formulated into a reference document which acts as a guide to what will be done, with the necessary flexibility to adapt to changing circumstances as needed. All the schools in this sample are acutely aware that a distinct educational project is being implemented, which will help continuous improvement and which involves challenge for the school's educational community as a whole. Learning leadership depends on a project, without necessarily planning what has to be achieved specifically for the school or for the people who make up that learning environment.

This project was done very differently in each of the situations studied. In some cases, it was summarised in a motto that binds together the vision and the mission. In some cases it took the form of strategic planning for the coming years (looking towards 2020, for example), establishing medium- and long-term objectives and agreeing on actions, resources, time frames and indicators to report on annual performance. In other cases, it involved the school's educational plan, which was reformulated as a vision of what should be in the medium- and long term. In another instance, although the plan was not formalised as a whole document, it was reported in significant detail by the school directors.

Each plan presents a different focus, and not all of them specifically mention the objective of improved learning (although this may be the final result), but in those in which this goal is not explicit, there are reasons behind it. In one case, the plan is based on the need to address the dynamics, relations and interactions between people and teams, on improving the professional life they share and how they treat one another, as a necessary condition to broach a second process focused on learning. In short, breaking down the barriers that prevent the school from progressing then allows it to focus on learning. One head teacher put it thus, "Up to now we've been leading an 'evolution'; now we're leading a 'revolution'".

The role of the management team

The management team is another key element with a central role in every case, although the distributed nature of leadership and collaborative leadership, based on the participation of the members of the team itself or on the creation of broader co-ordination teams, are also given recognition. In many cases, the team creates conditions that give rise to leadership in small teaching teams for a cycle or linked to a project.

In most cases, the team sees its task as part of a process that will continue for some time and, eventually, that team will have to be replaced by a new one that will continue and update the mission and the plan. In three instances, it has been possible to observe that the previous management teams continue at the school once they have left their management responsibilities and have carried on supporting the project as ordinary teachers. In one case, a former head remained in the management team.

Finding, involving, and training the staff who will take over is considered part of the management team's mission – progressively linking people to management or facilitating training (at a university postgraduate or master's level) in subjects of strategic interest to the organisation for people who will be brought into management positions. This awareness of the plan's sustainability and continuity has not been explicit in every case. Nevertheless, in those cases where sustainability is recognised as a top priority, steps have been taken to train new directors, with progressive delegation of responsibilities, intensive managerial training, etc.

The principals studied have also clearly shown an attitude of openness to learning new things and to new opportunities; they have been ready to be transparent about all the work they were doing. In almost all cases, they have viewed taking part in this study very positively, as it has been seen as an opportunity that fits closely their institutional plan to continue learning.

Teacher leadership

Teacher leadership is achieved in the change of role in the classroom and within the organisation. During a significant number of visits, it has been possible to observe the teacher as mediator and regulator of the dynamics of learning, rather than as the traditional transmitter of knowledge and content. Leadership actions have also been identified within teams related to levels, stages and other learner groupings, as well as within school-wide projects.

Some teachers have shown themselves to be highly competent at creating opportunities for learning in class by making the school's facilities (classrooms, laboratories, workshops, corridors, etc.) function as spaces for learning that combine openness, flexibility and autonomy in the learner's activity and interactions with an increased level of demand in terms of the objectives and the direction of the activity. It has been possible to observe the interaction of one or more teachers with one or more groups of learners through projects known to and shared by the learners. We have observed how teachers act as monitors of the process, regulators of the interactions and communication, and supporters and motivators in solving problems. They do this by carefully listening to requests, coming up with questions, making suggestions and proposing stimulating situations for the learners through various resources and supports.

Some teachers observed in action also explained their leadership vision for the group of learners: they feel they have to look after them, oversee their personal development and strive for each one to fulfil his or her potential. They have also shown a vision of teaching that is the continuous creation of opportunities to learn and improve personally, and opportunities to grow and mature, to advance in their development. Furthermore, they have shown that they are aware of simultaneously "learning from their pupils" and therefore growing themselves.

This can also be seen in the treatment of errors observed in some learning environments. In these, the learners have displayed a lack of fear about getting answers wrong. The teachers of these pupils have turned errors into an opportunity to intensify learning. As one learner stated: "we all get things wrong; sometimes the teacher does, too."

In all the cases studied, there exists a high and constant level of interest in the professional development of teachers. This interest is translated into seeking individual and collective training programmes related to managing knowledge, but it also involves mobilising internal and external resources in order to improve the quality of the teaching aimed at improvement.

At the end of each school year the management team of one of the schools in the study speaks with each of the teachers in connection with a satisfaction survey completed by the families and the learners. In accordance with the results and the teacher's own thoughts, he or she is asked what points for improvement in the form of objectives should be set for the following school year. Training or other resources are sought in order for the teacher to be able to meet the improvement objectives proposed. This formula combines formative assessment, reflection on the teacher's own practice, and support for professional development in a climate of high (self-) expectations and continued improvement.

There are also examples of interest in collective professional training and development. Various types are seen, in the organisation of space and time for all the teachers to meet and learn together: training workshops, internal training led by the teachers themselves, creating project teams, vertical and horizontal revision of the curriculum, and also the search for external training opportunities that are subsequently shared at the centre.

In some cases, the schools are particularly interested in hiring new teachers and involving them in the project. Mentoring ("assessor teachers") and special processes in the teaching departments are among the ways to add new teachers to the ongoing project and ensure its continuity. In the case of privately-owned schools, these methods also include selecting new teachers on the basis of strategic requirements, which forecast that they will be needed for the future development of the project. A good example of this would be requiring a higher qualification than that legally needed (a bachelor's degree in primary education, for instance) and knowledge of English, with a view to being able to give classes in that language, using specific methodologies such as Content and Language Integrated Learning (CLIL).

Learner leadership

The schools studied seek to make the most of the diversity of the learners. Whatever the level of education, a common characteristic was observed in all of the schools: the idea that the learner should, first, assume the leadership of their learning, and then assist with collective learning by contributing his or her personal traits or learning skills and techniques through group participation. This often takes the form of teamwork leading from proposals based on problems, projects or challenges, or work in the community as a team. Generally, the teams of learners, like their grouping, respond to criteria of inclusion, heterogeneity and growing autonomy. In some classes, the learners self-manage the task to be worked on individually or as small groups, and dynamics of running the activity and collaborative dynamics have been observed.

We should highlight two questions that have been systematically posed to the learners during the classroom visits at the learning environments observed: "What are you doing?" and "Why are you doing it?" This strategy has been adopted in order to gauge the degree of knowledge and awareness of the meaning and objectives of the activity taking place. The study group considered that if the emphasis was on learning (MacBeath, 2012; Salavert, 2012), it would be necessary to ask the pupils in a direct and simple manner about their degree of awareness and knowledge of their own learning. This should extend to the strategies used and even meta-cognition, as well as its meaning, utility and ultimate aim, the reasons for that activity and its connection with the subject, the course, the development process itself and the context. That is why these two questions were posed by each pair from the team in all the classes visited.

The responses have shown different learning realities which range from the mechanical and reproductive action of an instruction that is applied uncritically by the learner ("I'm doing it because the teacher said to, because it's time to, because now is the time that we do this activity"), to totally contextualised responses that demonstrate a learning process with meaning that is explained with enthusiasm and conviction. The team was aware that it is not always possible to ensure a response that shows an elevated level of awareness about the activity and its meaning, but the strategy of inquiry has provided valuable information. This strategy of inquiry has also been validated at the work team's workshops held at the Jaume Bofill Foundation with them and the school principals, leading the teaching and the management teams to revise the strategies that, at both the classroom and the establishment level, need to be strengthened in order to increase collective awareness of educational objectives.

Family and community participation

Family and community participation is a milestone that has only been partially achieved at the schools, but it is also clearly identified by the professionals who work there as on the horizon of the mission to be undertaken. The schools studied maintain a special relationship with their communities. In some of them, fathers and mothers (and even grandparents) have been brought in as "experts" to give explanations about things they have in-depth knowledge of to the pupils. They have also been brought in as conversation assistants for learning languages, especially English. In some cases, the initiative has come from the families themselves. Some schools have been able to mobilise community resources in a wider sense by strengthening and consolidating relations with neighbourhood organisations and groups, service learning activities, and taking part in community projects.

These experiences mean breaking the monopoly of teaching by teachers and helping learners to become aware that there are various sources of knowledge and learning: teachers, fathers, mothers, other adults from the community, or their own classmates, as well as other resources available in the networks.

The emphasis on learning means re-reading the curriculum

The curriculum needs to be revisited in a broad sense: programmes and content, of course, but also the classroom, the methodologies, the incorporation of information and communications technology (ICT), the spaces used, and learner groupings. In one learning environment, they referred to dedicating a substantial part of the teachers' preparatory work to re-reading the "official" programmes and content in order to favour learning by adapting the programmes to the learning environment's needs and opportunities, and to prune out everything that is marginal and unnecessary. This task is achieved through a new teacher programme focused on skills and the instrumental dimension of learning.

In other cases, the class dynamics have been redefined by approaching classwork as a series of projects, consequently altering the methodological strategies that have become subordinate to the needs of each phase of the project. In some learning environments, the presence of ICT in the classroom as an everyday resource was evident when some learners created content that they, independently, published on a class blog. Work with information and communication technologies is presented in various ways in the different schools, but in many it becomes an "invisible" element of classroom work, in the sense that it is assimilated and its use is natural, not considered exceptional or unique. However, they are all aware that there is still a long way to go in order to make the most of technology's potential. Several schools have carried on the work started during the "eduCAT 1x1" project (one pupil, one computer) that had to be stopped due to lack of funding (the programme envisaged providing primary schools and all public secondary educational schools with sufficient computers and interactive whiteboards).

In different schools, the team observed an interest in the continuous improvement in the ability to communicate what was being learnt by the pupils themselves so that, for example, they were invited from the first years to present in various ways (orally, in writing, in drawings, through the computer, etc.) what they had learnt, what they had researched, what they had found on the Internet or what they had read. This is in order to strengthen three skills: management of information and knowledge, communication, and leadership. In another case, two classes were merged so that groups of learners of two different levels – and thus of different ages – could work together, broadening the learners' vision of development and breaking the limitations of their location according to chronological age.

Effects identified

The effects have not always had to do with learning, as the initial situations that have created projects under the construct of "learning leadership" have been very different. As well as looking for specific effects in more formalised types of learning, other effects have been considered that are more relevant in a school and school-community context. These include improved attendance; positive coexistence between various groups, and especially relations with the learners and their families, as well as how they interact with the teachers; the public image of the school in the community; communicating and acknowledging the learning environment's mission; and also academic and school performance (expressed through marks, rates of graduation, results in external tests and continuation into post-compulsory studies).

In the cases studied, the team was able to establish the improvements in processes and results through the objective indicators provided by the management teams in the interviews. Not all the schools have achieved improvements in all the indicators, but they have all achieved trends of improvement in at least one of them, as summarised below:

- Levels of conflict have decreased; coexistence and a positive school atmosphere have improved.

- Student absenteeism has been reduced.

- Test results in basic skills established by the administration have improved.

- The number of students dropping out of school early as they turn 16, without finishing their studies or gaining the compulsory secondary education qualification, has decreased.

- The percentage of students with a school qualification on finishing compulsory education has increased.

- The retention rate for pupils who go on to post-compulsory education has increased.

Finally, regarding follow-up, assessment and sustainability, different realities were encountered. Some schools are already developing systems of assessment and accountability on a yearly basis, based on previously established indicators. They also reported that one of the mechanisms for developing improvements has been participatory assessment.

Research to promote learning leadership and innovation: key conclusions

The study into leadership for learning in six schools in Catalonia has made it possible to contrast practice with theoretical ideas suggested by various authors. It has been possible to see how the systematic vision of the school's reality and the removal of the barriers that hinder learning have created conditions conducive for learning (Senge, 1990). It has also been possible to show the importance of dialogue about the intentions and the importance of highlighting learning as the most important milestone that the whole educational organisation should pursue (MacBeath, 2012), and the importance of putting this emphasis into concrete terms as a plan and a motto that is constructed, known and shared by the whole community (Salavert, 2012). Various aspects related to leadership have also been revealed during the experience, such as the importance of the management team and its role in promoting processes, as well as in creating conditions that encourage collaboration and support for a project shared by the teachers and the rest of the community (Spillane, 2005; Fullan, 2002, 2009; Hallinger 2011).

The project has brought into relief practices in learning environments that, in the eyes of the team of experts, were previously understood only in very general ways. On some occasions, the discourse was rather more developed than the practices that could be expressed in concrete terms and followed. Some reference practices, congruent with the theoretical principles, were not sufficiently documented.

The strategy developed from the proposal by Salavert (2012) has been very useful for discerning elements of this leadership and has provided a simple and effective methodology: saving time, keeping interference in the school's dynamics to a minimum, and stressing that the study is research, rather than an assessment or judgement. This has been well received by both the study team and the principals and members of the schools visited.

Despite having selected schools that seemed *a priori* would present a considered reference scenario, the visits and the case studies have made it possible to add detail to this vision and identify different levels of development of many of the ideas collected in their theoretical contributions along a number of dimensions: formalising plans, distributing leadership, involving and communicating with the school community, assessment and follow-up systems, and impact on learning.

The different levels of development are also linked to different levels of sustainability among the projects studied. Thus in some cases we can identify situations of saturation of, or excessive dependency on, a small number of people, and this can endanger the continuity or sustainability of the project in the medium or long term, according to some of the leaders consulted.

The experience has made it possible to gauge the desire for permanent learning created by a school or other learning environment in which learning leadership is shared, and such a desire is indispensable for the leadership to be exercised and the wider project realised. The desire for learning that comes about through practices of leadership shared by an increased number of actors provides a context for building capacity, while also showing a horizon of innovation and research that is very healthy for the wider education system.

The research in this learning leadership initiative has been a crucial part of knowledge and legitimacy building, rather than an "assessment-judgement" strategy. As such it has very helpfully provided resources and knowledge to feed back into the change process, and will be used in the future through such ways as initial and continuing teacher education via partnerships with faculties of education.

The study group has acknowledged its desire to continue the task into the future. The objective is to prepare a text to explain the six cases as well as a series of guidelines to encourage schools and learning leaders to promote innovation in learning environments.

The group, through the leadership of the Jaume Bofill Foundation has also considered the possibility of inviting more schools to participate in a similar process during the next academic year in order to increase the knowledge on learning leadership and to promote better leadership for better learning.

Finally, one of the project's most important aims has been to create and spread knowledge in schools and in the system. To do so, the organisation of seminars and technical debates with stakeholders (in which the Foundation has a long experience), and publishing reports with the key findings and methodologies, are important strategies. The whole process will contribute to new international knowledge through the OECD channel, with the potential for setting in train a virtuous circle of positive change being tested in a local/ regional setting and then adapted and taken up elsewhere.

Note

1. The presentation of the project and its international connections has been primarily prepared by Anna Jolonch, while the research study has been primarily the work of Marius Martinez and Joan Badia.

References

Badia, J. and M. Martínez (2012), *Protocol per a l'observació de contextos de lideratge per a l'aprenentatge* (Observation protocol for learning leadership cases) Document for internal use, Fundació Jaume Bofill.

Fullan, M. (2009), *Motion Leadership: The Skinny on Becoming Change Savvy,* Joint publication of Corwin, Ontario Principals' Council, School Improvement Network, American Association of School Administrators and National Staff Development Council.

Fullan, M. (2002). *The Change Leader,* Center for Development and Learning, www.cdl.org/resource-library/articles/change_ldr.php.

Hallinger, P. (2011), "Leadership for learning: Lessons from 40 years of empirical research", *Journal of Educational Administration,* 49(2), 125-142.

Hargreaves, A. and D. Fink (2008), *El liderazgo sostenible. Siete principios para el liderazgo en centros educativos innovadores* (Sustainable leadership: seven principles for leadership in innovative schools), Morata, Madrid.

Jolonch, A. (2002), *Educació i infància en risc. Acció i reflexió en l'àmbit social* (Education and children at risk : action and reflection from the field), Proa-Centre d'Estudis de Temes Contemporanis, Barcelona.

Leithwood, K., K. Seashore, S. Anderson and K. Wahlstrom (2004), *How Leadership Influences Student Learning.* Center for Applied Research and Educational Improvement, Ontario Institute for Studies in Education, Toronto.

MacBeath, J. (2012), *Collaborate, Innovate and Lead: The Future of the Teaching Profession,* Debates on Education, Fundació Jaume Bofill, Barcelona.

MacBeath, J. (2005), "Leadership as distributed: A matter of practice", *School Leadership and Management,* 25(4), 349-366.

MacBeath, J. and Y.C. Cheng (eds.) (2008), *Leadership for Learning: International Perspectives,* Sense Publishers, Rotterdam.

Marsick, V.J., K.E. Watkins and S.A. Boswell (2013), "Schools as learning communities" in R. Huang et al. (eds.), *Reshaping Learning: Frontiers of Learning Technology in a Global Context*, Springer-Verlag Berlin Heidelberg, 71–88.

OECD (2010), *The Nature of Learning: Using Research to Inspire Practice,* OECD Publishing, Paris. http://dx.doi.org/10.1787/9789264086487-en.

OECD (2008), *Innovating to Learn, Learning to Innovate,* OECD Publishing, Paris. http://dx.doi.org/10.1787/9789264047983-en.

Salavert, R. (2012), *Metodologia per a l'anàlisi de contextos d'aprenentatge escolars* (Methodology for the analysis of the schooling cases), Document for internal use, Fundació Jaume Bofill.

Senge, P. (1990). *The Fifth Discipline: The Art and Practice of the Learning Organization,* Doubleday Currency, New York.

Seashore, K. et al. (2010), *Learning from Leadership: Investigating the Links to Improved Student Learning,* Center for Applied Research and Educational Improvement; University of Minnesota; Ontario Institute for Studies in Education; University of Toronto.

Spillane, J.P. (2006), *Distributed Leadership*, Jossey-Bass, San Francisco.

Spillane, J.P. (2005), "Distributed leadership", *The Educational Forum*, 69(2), 143-150.

ORGANISATION FOR ECONOMIC CO-OPERATION AND DEVELOPMENT

The OECD is a unique forum where governments work together to address the economic, social and environmental challenges of globalisation. The OECD is also at the forefront of efforts to understand and to help governments respond to new developments and concerns, such as corporate governance, the information economy and the challenges of an ageing population. The Organisation provides a setting where governments can compare policy experiences, seek answers to common problems, identify good practice and work to co-ordinate domestic and international policies.

The OECD member countries are: Australia, Austria, Belgium, Canada, Chile, the Czech Republic, Denmark, Estonia, Finland, France, Germany, Greece, Hungary, Iceland, Ireland, Israel, Italy, Japan, Korea, Luxembourg, Mexico, the Netherlands, New Zealand, Norway, Poland, Portugal, the Slovak Republic, Slovenia, Spain, Sweden, Switzerland, Turkey, the United Kingdom and the United States. The European Union takes part in the work of the OECD.

OECD Publishing disseminates widely the results of the Organisation's statistics gathering and research on economic, social and environmental issues, as well as the conventions, guidelines and standards agreed by its members.

OECD PUBLISHING, 2, rue André-Pascal, 75775 PARIS CEDEX 16
(96 2013 02 1 P) ISBN 978-92-64-18576-0 – No. 61067 2013